The Change I Believe In

## Also by Katrina vanden Heuvel

*Voices of Glasnost:*
*Interviews with Gorbachev's Reformers*
(coauthored with Stephen F. Cohen)

*The Best of the Nation:*
*Selections from the Independent Magazine of Politics and Culture*
(coedited with Victor Navasky)

*Taking Back America:*
*And Taking Down the Radical Right*
(coedited with Robert L. Borosage)

*Dictionary of Republicanisms:*
*The Indispensable Guide to What They Really Mean*
*When They Say What They Think You Want to Hear*

*Meltdown:*
*How Greed and Corruption Shattered Our*
*Financial System and How We Can Recover* (editor)

# THE CHANGE I BELIEVE IN

*Fighting for Progress in the Age of Obama*

Katrina vanden Heuvel

NATION
BOOKS
New York

For Steve,
who has helped me in so many ways,
with gratitude and love

Library of Congress Cataloging-in-Publication Data
Vanden Heuvel, Katrina
   The change I believe in : fighting for progress in the age of Obama / Katrina
vanden Heuvel.
      p. cm.
   Includes index.
   ISBN 978-1-56858-688-5 (alk. paper)—ISBN 978-1-56858-695-3 (ebook)
1. United States—Politics and government—2009- 2. United States—Economic
conditions—2009- 3. United States—Social conditions—21st century. 4. United
States—Military policy. 5. National security—United States. 6. Right and left
(Political science)—United States. 7. Obama, Barack. I. Title.

E907.V36 2011
973.932—dc23
                                                                    2011025291

10 9 8 7 6 5 4 3 2 1

# Contents

## PART III » HERDING ELEPHANTS

## PART IV » TOWARD A NEW NATIONAL SECURITY

# Introduction

As EDITOR OF A MAGAZINE founded by abolitionists in 1865—
a magazine committed to truth-telling, exposing injustice, rooting
out corruption, pushing transformative ideas, and fighting for a
more just and peaceful world—my work is often exhilarating,
usually meaningful and demanding.

Working at this rhythm, it's easy to lose a sense of possibility
and perspective—and certainly of idealism and hope—when
confronted by the forces of reaction and misinformation that
afflict our politics and media. To be editor at a time of radical
media transformation can sometimes lead to vertigo. But I've
tried to keep my balance, and worked (with a superb team) to
ensure that *The Nation* and TheNation.com engage the 24/7
media cycle with integrity—using all of the new media tools—
in order to better amplify our independent journalism. Yet I
also find ways to counter the frenetic pace and the occasional
dimming of spirits: dirty martinis (straight up), segments of
*Treme* and *True Blood*, listening to Aretha Franklin, Marvin Gaye
and Annie Lennox, long walks in Riverside Park with my husband and daughter (when she's home from college) and taking
the long view of Martin Luther King's arc of history that bends
towards justice.

Above all, I'm sustained by a core conviction—one articulated by both the poet Seamus Heaney and the people's bard Studs Terkel—that there is truth worth honoring. Studs, a regular *Nation* contributor, had a steely-sweet determination to tackle the odds and believed action engenders hope. Heaney wrote, "Hope is not optimism, which expects things to turn out well, but something rooted in the conviction that there is good worth working for." My hope is that the writing in this modest collection is infused with that spirit.

I've given this collection the title *The Change I Believe In* because these columns reflect how I've navigated the Obama era—as an editor and writer, a woman, a citizen of conscience and a small-"d" democrat. My journey has been similar to that of millions of Americans—from the exhilaration engendered by Obama's election and the first months of his presidency, which galvanized so much hope, through the disappointments.

The change I believe in is not one that happens in one or two or even three election cycles, or through a top-down approach—no matter who is president. The change I believe in will come largely from below, through determined idealism and grounded pragmatism. The change I believe in recognizes that we're living in a system hardwired to resist fundamental reform, in a political environment warped by corporate money and power. The change I believe in recognizes that it will take savvy organizing and smart inside-outside strategies by activists and principled political leaders to effectively counter and overcome the entrenched status quo. The change I believe in reflects candidate Obama's words in 2008 when he spoke of his hope for real change coming about by "imagining and then fighting and then working for what did not seem possible before."

Despite the fact that we might see few reasons for optimism, in contrast to the hope we felt during those early days of the Obama Administration, these columns reflect my abiding belief that we can indeed forge a politics of conviction. But it is not a project for the faint of heart: For me and those I consider allies, as well as those I hope to persuade, rebuilding our democracy is no short-term undertaking. It is an act of engagement that demands commitment and a steadfast belief that the forces of decency and humanity will prevail over those of reaction and division. As I write in "Hope in 2011": "Dark periods come and go. They can be overcome when those of us who are affronted by private greed and reactionary overreach stand together and fight for time-tested as well as innovative solutions to what plagues us, when we revitalize independent organizing and craft strategies to rebuild, revive and reclaim democracy."

»»»

My views on change and how to achieve it have evolved during my years at *The Nation*. In many ways, I embarked on my informal political education and found my voice at the magazine. I started as an intern in 1980, soon after Victor Navasky—a magnificent mentor—became *The Nation*'s editor. My stint was a kind of political and journalistic boot camp. The office was full of vivid characters, creative dissenters and shoe-leather journalists. Christopher Hitchens, freshly arrived from the UK's *New Statesman*, seemed to be a whirling dervish and brilliant writing machine. Andrew Kopkind, the model of a politically engaged journalist, inspired us with stories of his reporting from Washington to Hanoi, from Selma in 1965 to Prague in the wake of the 1968 Soviet invasion.

From 1984 to 1988 I was an associate *Nation* editor. Beginning in 1988, I became editor at large (and at liberty), spending a considerable part of that time with my husband, an exchange scholar, in Moscow—a city I first visited in 1978—reporting from the frontlines of Perestroika for *The Nation* and other outlets. In 1994, Victor took a sabbatical (at the Harvard Business School!) and asked me to sit in his chair as acting editor. A year later I became editor of *The Nation*.

My sixteen years as editor have also been turbulent times for America. I'm reminded of those events by the vast mountain of perilously stacked manila files behind my desk. These files stretch back in time: from the Clinton impeachment to the Supreme Court's selection of President George W. Bush in 2000; from 9/11 to the bombing of Afghanistan and the run-up to the Iraq War, and revelations of torture and abuse at Abu Ghraib; from Hurricane Katrina to America's worst financial crisis since the Great Depression and Obama's electrifying election. I have certainly never experienced a week like the one described by *The Nation's* founding editors, who wrote in the very first line of the magazine's first issue: "The week has been singularly barren of exciting events."

*The Nation's* coverage of all of those events and more has only increased my respect for this extraordinary institution and the debates—both civil and uncivil—that fill its pages and now its web pages. My work has many moving parts, but a central role for me is deciding (and occasionally drafting) a weekly editorial that speaks for the magazine, while also seeking an array of voices and ideas to challenge the limits of this country's political debate and lay out clear alternatives for the future. Over the years, I have sometimes struggled to respect and articulate conflicting views; but I have encouraged our contributors and columnists to disagree, argue and debate among themselves in our pages on matters of principle, practicality, politics, policy and even morality. I've usually reveled in our debates—over intervention, patriotism, Pacifica, pornography, religion, impeachment, Ralph Nader's candidacy (we urged him not to run in 2000—and again in 2004) and, more recently, Obama's presidency. Sometimes, however, debates at *The Nation* have descended to bickering, or ad hominem attacks, leading me to sympathize with a reader in Eugene, Oregon, who in 2003 asked, "can't you all just get along?" Or, as I like to say to my colleagues, paraphrasing the great singer Odetta: you might not agree with one another about everything, but can't you work together to turn this country around? (That said, I tend to agree with former *Nation* editor and publisher Oswald Garrison Villard, who remarked that if a week went by without the requisite number of cancellations, he felt his editorial hand might be slipping.)

I follow in the footsteps of remarkable editors who worked in that same spirit throughout *The Nation*'s history, including the magazine's first woman editor, Freda Kirchwey. Kirchwey, who was also publisher, led *The Nation* from 1937 to 1955. She was an early feminist, a fiercely principled and early opponent of fascism, and a foe of Mccarthyism and the civil liberties abuses it wrought. She was so tough and feisty a supporter of the World War II effort that after killing several columns by former editor and pacifist Villard, he wrote her a resignation letter the likes of which I've never seen (and as editor I've received my share of irate correspondence from columnists): "You have, according to my beliefs, prostituted *The Nation*, and I hope honestly that it will die very soon or fall into other hands."

But *The Nation* didn't die. It thrived. In fact, it's now America's oldest continuously published political weekly. Another former editor Carey McWilliams, who ran the magazine from 1955 to 1975, explained the secret of its longevity this way: "It is precisely because *The Nation*'s backers cared more about what it stood for than what it earned that the magazine has survived where countless other publications with circulations in the millions have gone under."

What *The Nation* stood for—and continues to stand for—is this: a belief that there are always alternatives—in history, politics and life—that would make our country and the world more humane, just and secure. I spoke of the magazine's fierce commitment to independent journalism when *The Nation* was honored by Global Green USA in 2002 for its coverage of the nuclear danger: "From the time *The Nation* was founded by abolitionists in 1865 . . . the magazine has tried . . . to challenge the prevailing orthodoxy and narrow consensus of our public debate by bringing minority ideas into the mainstream of American political life."

Former Soviet President Mikhail Gorbachev—Global Green's founder and a remarkable man my husband and I have come to know well—has long called for "new thinking": unshackling our imagination and casting off stale and discredited ideas. Gorbachev believes that all great reform ideas and movements, such as his own, begin as heresy and as a minority. The magazine has always embraced that conception, supporting peace and justice movements, opposing US intervention in Central America, sounding the alarm about US involvement in Vietnam and, decades later, being a leading voice against the Iraq War. Our consistent and early warnings about media conglomeratization, corporatization—dare I say Murdoch-ization—helped to launch the movement to reform and democratize the US media.

We have seen time and again during the Obama presidency the need for this kind of "new thinking," as progressive change has been thwarted by structural obstacles to healthcare and financial reform, energy and immigration legislation, and most recently, a national budget that puts the needs of wealthy special interests over the needs of the people.

Yet whether in dark political moments or more hopeful ones, I've tried to preserve my sense of outrage about injustice, while always remaining humane, engaged and curious. I like to say that there is a thin line between anger and passion. I much prefer passion. It's a mantra of sorts, even if I sometimes fail to live by it.

»»»

In 2006, moved by a sense of outrage at the Bush Administration's actions in the run-up to the Iraq War, I began to write a weekly web column called *Editor's Cut*. It quickly evolved into two or three posts a week. I found it liberating to have space in which to lay out my own views—propositions and prescriptions, proposals and reflections on events large and seemingly small—always trying to redefine the debate, provide a different narrative, look beyond our downsized politics of excluded alternatives—just as the magazine does.

In February 2010, Fred Hiatt of the *Washington Post* asked me to write a weekly web column for the newspaper. Life wasn't exactly slow-paced. But the idea of reaching a broader audience and engaging in a debate too often dominated by the mainstream media and inside-the-beltway pundits was too good an opportunity to let pass. I've always believed that those who call themselves liberals, progressives or small-"d" democrats should speak to as broad an audience as possible and be bold about taking our own side in an argument. Here was a chance to do that.

This collection is comprised largely of *Editor's Cut* and *Washington Post* columns that explore not only the Obama presidency, but also what real progressive change would look like and how it can be achieved. Whether examining how we lost the opportunity to restructure rather than resuscitate the big banks; challenging the deficit hawks and the savage impact of austerity in tough economic times; explaining why we desperately need a new national security policy that makes military intervention truly the last resort; putting forth pro-democracy ideas and rebuilding our fraying social contract. And, of course, overlaying all else: navigating between hope and realism in the aftermath of Barack Obama's historic election. As I wrote in "Let's Get Real About Obama": "I think that we progressives need to be as clear-eyed, tough and pragmatic about Obama as he is about us."

»»»

In 2010, in accepting an award for women's achievements in publishing, I reflected on how my experiences in Russia over the years have informed my admiration for women who take risks for just causes. While living in Moscow I saw the perils faced by my Russian colleagues in their efforts to report, publish, and speak out. During my years at *The Nation*, I have often thought of their courage. For me, *The Nation* is an essential source for the great political debates and fateful struggles that now face our own country. I hope this small book will play a role in the quest for the kind of society we have dreamed of but not yet achieved.

# Part I

# OBAMA AND PROGRESSIVE AMERICA

# Transformational Presidency
## *November 4, 2008*

Four years ago, we gathered at *The Nation* to watch the election returns. Around midnight we began to weep. But we had to put out an issue the next day. So, through the grim night and bleak day after, as the Election 2004 verdict became clear, we held our emotions in check and worked to make sense of the disaster that had befallen the country. The cover of our issue that week was of a black sky, dark clouds obscuring a slim and crestfallen moon, with a simple headline: "Four More Years."

Four years later, our offices are filled with editors, writers, interns and colleagues—some crying, this time with joy—all jubilant about the new era of possibility opened up by Barack Obama's victory. We know there is work ahead to build a politics of sanity and justice and peace. But tonight we simply celebrate.

Obama's election marks a remarkable moment in our country's history—a milestone in America's scarred racial landscape and a victory for the forces of decency, diversity and tolerance. As our editorial board member Roger Wilkins reminded us on the eve of the election, Obama's win "doesn't turn a switch that eradicates our whole national history and culture." But "win or lose, Obama has already made this a better country, made your children's future better."

This long and winding campaign has been marked by highs and lows, necessary and unnecessary divisions, indelible characters and high drama. For the first time in decades, electoral politics became a vehicle for raising expectations and spreading hope—bringing in millions of new voters. The Obama team's respect for the core decency, dignity and intelligence of the American people was reflected in the campaign's organizing mantra—"Respect-Empower-Include." In contrast, the McCain campaign chose to denigrate voters' intelligence, spread the smears and mock the dignity of work with its cynical celebration of a plumber who wasn't really a plumber.

Grassroots engagement and record-shattering turnout contributed mightily to Obama's decisive victory. Moving forward, this small-"d" democratic movement—broad-based and energized—will be critical in overcoming the timid incrementalists, the forces of money and establishment power, that are obstacles to meaningful change. And it will be needed to forge the fate and fortune of a bold progressive agenda.

Already we hear calls that the new Democratic majority must not "overreach." That is code for "do not use your mandate." Ignore those calls—this election was a referendum on conservatism that has guided American politics since 1980. Indeed, future historians may well view Barack Obama's victory as the end of the age of Reagan and the beginning of something substantially new. And progressives can justifiably claim that the election outcome was a clear repudiation of conservative economic ideas and absurd claims that a more egalitarian approach to growth constitutes "socialism." This ideological rejection, the sharp failures of the Bush administration and, perhaps most important, the shifts in public views on the economy and the war have led to this watershed moment—a historic opportunity for a progressive governing agenda and a mandate for bold action.

The great challenge for *The Nation* and other independent and progressive forces is whether we can harness the energy and idealism unleashed by Obama's candidacy—and the collapse of conservatism—to expand the limits of the current debate. *The Nation*, unmortgaged to any economic interest or political power, will continue to challenge our downsized politics of excluded alternatives, propose bold ideas, ferret out the truth, expose corruption and abuse of power, and hold our politicians accountable. We will work with grounded realism and determined idealism to broadly re-imagine the future.

For the first time in close to a decade, there will be sympathetic allies on the inside of the Executive Branch, and we will need to pepper them with smart and strategic ideas and offer clear alternatives. And working with allies—activists, thinkers, scholars, progressive members of Congress, the netroots, engaged citizens—*The Nation* will drive not-yet-ready-for-prime time ideas into the political arena and reset the valence of our politics. We know the Democratic Party is not the only vehicle for change. Historically, the party's finest moments have come when it was pushed into action from the outside by popular social movements. That same pressure is needed now. Retreat and timidity are losing strategies for addressing economic crisis, a shredded social compact, two wars which must be ended, and a damaged reputation abroad—especially with stronger majorities in Congress and a new president who has raised expectations and promised real change.

After years of playing defense, it is time to unshackle our imaginations, build coalitions and craft creative strategies that will move, persuade and push President Obama and a new Congress to seize the mandate they have been offered. We are not naive. We know there are formidable obstacles ahead. Without organizing and grassroots pressure, the corporate power over both parties will continue to suffocate possibilities. And despite the metastasizing financial crisis, the conservative assault on government still cripples our sense of what is fully possible.

With the country at an ideological watershed, Obama has a historic opportunity to reshape the ruling paradigm of American politics. The old order that has ruled for nearly thirty years has imploded. Building a new order will require continued mobilization and strategic creativity. It will be vital to sustain a reform politics and movement independent of the administration and the Democratic leadership in Congress.

Progressives in the Senate and the House, many grouped around the Progressive Caucus, can provide both leadership and a public forum for new ideas. Cutting-edge and independent organizations like the Apollo Alliance, the Campaign for America's Future, the Institute for Policy Studies and the Economic Policy Institute can help us think outside the establishment box. Independent media, new and old—and, as in the case of *The Nation*, new/old—can track the limits of the debate and give new ideas greater visibility. Reform leaders at the state and local levels can champion legislation that will be a model for the national agenda. And the emerging grassroots movements, supported by the idealism, energy and civic spirit of the young, will be crucial to tap and channel into postelectoral organizing work.

History tells us how Franklin Delano Roosevelt was compelled to abandon caution because of the great traumas of his day. The Great Depression gave him little choice but to be bold. But it was popular social movements working outside the administration and empowered unions of that time that put strong pressure on FDR to carry out bolder reforms. That outside force was disciplined, strategic and focused, and it made the FDR years much better than if people had just sat back and let the president fend for himself against special interests. There's a powerful lesson in there for the movements of our times.

Likewise, our hard times may push Obama to become a more boldly reformist president than he had envisioned—one who really does rearrange power on behalf of the people. But as we know from history and these last years—as progressives have driven the agenda on war, a green economy, trade and energy independence—Obama will need to hear from (and listen to) the millions of grassroots activists he has inspired if he is to overcome establishment power and well-funded lobbies.

I believe the fate of Obama's presidency will be determined by how bold he chooses to be. We may not agree with everything he will do, but he has a historic opportunity to be a truly transformative president and lead the country in a new direction.

He has run a brilliant campaign in which he has spoken eloquently of the power and promise of "change from below." Will that understanding lead him to re-envision a government that truly reorders America's priorities and values, and reconnects with the needs of people? After all, isn't it long past time to confront neglected social needs, tackle the deep corruption in our financial system and corporations, restore our civil liberties and respect for human rights, enact universal health care, protect a worker's right to organize, invest in renewable energy and a green economy, end the endless wars, and regain America's standing in the world?

Tonight we celebrate. Tomorrow we begin our work—with passion, conviction, hope and determination.

---

# The First 100 Days
## *November 7, 2008*

At the end of this remarkable week, we're starting to look ahead to the First 100 Days of the Obama presidency. Already, we're hearing calls in the mainstream media warning the new administration "not to overreach." And working overtime, the Inside-the-Beltway Punditocracy continues to reveal its ability to ignore reality—even while describing itself as "realist"—with its claims that this is still a center-right nation, despite all evidence to the contrary.

But as Nobel Prize–winning economist Paul Krugman writes in today's *New York Times*, "Let's hope that Mr. Obama has the good sense to ignore this advice . . . this year's presidential election was a clear referendum on political philosophies—and the progressive philosophy won."

Obama himself has talked about needing to measure his accomplishments over the first 1,000 Days, rather than 100, given the problems he has inherited from arguably the worst president ever (my words, not Obama's). Indeed, it will take years to undo the damage of the Bush administration and the conservative ideology that has dominated this country for nearly thirty years. But the First 100 Days are still crucial—not only in signaling to the American people and the world that the administration will take determined steps to repair this nation—but there is a historical precedent for the need to move forward expeditiously in order to seize the moment and the mandate.

President Obama will need to be bold to deal with the challenges he faces: a cratering economy, broken healthcare system, two wars, poverty and inequality, and the stained US reputation in the world. The millions who were mobilized and inspired by Obama's campaign and candidacy also have their work cut out for them—continuing to drive a bold agenda to respond to these crises—just as progressives have in recent years on the war, energy independence, trade, healthcare, and other issues that are defining the new "center" of American politics and hearts and minds.

Here is a list of actions—ones I care deeply about—that President Obama can take in the First 100 Days to immediately achieve real and significant change. Some of these he can literally achieve on Day 1 with the stroke of a pen, others will demand coalition building and an inside-outside strategy to push legislation.

**Bush Executive Orders:** As Obama himself said of his First 100 days when campaigning in Denver, "I would call my attorney general in and review every single executive order issued by George Bush and overturn those laws or executive decisions that I feel violate the constitution."

**Economic Stimulus:** Stop the bleeding—through expanded health and unemployment benefits and providing real aid to beleaguered state and local governments so they can sustain essential public services.

**Iraq:** Present a plan and hold to your timeline for withdrawal.

**Healthcare Reform:** Begin immediately by expanding health insurance to kids and passing the State Children's Health Insurance Program legislation vetoed by Bush.

**Women's Health and Reproductive Rights:** Repeal the Global Gag Rule that requires NGOs receiving federal funding to neither promote nor perform abortions in other countries.

**Energy and the Economy:** Announce a clean energy strategy that will reduce oil dependence, address global warming, create thousands of green jobs and improve national security. Groups like the Apollo Alliance, Center for American Progress and Natural Resources Defense Council have strong and concrete plans in this regard. Incorporate elements of this plan into a stimulus package.

**Bailout for Main Street:** Work to ensure that homeowners have real opportunities to renegotiate mortgages and remain in their homes.

**Poverty and Inequality:** Appoint a Hunger Czar—as Senator George McGovern and Congressman Jim McGovern call for in a recent op-ed—who would "coordinate the various food, nutrition and anti-poverty programs . . . to increase the independence, purchasing power and food security of every human being." Announce your commitment to the goal of cutting poverty in half in ten years.

**Labor and Trade:** Reject Colombia, Korea and Panama trade agreements as currently written and ensure future agreements promote the public interest. Work toward passage of Employee Free Choice Act.

**Science:** Allow federal funding of embryonic stem cell research.

**Global Warming:** Reverse the Bush EPA decision and allow California to regulate greenhouse gas emissions from cars and trucks. Call for a new climate treaty and ask Al Gore to lead that effort.

**Guantánamo:** Close it and try people in the United States or resettle them in countries where they face no risk of persecution or torture. *New York Times* columnist Nicholas Kristof offers a compelling idea to "turn it into an international center for research on tropical diseases that afflict poor countries . . . [serving as] an example of multilateral humanitarianism"

**Detention:** Close all CIA black sites and secret detention sites. End extraordinary rendition. Abolish preventive detention that allows people to be held indefinitely without charge. Initiate criminal investigations into programs of rendition and secret detention. End trials by military commission. End opposition to full habeas corpus hearings for detainees in Guantánamo and other similar situations. Make known the names and whereabouts of all those detained in rendition and secret detention programs.

**Torture:** End use in court of any evidence obtained through torture. Officially reject all memos, signing statements and executive orders that justify the use of torture. Establish an independent commission of inquiry into all aspects of detention and interrogation practices in the "war on terror." Announce your administration will work for redress and remedy for victims of human rights violations for which US authorities are found to be responsible.

**Protect Dissent:** Ensure that the FBI adheres to surveillance guidelines. Open Justice Department investigation into surveillance-related misconduct. Pledge to end all secret surveillance programs not reviewed by courts or Congressional committees.

**Limit State Secrets Privilege:** Issue new Executive Orders that reverse the expansion of state secrets privilege and the over-classification of documents. Pass legislation making it clear that military contractors are accountable for abuses.

**Roll Back Executive Power:** Repudiate the unitary presidency. Renounce use of signing statements as a tool for altering legislation. Pledge to abide by the War Powers Act and end abuse of Authorization to Use Military Force. (Or as Bruce Fein—a key player in the Reagan Justice Department—said, "Renounce presidential power to initiate war anywhere on the planet, including Iran.")

These are doable, and by taking these steps—with deliberate haste—President Obama would get a real start on repairing our nation and people's lives.

# How Audacious Will Obama Choose to Be?
*January 21, 2009*

President Barack Obama takes office at a time defined by hope and fear in equal measure. To confront this nation's many challenges he will need to act swiftly, show that he is on the side of people whose homes are being foreclosed and jobs lost, and invest political capital—along with trillions of dollars—in a sustained recovery program. While many caution our new president to tread carefully, the reality is that half-steps will not lay the groundwork for a new economy that is more just and fair. Only by effectively marshaling the power of government can Obama improve the actual conditions of peoples' lives—and consign antigovernment evangelists to the dustbin of history.

Fortunately, Obama has a mandate for change. People support reconstruction of America's crumbling physical infrastructure, and of our society. Here are a few steps I hope President Obama will take: reverse our deepening economic inequality by using this country's still immense wealth to assure that all Americans have the healthcare, housing and education they need; re-engage the world with wisdom and humility about the limits of military power; cut billions from wasteful defense budgets that empty our treasury without making us more secure; tackle the deep corruption in a financial system that consistently favors corporations over workers; respond with urgency to the climate crisis with an Apollo-like project to make America a clean-energy innovator; restore our tattered Constitution; protect a worker's right to organize; define a new spirit of sacrifice and service; clean up our elections; and reaffirm his campaign-trail commitment to end not just the war in Iraq but also "end the mindset that took us into" that war. Do not endanger the promise of this administration by escalating militarily in Afghanistan, further draining resources that are vital for rebuilding here at home and impede critical international initiatives such as renewing the Middle East peace process.

That's a bold agenda millions can believe in. In fact, it's what millions voted for. This new president does not have to pull his punches, and Americans do not have to settle for less. As the first Community-Organizer-in-Chief, Obama understands the power of change from below. He has oxygenated the grassroots and got people believing and dreaming again. But he will only be as brave as ordinary citizens move him to be. That's why independent small-"d" democratic movements, grassroots organizing, online and offline, will be vital to pushing the limit of Obama's own politics and countering the forces of money and establishment power which remain obstacles to meaningful reform. A savvy inside-outside political strategy, engaging the new administration and Congress constructively, even as progressives push for solutions on a scale necessary to deliver, will be critical if we are to fulfill the promise of relief, reform and reconstruction.

We celebrate the beginning of a new era, and we recognize that the fate of an Obama presidency may well be determined by how audacious he chooses to be. During the campaign, our new president told us that real change comes about by "imagining and then fighting for and then working for what did not seem possible before." If Americans keep fighting for that change, we can reaffirm our expectations of our new president, and together complete the unfinished work of making America a more perfect union.

# 100 Down, 900 to Go
## *April 22, 2009*

As we mark the first 100 days of his presidency, it is staggering to consider the enormous challenges President Obama inherited from his predecessor, arguably the worst president ever. Can the devastation wrought by an eight-year nightmare be sorted out in 100 Days? Of course it can't. That's why Obama himself talked about needing to measure his accomplishments not by the first 100 days, but by the first 1,000.

Yet as we near this iconic marker—whether one is disappointed by some key appointments (read on), the size of the recovery bill, escalation in Afghanistan, the bank bailout plan or other issues—this president must be given credit for hitting the ground running and confronting challenges head on. Brutal and fundamental fights still lie ahead—on energy, healthcare, the budget, to name a few.

Obama understood the power—both symbolic and real—of swift, smart action, even within the first 100 hours of his inauguration. He pledged to close Guantánamo and the CIA black sites. He quickly passed a strong recovery bill—even if it was smaller than it should have been; that bill and his proposed budget begin to lay out a new blueprint for economic recovery and reconstruction, and a break with ill-conceived dogma about deficit reduction that has defined and limited economic policy for thirty years. He repealed the global gag order, took steps to restore science to its proper place with regard to stem cell research and addressing climate change, and has embarked on a substantive transformation to a clean energy economy.

On diplomacy, Obama has shown a willingness to engage with countries that may have interests and ideas that diverge from those of the United States. He's expressed support for a more central US role in global alliances, including a firm endorsement of the UN, and on recent trips to Europe and Latin America he's set a new tone of respect and listening. He's declared his commitment to nuclear abolition and, in doing so, has opened the door to a renewed and wiser nuclear nonproliferation framework. He has begun to reset the relationship with Russia, reexamining the folly of missile defense, putting NATO expansion on the back burner, and cooperating on regional diplomacy to stabilize Afghanistan. After years of failed policy toward Cuba, the administration has created new possibilities for cooperation by lifting restrictions on Cuban Americans' visits to relatives and the amount of money they can send to them. Diplomatic overtures to Iran have also opened new windows of possibility. Obama has committed to withdrawing from Iraq on a faster timetable—and we need to push him to adhere to his commitment to security through withdrawal. It's disappointing to see his support for increasing the defense budget with a new focus on counterinsurgency and low-intensity conflict. But, in all, we see in Obama a sense of responsibility and a desire to reengage the world on new terms, following eight years of arrogance and swagger. We see the rough outline of an Obama Doctrine—progressive realism—a belief, as the president stated, that "we do our best to promote our ideals and our values by our example." What will be the real test, however, is the one Obama recently described at the Summit of the Americas, "The test for all of us is not simply words, but also deeds."

But there are two areas which I fear could endanger the Obama presidency: military escalation in Afghanistan and the bank bailout. With the cratering economy, and most projections indicating double-digit unemployment through 2011, there is a sense that he has given with one hand through his recovery plan and budget proposal, but tied the other with a bank bailout that could undermine much of the good in his economic plan. The contrast between the treatment of the auto industry, where workers and managers and creditors and shareholders are taking the hits, and the bailout of banks is corrosive. The selection of the Summers/Geithner team was a huge missed opportunity and misstep. When more bonuses are paid out, and more self-dealing exposed, we may see more anger—especially right-wing populism. On Afghanistan, I am concerned that it will bleed us of the resources needed for economic recovery, further destabilize Pakistan, open a rift with our European allies, and negate the positive effects of withdrawing from Iraq on our image in the Muslim world.

Alternatively, there is reason for optimism. The president's commitment to pragmatism and experimentation suggests that—if the bank bailout doesn't work, and he's confronted by mobilized citizens and thinkers who understand the endemic problems of the Summers/Geithner approach—he may ultimately move to a Plan B or even a Team B in order to maintain his popularity and credibility, and keep his agenda alive.

We can also hope that hearings in Congress, and pressure from citizens who seek a non-military path to security in Afghanistan and Pakistan, will push the administration to bear down on regional diplomacy, commonsense counter-terrorism measures, and targeted development aid as the most effective security policies to stabilize the region.

Other issues will measure not only Obama's fighting spirit, but whether this Congress has the spine to be a reform Congress, and whether progressives can mobilize to create space in a system hardwired to resist change.

Key challenges lie ahead. Healthcare will be a brutal battle, as will the energy and climate bill. The gloves are already off over the Employee Free Choice Act, and we can't afford to lose that fight—even if it means a compromise, but one that retains key elements of the bill. Will Obama stand for universal healthcare with an option for a public plan? Without that option, meaningful healthcare reform is in real trouble. On these issues and others, will the president temper one of his favorite phrases—"don't let the perfect be the enemy of the good"—in order to push the limits of the possible? There is a fine line between necessary compromises in order to achieve profound change and watering down polices to appease for-profit special interests.

With regard to torture—Obama took the much needed step of immediately renouncing it, ending its use, and releasing the memos. But we need to hold not only the architects of illegal activity responsible but also those who implemented it. Torture remains a sore on the body republic, and Congress needs to ensure accountability for the future of our democracy and our reputation in the eyes of the world.

But the defining political struggle ahead is the budget. President Obama knows that the right isn't going to give an inch, that members of his own party are turning tail and fixating on deficits instead of investment, and that some of the missteps of his own economic team have made the budget debate even more difficult. Progressives will need to confront lobbies mobilized to halt essential reforms. For better or worse, this president has shown himself as open to influence—he's malleable—and progressives need to keep that in mind as we fight for an agenda that is just, sustainable and real.

## Let's Get Real about Obama
### *August 13, 2009*

It's been a rough and tough few months. And this August is making a bid to replace the Ides of (is it?) March as the meanest month in our calendar. From a slew of intense late night and early morning calls, I know that many progressives are wondering: Who did we vote for? (And I won't pose the David Axelrod question: Are you Muhammad Ali or Sonny Liston? Though I confess I think it's one worth asking right now.)

Now, no one on the left with any savvy or knowledge of history believed we wouldn't live—and learn—through disappointment. Isn't that what politicians are for? And anyone who believed Obama was going to remain an idealistic community organizer, well—I got a bridge to sell you.

Still, questions remain: Couldn't he have picked a cabinet filled with that real team of rivals? Why not include a Joseph Stiglitz along with a Larry Summers and let the sparks fly? It might have led to a kind of creative de/construction. Where is the organizing out of the White House—committed to overtaking those who would undermine its message and policies? And couldn't Obama, like FDR, have used this moment of crisis, admittedly not as severe as 1933, but still as severe as many living have experienced, to restructure—not simply resuscitate—the smug financial sector? Couldn't he have used his pulpit and brilliant speaking skills to explain that what we need to fear is joblessness—not deficits? Or as one of the great historians of the New Deal, David Kennedy, argued, Obama "will be judged not simply on whether he manages a rescue from the current economic crisis but also on whether he grasps the opportunity to make us more resilient to face those future crises that inevitably await us."

The healthcare fight is still up for grabs, yet the emerging stories of White House deal-making with the drug and insurance industries—and with the heavily mortgaged Max Baucus and the Senate Finance Committee—are more than dispiriting. Yet we also confront a political landscape filled with those who fulminate at rallies about government overreach—the very same folks who should stop, take a deep breath and understand what their lives would be like without government programs like Social Security and Medicare. These are the very programs that Roosevelt, and then Lyndon Johnson, and subsequent Democratic and, yes, Republican presidents and Congresses put in place to temper for generations what FDR liked to call the "hazards and vicissitudes" of life.

In this hot month of town halls filled with raging, often inchoate, anger on the right—and a season of disappointment among progressives, I wanted to repost what I wrote just a few days after that glorious election night in 2008—a night in which the forces of decency and dignity vanquished those forces which hate and demean the possibilities of government and cheer on the forces of reaction at home and abroad. Let's not forget that as we move forward.

Here's what I wrote on November 23, 2008:

I think that we progressives need to be as clear-eyed, tough and pragmatic about Obama as he is about us.

President-elect Obama is a centrist at a time when centrism means energy independence and green jobs and universal healthcare and massive economic stimulus programs and government intervention in the economy. He is a pragmatist at a moment when pragmatism and the scale of our financial crisis compel him to adopt bold policies. He is a cautious leader at a time when, to paraphrase *New York Times* columnist Paul Krugman, caution is the new risky. The great traumas of our day do not allow for cautious steps or responses.

At 143 years old (that's *The Nation*'s age, not mine), we like a little bit of history with our politics. And while Lincoln's way of picking a cabinet frames this transition moment, it's worth remembering another template for governing. Franklin Delano Roosevelt was compelled to become a bolder and, yes, more progressive president (if progressive means ensuring that the actual conditions of peoples' lives improve through government acts) as a result of the strategically placed mobilization and pressure of organized movements.

That history makes me think that this is the moment for progressives to avoid falling into either of two extremes—reflexively defensive or reflexively critical. We'd be wiser and more effective if we followed the advice of one of *The Nation*'s valued editorial board members who shared thoughts with the Board at our meeting on Friday, November 21, 2008.

1. It will take large-scale, organized movements to win transformative change. There is no civil rights legislation without the movement, no New Deal without the unions and the unemployed councils, no end to slavery without the abolitionists. In our era, this will need to play out at two levels: district-by-district and state-by-state organizing to get us to the 218 and sixty votes necessary to pass any major legislation; and the movement energy that can create public will, a new narrative and move the elites in DC to shift from orthodoxy. The energy in the country needs to be converted into real organization.

2. We need to be able to play inside and outside politics at the same time. I think this will be challenging for those of us schooled in the habits of pure opposition and protest. We need to make an effort to engage the new administration and Congress constructively, even as we push without apology for solutions at a scale necessary to deliver. This is

in the interest of the Democratic Party—which rode the wave of a new coalition of African Americans, Latinos, young people, women, etc.—but they have been beaten down by conservative attacks, and the natural impulse will be caution and hiding behind desks.

3. Progressives need to stick up especially forcefully for the most vulnerable parts of the coalition—poor people, immigrants, etc.—those who got almost no mention during the election and will be most likely to be left off the bus.

# Obama Must Reclaim the Debate
## *September 8, 2009*

Barack Obama's genius was to run a campaign that understood how much Americans wanted change. On Wednesday evening, when he speaks to a joint session of Congress, President Obama will need to reclaim that genius. And he will need to reclaim the debate from those who would deny the urgency of real healthcare reform for the millions insured, underinsured and uninsured.

Obama will be most persuasive if he speaks with passion about his principles and priorities—and draws some lines in the sand. A key line is support of a strong public option—not as a liberal litmus test but as a critical part of expanding coverage, reining in costs and disciplining rapacious insurance companies. He must explain in clear and simple language that the alternative—a "trigger"—is a trap to kill healthcare reform; and that even if "trigger" conditions are met years from now, big insurance companies will start the fight all over again to stop the public option from going into effect. And by any reasonable measure conditions for triggering a public plan have already been met because insurance companies have failed to rein in costs and expand coverage! As for those ballyhooed nonprofit coops, Obama should explain why they won't have any real bargaining leverage to get lower prices because they'll be too small. Define the public plan for what it is: pragmatic, principled and all-American in how it privileges choice and competition.

Obama must invoke history. He should place himself squarely in the tradition of those reform presidents—Roosevelt, Truman, Johnson—who labored hard for universal healthcare. Remind people that the Democrats are the party which brought them the two most popular domestic government programs—Social Security and Medicare—which have improved the condition of their lives in the 20th century. Tell people: "We brought you Medicare. They opposed it. Now we're trying to fix the healthcare system. And—sound familiar? Once again, they are opposing it."

Obama should also explain why bipartisanship ain't what it used to be. This GOP is a party out to cripple or kill reform, and with it the future success of Obama's presidency. As the eminent Roosevelt scholar Jean Edward Smith recently argued, "This fixation on securing bipartisan support for healthcare reform suggests that the Democratic party has forgotten how to govern and the White House has forgotten how to lead."

The president should challenge the Blue Dogs. Place the burden on them to get out of the way of the majority in favor of a comprehensive plan. The question isn't whether the progressive majority is unreasonably resisting reform to save the public option. The question is whether a small minority of conservative Democrats will sabotage reform simply to stop the public option. Do the Blue Dogs wish to cripple their own president in his first year in office for seeking an objective that has been the stated goal of their party since the Truman administration?

Obama must lead the charge and rally the people who swept him into the White House. And challenge the Democrats. Make it clear to the Democratic Caucus in general, and to the Blue Dogs in particular, that for the sake of the country they must vote for cloture so that a bill that will accomplish substantive reform can have an up-or-down vote on the floor. Don't heed those who counsel incrementalism or bipartisanship at all cost. The art of the possible is not the same as the art of incrementalism. And healthcare reform enacted by a Democratic majority is still meaningful reform.

If President Obama can boldly lay out those principles and priorities that inspired the movement which swept him into office, Americans will stand and fight with him to make the changes this nation so desperately needs.

# The Burden and The Nobel
## October 11, 2009

The choice has always been, as a former chair of the Nobel Peace Prize judging committee explained in 2001, "a political act." This year it was also an ingenious leap of faith—the endorsement of the hope and the promise represented by America's new president. Of course, it was also a pointed rebuke to the unilateral recklessness of the Bush administration, with its aversion to international organizations and diplomacy. (As were the awards given to former President Jimmy Carter and Vice President Al Gore.)

Perhaps the committee, in welcoming Obama's re-embrace of the global community, should have also honored the millions of Americans who voted for Obama—and who, in so doing, helped redeem America's image.

I think those who argue that the Prize is cheapened are just plain silly. The Prize doesn't go to only those who have succeeded in their efforts, nor is it a lifetime achievement award. Instead, it is often and wisely given to endorse and encourage those who are working to bring about a better and more peaceful world. As Thorbjorn Jagland, the committee's new chair, said: "It's important for the committee to recognize people who are struggling and idealistic, but we cannot do that every year. We must from time to time go into the real of realpolitik. It is always a mix of idealism and realpolitik that can change the world."

Finally, for those who are really worried about the devaluing of the Peace Price (and this crowd includes people who've been bashing peace for decades), remember that Henry Kissinger is a previous winner. (Or, as Maureen Dowd put it, "Any peace prize that goes to Henry Kissinger but not Gandhi ain't worth a can of Alpo.")

Many domestic commentators have also obsessed over the Peace Prize's political liability for Obama. A cynical type, arguing in the *Washington Post*, wrote, "if the international community thinks so highly of him, perhaps it is because he shares their ultra-liberal agenda; perhaps it is because he cares more deeply about global causes than vital US interests." This kind of thinking reveals the zero-sum mindset—the dangerous fusion of US exceptionalism and provincialism—which has caused this country and the world so much trouble and insecurity.

In other parts of the world, more humane and wiser comments have been circulating. The other evening, I received some optimistic, insightful thoughts from Pierre Schori, the former UN Ambassador from Sweden and Olof Palme's close adviser:

I think this decision was bold and ingenious. Obama gives us breathing-space in a dangerous world where there are too many trigger-happy people. He inspires hope for the many dispossessed, but also to us who are worried about how dangerous crises are handled. While meeting resistance at home from some quarters, the governments of Europe keep their mouth shut when he is trying to dialogue with Iran, Cuba and Venezuela and deal with the Middle East, etc. He has started the exit from Iraq. He is a new kind of American President, a cosmopolit [sic] with the world on his mind. While sitting in meetings with his advisers on Afghanistan, the Prize will hopefully help him to a wise decision. He did a great thing for peace beating Bush and McCain. . . . Now America, with Obama in the White House, we are all better off and safer. His visit to the UN bears evidence of this—he has paid all debts to the UN, he got the Security Council to adopt a statement on nuclear-free world and promised support to UN peace-keeping which is in deep crisis. He has started processes that we all now need to support as world citizens.

I value Schori's thoughts. Of course, there are people who are angered by this decision because they rightly worry that the president is poised to further escalate an unnecessary and destructive war in Afghanistan. They believe he is all words and, as of yet, very few deserving deeds. What seems clear is there is much ahead to do—and much to earn—if the committee's decision is to be validated. Obama himself acknowledged the roads not yet taken in his graceful acceptance remarks: "Let me be clear, I do not view this award as a recognition of my own accomplishments, but rather as an affirmation of American leadership on behalf of aspirations held by people in all nations. . . . I will accept this award as a call to action."

Perhaps we should think of this year's Nobel Peace Prize as the strategic Nobel. Its strategy is to strengthen Obama's resolve to work for a nuclear weapons–free world; strengthen his campaign promises to engage Iran and North Korea; and provide momentum to find a non-military path to ending the war in Afghanistan.

# Give Up on Postpartisanship
## *January 21, 2010*

Election results rarely have a single explanation. Yet it's pretty clear that Scott Brown's win in a state that last sent a Republican to the Senate in 1972 is an indicator of the anti-establishment anger sweeping through this country. It has only been reinforced by a White House that has delivered for Wall Street, but hasn't done enough for Main Street's hurting communities. And it is an anger that is fueled by savage right-wing antigovernment attacks.

Massachusetts' special election is a wake-up call. The Democratic Party can no longer run as a managerial and technocratic party. Going populist is now smart politics and good policy.

The Obama White House needs to take immediate, bold action to show that it stands squarely with the working people of America. It needs to fight hard for jobs and a just economy of shared prosperity.

Here's a symbolic, but smart start: jettison those on the White House economic team whose slow, timid response to the crisis of unemployment and to Wall Street's obscene excesses helped create the conditions for the Tea Party's inchoate right-wing populism.

The Bay State offers another lesson. Barack Obama's decision to demobilize his base after his victory, in favor of an insider approach to governing, was a big mistake. I'm not a political strategist, but I don't know how you win elections by failing to rally the people who've worked so passionately at the grassroots to get you elected. It's time to re-mobilize the base.

And here's a no-brainer: after a year of being knifed by the GOP at every turn, isn't it time to give up on faith in genteel postpartisanship? Go after those who oppose your common-sense tax on big banks to recoup the taxpayer-funded bailout money.

Getting the strongest possible healthcare bill as quickly as possible is now key. Passing the Senate bill first, and then quickly fixing it through the reconciliation process, could create strong political pressure for reviving the public option or Medicare buy-in.

Passing a bill won't be the Democrats' political salvation. But if Mr. Obama and his party fail, it may well snuff out any chance for reform in other areas like financial regulation, immigration and labor rights.

President Obama warned us that change wouldn't come easy. Many believe he hasn't held up his end in fighting hard enough for key progressive priorities. What comes next will be a real test of his willingness to learn lessons from this past year.

President Obama: don't pay attention to those who counsel going slow. The only thing you have to fear is caution itself.

# Obama, One Year On
*November 4, 2009*

Barack Obama was elected president at a time defined by hope and fear in equal measure. It was a remarkable moment in our country's history—a milestone in America's scarred racial landscape and a victory for the forces of decency, diversity and tolerance. For the first time in decades, electoral politics became a vehicle for raising expectations and spreading hope while it mobilized millions of new voters. Obama's was a campaign built on the power and promise of change from below. At the same time, he was elected as the nation was rapidly sinking into the worst economic downturn since the Great Depression.

The night Obama was elected, relief was felt around the world. There was a widespread feeling that the United States had turned its back on eight years of destructive, swaggering unilateralism and was re-embracing the global community. In many ways, the election was a referendum on an extremist conservatism that has guided (and deformed) American politics and society since the 1980s. The spectacular failures of the Bush administration and the shifts in public opinion on the economy and the Iraq War presented a mandate for bold action and a historic opportunity for a progressive governing agenda.

A year later, it's clear we are a long way from building a new order and transforming the prevailing paradigm of American politics. That will take more than one election. It requires continued mobilization, strategic creativity and, yes, audacity on the part of independent thinkers, activists and organizers. The structural obstacles to change are considerable. But at least we now have the political space to push for far-reaching reforms.

Whatever one thinks of Obama's policy on any specific issue, he is clearly a reform president committed to the improvement of people's lives and to the renewal and reconstruction of America. Yes, his economic recovery plan was too small and too deferential to the Republican Party and tax cuts. But it has kept the economy from falling into the abyss, and it includes more new net public investment in anti-poverty measures than any program since Lyndon Johnson's Great Society.

We need a much more robust jobs program—without one, Americans will not believe this president stands with the working people. Obama would be wise to use his presidential pulpit and brilliant oratorical skills to explain that when one out of six Americans is unemployed or underemployed, our greatest fear should be joblessness, not deficits.

Still, there's much to be praised. Obama has spoken eloquently of a new and progressive role for government. His first appointment to the Supreme Court, Sonia Sotomayor, was a strong choice—the first Latina on the Court and a powerful progressive jurist. In selecting Sotomayor, Obama has finally halted the Court's long drift to the right. The president says the labor movement is the solution, not the problem. (If he really believes this, he should act on it by pushing for speedy passage of the Employee Free Choice Act.) He has reinvigorated the regulatory agencies in Washington, from the EPA to the FCC (in doing so he has, ironically, fueled a full-employment program for K Street lobbyists). He has repealed the global gag rule on abortion, has spoken of the urgency of climate crisis and has restored integrity to the government's scientific research programs.

The president's quartet of major speeches abroad—in Cairo, Prague, Moscow and Accra—began to lay out an Obama Doctrine in international affairs: support for diplomacy and the UN; commitment to a nuclear-free world; a belief that democracy is strengthened not through US intervention but when people win for themselves their rights and liberties; and engagement and cooperation with, rather than antagonism toward, the Muslim world. However, the military-industrial complex Eisenhower warned against grows ever stronger. And so far Obama has been unwilling to rethink skewed priorities in this arena; he just approved a bloated military budget despite his rare cancellation of several costly weapons programs.

And then, of course, there is Afghanistan. Historians have warned that wars kill reform presidencies. The most recent, and perhaps most relevant, example is the Vietnam War's undermining of the Great Society. Obama is wisely taking his time to make a decision about Afghanistan, but he appears to have excluded the one option that makes the most sense—a responsible exit strategy—and seems poised to escalate this unnecessary war. If he does so, he will endanger his reform presidency and squander funds needed to rebuild and renew our country.

Obama could have used the moment of economic crisis to restructure the economy and rein in the financial sector, not simply resuscitate it. The taxpayer-funded bailout of the banks has contributed to a popular backlash. If Obama doesn't respond to the widespread anguish and anger with constructive support for those in need, the GOP will continue to channel it in destructive directions.

There are other disappointments. I am sure you have your list. At the top of mine is Obama's failure to end the excesses and abuses associated with the Bush/Cheney national security apparatus; also on it is his unwillingness to push more strongly for a public option on healthcare reform. But instead of playing the betrayal sweepstakes, which promotes disappointment and despair, we'd be smart to practice a progressive politics defined by realistic hope and pragmatism. That is, simply denouncing the administration's missteps and failures doesn't get us very far and furthers what our adversaries seek: our disempowerment. We can't afford that. These are times to avoid falling into either of two extremes: reflexively defensive or reflexively critical.

Remember that throughout our history, it has taken large-scale, sustained organizing to win structural change. There would have been no New Deal without the vast upsurge in union activism and unemployed councils, no civil rights legislation without the mass movement. We need to learn from those inspiring examples and build our own movements. And we need to start playing inside-outside politics, too: engage the administration and Congress, even as we push without apology for bolder solutions than the ones Obama has offered.

Progressives should focus less on the limits of the Obama agenda and more on the possibilities that his presidency opens up. Like all presidents, Obama is constrained by powerful opponents and deep structural impediments. Independent organizing and savvy coalition-building will be critical in overcoming the timid incrementalists of his own party and the forces of money and establishment power that are obstacles to change. But if we work effectively, we can push Obama beyond the limits of his own politics and create a new progressive era.

# Obama Can't "Plug the Damn Hole," but He Can Seize the Damn Crisis
### *June 7, 2010*

There's no question that the Obama administration was slow to get on top of the BP Oil Disaster. But not because President Obama didn't show enough emotion or anger—a lame line pushed by too many pundits—or because this crisis has hijacked his legislative agenda (which it hasn't—yet).

Where Obama screwed up was in ceding the lead in the recovery effort to an oil company—a private corporation that was never going to see protecting the public interest as its top priority. That decision was a blown call akin to umpire Jim Joyce's denying Detroit Tigers pitcher Armando Galarraga a perfect game in the final out of the ninth—only with far more severe consequences, obviously.

Indeed, given BP's ugly record of environmental, safety and antitrust abuses, entrusting them with this cleanup was like outsourcing human rights policy to Dick Cheney. But the problem is greater than just BP. As Michael Klare writes in *The Nation*, it's "a corporate culture that favors productivity and profit over safety and environmental protection."

There are signs in these last few days that the administration now gets it. President Obama seems to have a new sense of urgency—and action. There's a movement to begin criminal and civil investigations. The president has started to make the case for a more active and less corrupt government, and ending tax breaks for oil and gas companies. (He should also end all Big Oil and Gas subsidies so that more governmental resources are available for R&D in renewable energy technologies.) His call to raise fuel efficiency standards for cars and trucks to 35.5 miles per gallon by 2016, and to work on higher standards for 2017, is a step toward ending our addiction to oil.

He also seems to better understand the bigger picture—that there was a systems breakdown that led to this disaster and now must be fixed. Regulations didn't keep pace with the risks posed by deepwater drilling; and drilling technology outpaced advances in safety equipment (if it's too deep to fix, it's too deep to drill). Obama has the capacity to take on that corroded system. Breaking up Mineral Management Services into three parts is a start, but much more needs to be done if we're to avoid these disasters in the future.

What Obama really needs to do isn't get mad at BP; he needs to get even on behalf of the American people—especially the workers who lost their lives, those injured, and the Gulf Coast residents who will be hugely impacted by this disaster for years to come, if not generations. He must seize this crisis as a transformative moment to lay out a new and sane energy policy—one that will protect environmental and public health, create jobs and break our addiction to fossil fuels. If he has the political will and courage (the emotion this nation needs most right now), the legislation just introduced by Senator Bernie Sanders is a good starting point.

The senator's bill would set fuel standards at fifty-five miles per gallon by 2030 and prohibit drilling in the Pacific and Atlantic oceans and along Florida's gulf coastline. A moratorium on drilling in those areas was approved by Congress every year since 1982 and lapsed in 2008.

Sanders points out that his fuel efficiency standards "would eliminate the need for 3.9 million barrels of oil per day, more than double the amount we now import from Persian Gulf nations like Saudi Arabia." He also argues that it is in line with what other nations are achieving—the EU currently gets forty-two miles per gallon and has set its sights on achieving sixty-five miles per gallon by 2020. China, Canada, Japan and South Korea all have stronger fuel economy standards than the United States.

It's certainly no radical idea to reinstate a ban on drilling that was in place until 2008. What was radical (and reckless) was to open new areas to offshore drilling in the hope of winning over Republicans—who were never going to move—on climate change. Like umpire Joyce after his blown call in Detroit, Obama now has a chance to reassess the facts and say, "We need to chart a new course, and I'm going to lead it."

"If we take bold action in energy efficiency, public transportation, advanced vehicle technologies, solar, wind, biomass, and geothermal," Senator Sanders writes, "we can transform our energy system, clean up our environment, and create millions of new jobs in the process."

I think Sanders gets it. The question remains: Does President Obama have the cool, conviction and courage to correct his blown call?

# An Undeserved Win for the GOP
## November 5, 2010

This was an unearned win for the Republican Party. The election was fundamentally about one thing—the rotten economy—and Democrats paid the price as voters expressed their discontent. Conservatives in both parties who claim the vote represented an ideological shift to the right are plain wrong.

The quickly congealing conventional wisdom is that President Obama tried to do too much and was too liberal. The opposite is true: Voters were alienated because they didn't believe his team had fought aggressively enough for the interests of working- and middle-class citizens.

For thirty years, these Americans have seen their incomes stagnate as the top 1 percent accrued a staggering percentage of the nation's wealth. By rescuing the big banks and failing to place demands on them, the White House economic team, led by Larry Summers and Tim Geithner, ceded populist energy to the Tea Party. The inadequacy of the recovery program—largely a result of concessions to the GOP—became a political catastrophe for the White House.

In the face of this anemic economy, the president failed to convince voters he was on a consistent course that would turn things around. Furthermore, the absence of a clear explanation about how conservative policies have failed in the past and will continue to fail allowed a right-wing narrative of empty slogans to gain traction. Mr. Obama abandoned his smart argument about building a new foundation for the economy, embracing deficit reduction instead. This only left voters confused about the White House's recovery plan.

Going forward, Mr. Obama would be wise to lay out a bold plan to create jobs. He should take the advice of the more than

300 economists, including former Clinton labor secretary Robert Reich, who have urged his administration not to undercut the recovery by focusing prematurely on deficit reduction. Joining Republicans' embrace of Social Security cuts and austerity makes for bad policy and bad politics. Instead, Mr. Obama and Democrats should promote sensible investments, particularly in vital infrastructure like roads and rail, as well as green energy initiatives.

If, as University of Massachusetts economist Robert Pollin and others argue, the single most important reason for the failure of economic recovery is that private credit markets are locked up, especially for small businesses, then the federal government could help by expanding existing federal loan guarantees by $300 billion. Meanwhile, excess cash reserves held by banks—now estimated at an unprecedented $1.1 trillion in Federal Reserve accounts—should be taxed an initial 1 to 2 percent. Mr. Pollin estimates that this combination could generate about three million new jobs if it succeeds in pumping about $300 billion into productive investments. This plan should get bipartisan support.

As the president made clear in his press conference Wednesday, he remains committed to a politics of "civility and common ground." Common ground is fine, so long as it makes the government more responsive to the needs of the majority of Americans. This means investments in people and deteriorating infrastructure; ending a wasteful and futile war in Afghanistan; and enacting ethics and campaign finance reform that levels the playing field so ordinary Americans' voices aren't drowned out by covert political money. If this sensible agenda is met with Republican obstruction, as is likely, Mr. Obama should channel Harry Truman and come out fighting against a know-nothing, do-nothing GOP.

Common ground and common sense also demand that the president listen to and remobilize the base that is the heart of his party. An empowered Democratic electorate—the young, Latinos, African Americans, single women, union folks—will be an effective counterweight to the assaults of the GOP and its corporate funders.

The Republicans have won control of the House, but they do not have a mandate to dismantle government. According to many polls, majorities across party lines want government to work. They aren't interested in rolling back decades of social and economic progress, abolishing the Education Department and the minimum wage, or privatizing Social Security and Medicare—issues that many Tea Party candidates touted.

More than 20 million Americans are out of work or under-employed. These people are interested in real solutions. They will not find them with a GOP committed to slashing billions from key domestic programs even as they make tax cuts for the rich permanent.

All of this presents an opportunity for Mr. Obama to show he stands with working people and the middle class. This is not a time to retreat. This is a time for the politics of conviction that Mr. Obama has said so many times he believes in.

# Obama: On the Way to a Failed Presidency?
*December 7, 2010*

Ronald Reagan famously quipped that the Democratic Party left him before he left the party. Like many progressive supporters of Barack Obama, I'm beginning to have the same feeling about this president.

Consider what we've seen since the shellacking Democrats took in the fall elections.

On Afghanistan, the administration has intimated that the 2011 pullout date is "inoperable," with the White House talking 2014 and Gen. David H. Petraeus suggesting decades of occupation. On bipartisanship, the president seems to think that cooperation requires self-abasement. He apologized to the obstructionist Republican leadership for not reaching out, a gesture reciprocated with another poke in the eye. He chose to meet with the hyper-partisan Chamber of Commerce after it ran one of the most dishonest independent campaigns in memory. He appears to be courting Roger Altman, a former investment banker, for his economic team, leavening the Goldman Sachs flavor of his administration with a salty Lehman Brothers veteran.

On the economy, the president has abandoned what Americans are focused on—jobs—to embrace what the Beltway elites care about—deficits. His freeze of federal workers' pay, of more symbolic than deficit-reducing value, only reinforced right-wing tripe: that federal employees are overpaid; that overspending is our problem, as opposed to inane tax cuts for the top end; that we should impose austerity now, instead of working to get the economy going.

Now the not-so-subtle retreats are turning into a rout. The president is touting a NAFTA-like corporate trade deal with South Korea. He appears to be headed toward supporting cuts in Social Security and Medicare and irresponsible reductions in domestic investment. And he's on the verge of kowtowing to Republican bluster and cutting a deal to extend George W. Bush's tax cuts for the rich in exchange (one hopes) for extending unemployment insurance and possibly getting a vote on the New START treaty.

This is political self-immolation. Blue-collar workers abandoned Democrats in large numbers in the fall; wait until they learn what the trade deal means for them. Seniors went south, probably because of Republican lies about cuts in Medicare; wait until anyone over forty who's lost their savings hears about

Alan Simpson's plan to take it to the "greedy geezers." The $60 billion each year in Bush tax cuts for the richest Americans could pay for universal preschool for America's children, or tuition and board for half of America's college students.

The stakes are much higher than the distant election. The president has suggested unconvincingly that he'd prefer to be a successful one-term president than a two-term president who didn't get anything done. But there are other alternatives. If the president continues on his current course, we're looking at a failed one-term presidency that the nation cannot afford.

Forget about electoral mandates or campaign promises. This president has a historic mandate. Just as Abraham Lincoln had to lead the nation from slavery and Franklin Roosevelt from the Depression, this president must lead the nation from the calamitous failures of three decades of conservative dominance. This requires beginning to reverse the perverse tax policies that have contributed to gilded-age inequality and starved the government of resources needed for vital investments. This demands correcting destabilizing global imbalances, laying a new foundation for reviving American manufacturing and shackling financial speculation. It means ensuring the United States leads rather than lags in the green industrial revolution. And it requires unwinding the self-destructive military adventures abroad. The president must strengthen America's basic social contract in a global economy, not weaken it.

This daunting project is not a matter of ambition or appetite—or even unconscious Kenyan socialism. It is the necessary function of a progressive president elected in the wake of calamitous conservative misrule. Every entrenched corporate and financial interest stands in the way; it is easier to take a less confrontational path. President Bill Clinton, for example, found it convenient to join in the conservative project of corporately defined trade, financial deregulation and social welfare constriction. From NAFTA to the repeal of welfare and the failure of labor law reform, to deregulating derivatives and repealing Glass-Steagall, he got his agenda wrong. He was seduced far more by Wall Street's Robert Rubin than by Monica Lewinsky. Now Obama faces the same challenge. This isn't about conventional politics. This is simply about the fate and future of our country. This president has a clear and imperative historic mandate. If he shirks it, he risks more than failing to get reelected. He risks a failed presidency.

# A Progressive's Answer to Obama
## December 14, 2010

"This country was founded on compromise," remarked the president toward the end of last week's tax deal press conference. "My job is to make sure that we have a North Star out there." Perhaps Barack Obama is right to define his job that way. But in light of the negotiations that led up to this claim, it's hard to see what he has done to truly illuminate that North Star.

There is no question, in a political system warped and broken by corporate money and lobbyists, that a president intent on achieving "victories for the American people," as he described them, would require a sense of pragmatism and a willingness to accept the compromises that, at times, will flow from it.

But too often, this president is so singularly focused on seeking common ground that he fails to define his—and our—principles. The tax cut deal is just the most recent example. Obama began those negotiations telegraphing his endgame, with eyes set unwaveringly on resolution. He chose not to passionately articulate his values or to define the GOP's, and in the aftermath of the battle, he refused to explain where it's all meant to lead us.

This, he might conclude, is a minor complaint from a dismissible left. But the truth is, without a president who is able—and willing—to lay out a clear, strong and principled argument, without a president who will stand up for the ideals he ran on, even as he seeks resolution, the progressive worldview becomes muted, and the conservative worldview validated.

Obama has reinforced the notion, not by compromise but by relative silence, that we should fear changing tax rates in a time of economic crisis, even when economists of all stripes tell us that tax cuts for the wealthy offer extraordinary cost and zero benefit to the nation. He speaks most passionately not while lambasting a Republican Party that would drown the middle class on behalf of the wealthy, but when criticizing the left for not offering support at a time when he doesn't deserve it. Because he rightly expects the worst from the far right, he seems to have lost his sense of outrage toward them. The left, in turn, receives his overcharged and misplaced anger—suggesting an equivalence between the two when, in truth, there is none.

The fact is, there is no monolithic left of the type Obama imagines. That a number of progressive economists are supportive of the tax deal is, in itself, proof of that reality. There are few on the left who expect unwavering ideological purity, few who reject the notion of compromise at any time. Most of us understand the structural limitations of our political system and the need to achieve what is possible.

I met Obama once when he was a candidate for president. On learning that I was editor of *The Nation*, he said to me, "The perfect is the enemy of good." Perhaps he expected me to disagree. I don't.

I don't disagree with the need to find balance, the need, at times, to compromise on policy. What I disagree with—and what I will never shy away from criticizing the president for—is his willingness to compromise on principle. Real leadership might require compromise, but it cannot be defined by compromise.

It must instead be defined by a clear vision for the future, and most important, a willingness to defend it. It should be focused not on what is possible but, instead, on the most that is possible; not the path of least resistance but the path of maximum potential benefit. That path doesn't trade away a federal pay freeze or a public option or more stimulus dollars for too little—or worse, for nothing. It doesn't begin with a willingness to relent.

A more aggressive stance from the president might not have substantially changed the contours of the ultimate tax deal, but it would surely have changed the narrative. It would have defined the Republican stance as morally indefensible.

Real leadership, too, should not be about merely accepting that you have popular support. It should be about mobilizing that support. "The fact of the matter is the American people already agree with me," said the president at his press conference. But he did not—and perhaps cannot—explain why he refused to use their support as a point of leverage.

These next two years present a daunting challenge. Once the new Congress is sworn in, any legislative movement forward on the progressive agenda (if any is possible) will require some form of compromise with an increasingly loathsome opposition. This is not a reality lost on any of us. But if reaching those compromises means a continued berating of the left, a continued lack of outrage toward the right and a continued willingness to strike deals without defining principles, then in the end, the president may well find himself with a modest list of achievements, a deeply demoralized base and a party that seemingly stands for nothing.

# Hope in 2011
*January 6, 2011*

As we head into another year in the long struggle between reform and reaction in our country, with conservatives and the Tea Party wielding new power in Washington, history offers some solace. Dark periods come and go. They can be overcome when those of us who are affronted by private greed and reactionary overreach stand together and fight for time-tested as well as innovative solutions to what plagues us, when we revitalize independent organizing and craft strategies to rebuild, revive and reclaim democracy.

The Rev. Martin Luther King Jr., who wrote an annual essay on civil rights for this magazine from 1961 to 1966, often spoke of how the arc of history, while long, bends toward justice. But King understood that it did not bend by itself. Social, cultural and political activism is what forces change, even in the most difficult times. We should not forget that when King began to emerge as a national figure, Republicans held the White House, Joe McCarthy still served in the Senate and almost every office in Alabama was held by a segregationist. Nothing about our moment is as daunting as that—except, perhaps, the challenge posed by the Supreme Court's *Citizens United* ruling, which will only strengthen the domination of money and corporate power over our politics. But there, too, history provides inspiration: in the latter part of the 19th century, the Senate was almost wholly owned by the railroad and other trusts. Still, the Progressive movement followed, taming them.

If the Progressives could tame the forces of money a century ago, and if King and his allies could bend the arc of history, so can we.

Gazing out over our current political terrain, it's clear that we have a lot of work ahead of us. We've helped build a society that is more socially tolerant than it was a quarter-century ago, but when it comes to public policy, economic outcomes and control of government, the story is different. The broad movement of American politics in recent decades has been toward greater inequality, the discrediting of public institutions and a near idolatry of private markets at the expense of corporate accountability.

I believe this is a pivotal moment for *The Nation*. Launched in the days after the Civil War, in July 1865, this magazine is one of the few longstanding media institutions that have worked to bring about lasting social and political change. In the time ahead, we will need to rededicate ourselves to our mission by confronting and countering misinformation, bigotry and greed with tough, intelligent and principled journalism while sowing new and alternative—often heretical—ideas.

In every part of our nation and world there are people engaged in courageous activism, and they are brimming with good ideas. But too often they are not well connected to one another, or they lack a larger vision or strategic purpose. *The Nation* and TheNation.com will seek to act as a forum for strategic thinking—connecting movements and their members with ideas and strategies while providing a long-term vision of a more just and peaceful society and world.

In some ways, this work will necessarily be defensive or oppositional. We will have to protect Social Security, Medicare and other civilizing reforms and prevent them from being slashed at the national and state levels. We will have to defend the public sphere from assault. We must oppose an unwinnable war in Afghanistan, and we must expose the depredations and fallacies of the global "war on terror." And we will have to fight corporatist and callous Republicans, as well as those in the Democratic Party, who would diminish working-and middle-class security and increase inequality and poverty.

In fighting these battles, we should also be challenging the limits of debate, laying down clear alternatives for the future of our economy and politics, and galvanizing broader support. New coalitions and a reinvigorated inside-outside strategy could move public opinion across a transpartisan spectrum. There remain strong allies within this administration and Congress with whom we can work. The consequences of inhumane cuts in state and city budgets—ravaged pensions, gutted schools, mass unemployment—could lead people of all parties to a renewed understanding and appreciation of government's role. All the while, we can do a better job of mobilizing people who are demoralized and fearful about their future but not yet ready to give up on the promise of democratic politics.

Legislative gridlock is likely at the federal level, but we should pressure the president to make deft use of the executive's regulatory and rule-making powers—by, for example, empowering workers, advancing immigration reform and strengthening the EPA's mandate. Despite Republican gains at the state level, many cities and states remain our laboratories of democracy. In Vermont, for example, the new governor, Peter Shumlin, is working with a citizens' coalition to support "Medicare for All." California is slashing greenhouse gas emissions and creating jobs through renewable energy, retrofitting, transit and infrastructure.

Building stronger coalitions around issues like drug and prison reform, living-wage campaigns, food justice and security, and environmental sustainability will lay the groundwork for progress in the years ahead—and engage a younger generation seeking a more humane and equitable politics. And we should not forget that some of the most inspiring ideas and movements for democratic renewal will come from abroad. These are also times when we'll need more creative strategies, including civil disobedience, to confront the climate crisis, joblessness, foreclosures and the war in Afghanistan.

Joining the battle of ideas and taking on a status quo that is not working will be key. Challenging the limits of austerity and the ideology of budget-balancing with alternative proposals and ideas will be a central part of our work. As long as a suffocating establishment consensus on deficit-slashing and tax cuts for the wealthy holds, America's politics is reduced to posturing.

The times demand a balance between short-term actions and long-term strategic thinking. Just as, in years past, the right has built movements around long-term causes in the face of great odds, we must be patient, stay committed to our principles and work for victory and not fear defeat. And as we do, we'll build a humane politics of passion and conviction that will re-connect with people where they live and work.

The late Studs Terkel, a true friend of *The Nation*, believed that hope was not simply optimism, which expects things to turn out well, but something rooted in the conviction that there is good worth working for. For 145 years, *The Nation* has sub-scribed to that belief. It is time to summon the spirit of hope Studs spoke of, never underestimating the tough landscape we live and work in but also remembering that in the past we have overcome more formidable obstacles.

# Obama Needs a Budget to Match His Progressive Ideals
*April 19, 2011*

For perhaps the first time since being sworn into office, President Obama has articulated, in eloquent terms, what it means to be a progressive. In his budget speech last week, he spoke of our obligation to the broader community to provide a basic level of security and dignity. Speaking of programs such as Medicare, Medicaid and Social Security, he said what every good progressive believes: "We would not be a great country without those commitments."

He fused a defense of progressive governance with a scathing critique of Paul Ryan's cruel budget, which all but four Republican House members have now voted for. And he demanded that the rich finally pay their fair share, vowing to let the Bush tax cuts expire. It was a powerful speech, in many ways reassuring to progressives who have been demoralized by a president who appeared missing in action.

But rhetoric and policy are not the same thing. And in this case, as in far too many, the policy agenda the president has laid out is not worthy of, in his words, "the America we believe in."

To begin with, the president continues to let Republicans define the playing field in almost every instance. Why is the debate we are having not about whether to cut, but how much to cut? Why isn't it about the urgency of joblessness instead of the perils of deficits? The budget the president proposed is clearly influenced by a discredited conservative economic worldview. It shouldn't be accepted as the "progressive" alternative in the negotiations soon to come.

What's worse is that, even on this narrow playing field, the president isn't fighting harder for those who need government's support the most. He has jettisoned the Keynesian thinking this era demands, prematurely embracing what might be described as austerity-lite policy, one that all but guarantees mass unemployment as the new normal.

In his speech, he spoke eloquently of how there was "nothing courageous about asking for sacrifice from those who can least afford it and don't have any clout on Capitol Hill." Nothing courageous, indeed. And yet it is President Obama who has said that for every $1 in tax increases, we should create $2 in spending cuts. Faced with the choice between new cuts to the social safety net and new taxes for the richest few, it is not just Paul Ryan but President Obama whose acceptance of the way this choice is framed leaves the poor shouldering most of the burden.

The most progressive president since Lyndon Johnson should be willing to embrace a bolder opening gambit. He should not be so willing to compromise on principle, even when ultimate compromise may be necessary. Real leadership might require compromise, but it cannot be defined by compromise. It must instead be defined by a clear vision for the future, and most important, a willingness to defend it. It should be focused not on what is possible, but instead, on the most that is possible; not the path of least resistance, but the path of maximum potential benefit.

Failing to do so is what can produce a Tea Party budget, such as the one adopted last week. As Paul Krugman put it in his column this week, the two parties "don't just live in different moral universes, they also live in different intellectual universes." Any embrace or acceptance of that Republican universe by the White House is a retreat from the reforms this country desperately needs—and was promised.

Yet the president has again telegraphed his willingness to compromise, admitting in his speech that he did not "expect the details in any final agreement to look exactly like the approach" he laid out. What, then, does he expect it will look like?

The further right this process moves—whether as a result of a political system warped and broken by corporate interests protecting their privilege, or lobbyists actively gutting reform— the more disheartening the definition of victory becomes. Is merely preventing Republicans from ending Medicare what victory looks like now? Yes, we need a defensive opposition, but while Democrats control the Senate and the White House, they cannot act merely as a minority party. Shouldn't they be laying out a clear vision of a sustainable and fair economy? As the extremists take over the GOP, is the Democratic Party really going to be content to define success so modestly?

There are at least eighty-three Democratic members of the House who believe that we cannot exclude alternatives that would solve this economic challenge more justly and fairly. They believe we must challenge the limits of our narrowing debate and expand, as President Obama once called it, "our moral imagination."

They are the members of the Congressional Progressive Caucus (CPC), who last week introduced what they are calling the "People's Budget," an alternative both to President Obama's proposal and the unconscionable Ryan Budget.

It lays out what a robust progressive agenda should look like. It protects the social safety net, promotes a progressive tax policy and makes significant cuts to the Pentagon by bringing our troops home from Iraq and Afghanistan. It actually generates a surplus by 2021, according to Rep. Raúl Grijalva, co-chair of the CPC.

This is the kind of budget our president should be proposing. This is the kind of budget the progressive community should be rallying around. One that makes millionaires, billionaires and corporations pay their fair share. One that protects the poor and middle class. But it is the kind of budget that establishment Democrats and media elites are inclined to ignore and dismiss.

We can be, as Nobel Prize–winning economist Joseph Stiglitz recently put it, a country "of the 1%, for the 1%, by the 1%." Or we can be a country that believes in—and embraces—shared sacrifice. A country not defined by the greed of the few but by the needs of the many.

That's the only kind of America really worth believing in.

*Part II*

## A NEW ECONOMIC NARRATIVE

# The Bailout and Small-"d" Democratic Capitalism

*October 2, 2008*

The Bailout Bill was passed by the Senate last night, 74–25. Though it was an improvement from the original plan that the Bush administration tried to ram through last week, it's still an extremely flawed bill. There is a need for an effective, just and equitable intervention, and that's not what this bill represents. It rewards the worst actors in the financial industry while doing little to nothing for working people—people who are being asked nevertheless to pick up the tab for Wall Street's recklessness. (And, yes, it's true that taxpayers will get some stake in the companies now, but there is no telling what, if any, return there will be on these toxic assets).

The action moves to the House now, where a truly progressive bill could be crafted with key elements like: bankruptcy reforms and loan modifications to keep people in their homes; a surtax on the wealthy as proposed tonight in an amendment offered by Senator Bernie Sanders; re-regulation of Wall Street to curb the casino/bandit economy that got us into this mess; direct recapitalization of banks; and an economic stimulus package that includes extension of unemployment insurance and infrastructure investment that rebuilds our nation and creates jobs.

Of course, we are unlikely to see this kind of bill because it doesn't have the needed votes—certainly not in the Senate and probably not in the House, where the Blue Dog Dems would be needed. But at the very least, one wonders why Democratic leadership didn't push harder for an economic stimulus for Main Street at a time when Wall Street and the Bush administration are begging for taxpayer help? If they truly need

$700 billion to save the global economy, would they really have thrown that away over—for example, a $60 billion stimulus package?

Although Senator Barack Obama spoke eloquently about the need for Congress to focus on Main Street—and his words made clear that he understands the pain people are feeling and what's at stake in this Bush economy—he was willing to put off the fight for bankruptcy reforms, loan modifications and a stimulus package. He said:

> As soon as we pass this rescue plan, we need to move aggressively with the same sense of urgency to rescue families on Main Street who are struggling to pay their bills and keep their jobs. They've been in crisis a lot longer than Wall Street has. I've said it before and I say it again: We need to pass an economic stimulus package that will help ordinary Americans cope with rising food and gas prices, that can save 1 million jobs rebuilding our schools, and roads, and our infrastructure, and help states and cities avoid budget cuts and tax increases, a plan that would extend expiring unemployment benefits for those Americans who've lost their jobs and cannot find new ones. . . . We also must do more in this rescue package in order to help homeowners stay in their homes. I will continue to advocate bankruptcy reforms.

Another Senator—Bernie Sanders of Vermont—believes now is the time to fight for working families. Majority Leader Harry Reid gave him one hour to introduce the sole amendment to the bailout bill. It called for a 10 percent surtax on couples with an income over $1 million a year or $500,000 for single taxpayers, raising $300 billion in revenues over five years to go toward the bailout. The amendment was defeated by a voice vote, but in introducing it, Senator Sanders captured the frustration and outrage of people who have been shafted for eight years under

George Bush, and who continue to receive the short end of the stick with this bailout.

It's clear that the ideology of unfettered, unregulated capitalism is dead. The fight for small-"d" democratic capitalism that puts the public interest first while investing in people, productivity and opportunity is on. In his speech tonight, Senator Sanders gives us a glimpse of that fight and a glimpse of what a more democratic economy might look like.

Here are Senator Sanders' remarks on the Senate floor:

This country faces many serious problems in the financial market, in the stock market, in our economy. We must act, but we must act in a way that improves the situation. We can do better than the legislation now before Congress.

This bill does not effectively address the issue of what the taxpayers of our country will actually own after they invest hundreds of billions of dollars in toxic assets. This bill does not effectively address the issue of oversight because the oversight board members have all been handpicked by the Bush administration. This bill does not effectively deal with the issue of foreclosures and addressing that very serious issue, which is impacting millions of low- and moderate-income Americans in the aggressive, effective way that we should be. This bill does not effectively deal with the issue of executive compensation and golden parachutes. Under this bill, the CEOs and the Wall Street insiders will still, with a little bit of imagination, continue to make out like bandits.

This bill does not deal at all with how we got into this crisis in the first place and the need to undo the deregulatory fervor which created trillions of dollars in complicated and unregulated financial instruments such as credit default swaps and hedge funds. This bill does not address the issue that has taken us to where we are today, the concept of too big to fail. In fact, within the last several weeks we have sat idly by and watched gigantic financial institutions like the Bank of America swallow up other gigantic financial institutions like Countrywide and Merrill Lynch. Well, who is going to bail out the Bank of America if it begins to fail? There is not one word about the issue of too big to fail in this legislation at a time when that problem is in fact becoming even more serious. This bill does not deal with the absurdity of having the fox guarding the hen house. Maybe I'm the only person in America who thinks so, but I have a hard time understanding why we are giving $700 billion to the Secretary of the Treasury, the former CEO of Goldman Sachs, who, along with other financial institutions, actually got us into this problem. Now, maybe I'm the only person in America who thinks that's a little bit weird, but that is what I think.

This bill does not address the major economic crisis we face: growing unemployment, low wages, the need to create decent-paying jobs, rebuilding our infrastructure and moving us to energy efficiency and sustainable energy.

There is one issue that is even more profound and more basic than everything else that I have mentioned, and that is if a bailout is needed, if taxpayer money must be placed at risk, whose money should it be? In other words, who should be paying for this bailout which has been caused by the greed and recklessness of Wall Street operatives who have made billions in recent years?

The American people are bitter. They are angry, and they are confused. Over the last seven and a half years, since George W. Bush has been president, 6 million Americans have slipped out of the middle class and are in poverty, and today working families are lining up at emergency food shelves in order to get the food they need to feed their families. Since President Bush has been in office, median family income for working-age families has declined by over $2,000. More than 7 million Americans have lost their health insurance. Over 4 million have lost their pensions. Consumer debt has more than doubled. And foreclosures are the highest on record. Meanwhile, the cost of energy, food, healthcare, college and other basic necessities has soared.

While the middle class has declined under President Bush's reckless economic policies, the people on top have never had it so good. For the first seven years of Bush's tenure, the wealthiest 400 individuals in our country saw a $670 billion increase in their wealth, and at the end of 2007 owned over $1.5 trillion in wealth. That is just 400 families, a $670 billion increase in wealth since Bush has been in office.

In our country today, we have the most unequal distribution of income and wealth of any major country on earth, with the top 1 percent earning more income than the bottom 50 percent and the top 1 percent owning more wealth than the bottom 90 percent. We are living at a time when we have seen a massive transfer of wealth from the middle class to the very wealthiest people in this country, when, among others, CEOs of Wall Street firms received unbelievable amounts in bonuses, including $39 billion in bonuses in the year 2007 alone for just the five major investment houses. We have seen the incredible greed of the financial services industry manifested in the hundreds of millions of dollars they have spent on campaign contributions and lobbyists in order to deregulate their industry so that hedge funds and other unregulated financial institutions could flourish. We have seen them play with trillions and trillions dollars in esoteric financial instruments, in unregulated industries which no more than a handful of people even understand. We have seen the financial services industry charge 30 percent interest rates on credit card loans and tack on outrageous late fees and other costs to unsuspecting customers. We have seen them engaged in despicable predatory lending practices, taking advantage of the vulnerable and the uneducated. We have seen them send out billions of deceptive solicitations to almost every mailbox in America.

Most importantly, we have seen the financial services industry lure people into mortgages they could not afford to pay, which is one of the basic reasons why we are here tonight. In the midst of all of this, we have a bailout package which says to the middle class that you are being asked to place at risk $700 billion, which is $2,200 for every man, woman, and child in this country. You're being asked to do that in order to undo the damage caused by this excessive Wall Street greed. In other words, the "Masters of the Universe," those brilliant Wall Street insiders who have made more money than the average American can even dream of, have brought our financial system to the brink of collapse. Now, as the American and world financial systems teeter on the edge of a meltdown, these multimillionaires are demanding that the middle class, which has already suffered under Bush's disastrous economic policies, pick up the pieces that they broke. That is wrong, and that is something that I will not support.

If we are going to bail out Wall Street, it should be those people who have caused the problem, those people who have benefited from Bush's tax breaks for millionaires and billionaires, those people who have taken advantage of deregulation, those people are the people who should pick up the tab, and not ordinary working people. I introduced an amendment which gave the Senate a very clear choice. We can pay for this bailout of Wall Street by asking people all across this country, small businesses on Main Street, homeowners on Maple Street, elderly couples on Oak Street, college students on Campus Avenue, working families on Sunrise Lane, we can ask them to pay for this bailout. That is one way we can go. Or, we can ask the people who have gained the most from the spasm of greed, the people whose incomes have been soaring under President Bush, to pick up the tab.

I proposed to raise the tax rate on any individual earning $500,000 a year or more or any family earning $1 million a year or more by 10 percent. That increase in the tax rate, from 35 percent to 45 percent, would raise more than $300 billion in the next five years, almost half the cost of the bailout. If what all the supporters of this legislation say is correct, that the government will get back some of its money when the market calms down and the government sells some of the assets it has purchased, then $300 billion should be sufficient to make sure that 99.7 percent of taxpayers do not have to pay one nickel for this bailout.

Most of my constituents did not earn a $38 million bonus in 2005 or make over $100 million in total compensation in three years, as did Henry Paulson, the current secretary of the Treasury, and former CEO of Goldman Sachs. Most of my constituents did not make $354 million in total compensation over the past five years as did Richard Fuld of Lehman Brothers. Most of my constituents did not cash out $60 million in stock after a $29 billion bailout for Bear Stearns after that failing company was bought out by JPMorgan Chase. Most of my constituents did not get a $161 million severance package as E. Stanley O'Neill, former CEO Merrill Lynch did.

Last week I placed on my website, www.sanders.senate.gov, a letter to Secretary Paulson in support of my amendment. It said that it should be those people best able to pay for this bailout, those people who have made out like bandits in recent years, they should be asked to pay for this bailout. It should not be the middle class. To my amazement, some 48,000 people cosigned this petition, and the names keep coming in. The message is very simple: "We had nothing to do with causing this bailout. We are already under economic duress. Go to those people who have made out like bandits. Go to those people who have caused this crisis and ask them to pay for the bailout."

The time has come to assure our constituents in Vermont and all over this country that we are listening and understand their anger and their frustration. The time has come to say that we have the courage to stand up to all of the powerful financial institution lobbyists who are running amok all over the Capitol building, from the Chamber of Commerce to the American Bankers Association, to the Business Roundtable, all of these groups who make huge campaign contributions, spend all kinds of money on lobbyists, they're here loud and clear. They don't want to pay for this bailout, they want middle America to pay for it.

# A Trillion Dollar Recovery
## December 30, 2008

Poverty is on the rise, record numbers of people are relying on food stamps and we've seen no relief from the foreclosure crisis. There are increasing rates of child abuse and domestic violence linked to this recession. State governments don't have financial resources to cope at the exact moment when those resources are most needed. Nineteen states and the District of Columbia have lowered Medicaid payments or eliminated people from eligibility. The senior economist of the International Monetary Fund recently warned of another Great Depression.

We don't need a stimulus, we need a recovery. And that means investing $1 trillion over the next two years.

The Congressional Progressive Caucus (CPC) has proposed a plan to do just that—a detailed $1 trillion recovery plan to kick-start the economy, invest in sustainable, long-term growth and target individuals and communities that are most desperate for resources.

Obama political adviser David Axelrod said this weekend that the new administration is looking at a stimulus bill in the range of $675 to $775 billion over two years. But is that enough at this moment of metastasizing economic pain and deepening recession? Not according to CPC co-chair, Representative Lynn Woolsey of California, who said, "anything much less than $1 trillion would be like trying to put out a forest fire with a squirt gun."

In addition to much needed investments which have already been laid out—like the extension of unemployment insurance while joblessness soars, increasing food stamps, and assisting cash-strapped states with Medicaid—the CPC plan goes a step further. It takes a holistic approach to economic recovery and the needs of ordinary Americans by addressing infrastructure, human capital, keeping people in their homes, job creation, fiscal relief for state, local and tribal governments, education and job training and tax relief for lower-income families.

There are smart commitments in the CPC plan that deserve real attention, such as:

- A percentage of the infrastructure work would be performed by veterans, low-income and homeless individuals, out-of-school youth, and others facing multiple barriers to employment
- Green technologies to weatherize the nation's homes and small businesses
- Grants to the neediest schools for modernization, renovation, energy efficiency and investing in educational technology
- Construction of libraries in rural communities in order to expand broadband access

- Capital improvements and short-term operating funds for federally qualified health centers
- Boost funding for National Health Service Corps to produce more doctors, dentists and nurses to provide healthcare in underserved areas
- Expand sustainable food systems at the local community level
- A moratorium on home foreclosures
- At least $100 billion allocated to "green jobs creation," including at the community level and in Indian Country
- Creation of a new energy block grant to transition to green energy sources
- Re-establish Youth Conservation Corps to eliminate a backlog of work projects in national, state and local parks
- Federal Arts and Writers Project to create jobs for American artists, writers, editors, researchers, photographers and others
- Triple funding for the Community Development Block Grant Program
- Make the child tax credit fully refundable, lifting 2.7 million people—including 1.7 million children—above the poverty line
- Expand the earned income tax credit for families with three or more children

"The Progressive Caucus is determined to bring justice and prosperity to the American economy, and this proposal does both," CPC Co-Chair, Rep. Raúl Grijalva of Arizona, said in a released statement.

"The American people's urgent needs in healthcare, employment, education and infrastructure have been neglected for so very long that the basic structure of our economic system has been undermined. Now that the American people have the attention of Wall Street and Washington, we intend to lift their voice and demand the profound change the people voted for."

There is a groundswell of support for massive action along these lines. More than twenty progressive groups and unions are spearheading the Jobs and Economic Recovery Now campaign, building grassroots support for a bold recovery program of $850 billion or more. At events across the nation, supporters urged quick passage of the legislation so that it is waiting on President Obama's desk the day he takes office.

The campaign is also targeting moderate Republicans in the Senate in order to avoid a filibuster. It was just three months ago, after all, that Republicans successfully filibustered a stimulus that targeted unemployment insurance, food stamps and "shovel-ready" infrastructure projects—and that was only $56 billion.

At this moment, a massive recovery along the lines of what the country needs is far from a done deal. The Congressional Progressive Caucus has done a great service with its plan, showing us what a comprehensive approach to economic recovery looks like—addressing the needs of ordinary Americans who have been left behind by the Wall Street Bailout Bonanza and eight years of greed and deregulation.

# Obama's Economic Sermon on the Mount
## April 14, 2009

As President Obama approaches the 100-day mark of his presidency, he delivered a speech Tuesday at Georgetown University in which he laid out what he sees as the foundation of a new economy. Using this crisis—and his gift of oratory—Obama signaled that the fight for the next economy begins now.

He alluded to the Sermon on the Mount to describe the stronger, more fair economy he envisions: "There is a parable at the end of the Sermon on the Mount that tells the story of two men," he said. "The first built his house on a pile of sand, and it was destroyed as soon as the storm hit. But the second is known as the wise man, for when '. . . the rain descended, and the floods came, and the winds blew, and beat upon that house . . . it fell not: for it was founded upon a rock.' We cannot rebuild this economy on the same pile of sand. We must build our house upon a rock."

I think the speech is important for what it reveals about Obama's understanding of the task ahead—building a new economy out of the ashes of our failed one.

But real and grounded concerns about the administration's bank bailout plan remain. As Nobel prize–winning economist Joseph Stiglitz wrote recently in a *New York Times* op-ed, the Obama administration's plan is "far worse than nationalization: it is ersatz capitalism, the privatizing of gains and the socializing of losses . . . the kind of Rube Goldberg device that Wall Street loves—clever, complex and nontransparent, allowing huge transfers of wealth to the financial markets." Other good thinkers share this view, including Paul Krugman, Simon Johnson, William Greider and Robert Reich.

While Obama's speech lays out some strong principles for a new foundation, the administration's financial team remains unwilling to understand that we're not just going through a financial crisis or a panic, but the failure of a whole model of banking. We are living amid the blowback of an overgrown financial sector that did more harm than good.

As *The Nation*'s Greider has argued, we need a new banking system—smaller and more diverse and responsible to the public interest. Creating this new system is where public resources should be committed, not to saving banks that are "too big to fail." We should create public banks and non-profit savings and lending cooperatives to serve as an important check on private commercial banks. We need to make banks the servants—not the masters— of our economy. Only when we do that will a new regulatory framework do what's needed; it would be a mistake to simply re-regulate the shadow banking system which got us into this mess.

If this realization begins to sink in through the failure of the current plan—and Obama's commitment to pragmatism and experimentation suggests he might be willing to move to Plan B with sufficient pressure from mobilized citizens and thinkers who envision a different model than the Summers/Geithner approach—then we're on the road to laying the foundation, the rock, for a new economy.

But creating that new economy will require what Obama himself might call "tough choices"—and some different "pillars" from the ones he outlined today. We need affordable healthcare; pensions above Social Security; and sustained public investment in areas vital to high wages in a global economy—affordable colleges, world-class public schools, and a 21st-century infrastructure. We need to restructure—not just re-regulate—the financial sector so that banking is once again a "boring" occupation devoted to making loans to the real economy, not peddling exotic and (as we now know) toxic instruments. We need to break up and restructure major banks that are on life support and "too big to fail." And we need to fight for the Employee Free Choice Act—so that workers are able to organize and bargain collectively, and the middle class is rebuilt and strengthened.

The mother of all fights lies ahead—beyond the first 100 days—as lobbies mobilize to halt the reforms needed to rebuild and reconstruct a new economy of shared prosperity. The drug and insurance companies, the business lobby, multinationals that seek to retain tax havens—they will all warn ominously of massive job losses, failed businesses and much suffering for each and every needed reform offered.

Despite the flaws of the bank bailout, President Obama has signaled that we can work toward a new economy. But it will require a massive mobilization of citizens. We've had thirty years of the markets-know-best-and-are-self-correcting, government–get-out-of-the-way, let-CEOs-rule, maximize-executive-profits dogma. The catastrophic results are in. Now begins the fight to rebuild a balanced economy in which government is on the side of the people, corporations are held accountable and workers are empowered.

Long-term challenges should be seized, not ignored—lest we remain on shifting sands.

# The Front Lines of the Economic (and Democracy) Crisis
## May 26, 2009

On May 12, in a packed hearing room on Capitol Hill, the Congressional Progressive Caucus (CPC) held a spirited briefing for its Members and their staffs—"Voices from the Front Lines of the Economic Crisis: A Bold Agenda for Change."

CPC Co-Chair Raúl Grijalva and Congressman John Conyers, as well as about thirty Congressional staffers and other allies, heard testimony from members of the Inter-Alliance Dialogue—an emerging coalition of networks representing domestic workers, janitors, day laborers, housing activists, worker rights advocates, and others hit hardest during these times. The event was co-sponsored by the Institute for Policy Studies, a progressive multi-issue think tank in Washington, DC.

Witnesses painted a vivid picture of the current struggles too many workers and communities face, and described their vision for addressing short-term needs as well as long-term systemic change.

Joycelyn Gill-Campbell of the National Domestic Workers Alliance discussed the domestic worker workforce "of over 2 million, mostly women of color who come to this country because the economic policies around the world force us abroad to [find] work to support our families. Globalization has hurt us." She said before the crisis, a survey showed that of 200,000 domestic workers in New York, 18 percent lived below the poverty line, and only 13 percent earned a living wage. One in five reported "sometimes or often not having enough to eat. . . . One-third of all domestic workers and one-half of live-in domestic workers experience verbal or physical abuse."

With the economic collapse these conditions have only grown worse.

"The fear of losing their jobs is silencing [domestic] workers who are facing abuse and exploitation," Gill-Campbell said. "They are so afraid of losing their jobs that they are accepting worse and worse conditions. This is driving down conditions for everyone."

Her colleague, Antonia Pena of Casa de Maryland agreed. "It is difficult to honestly say that if you leave your abusive employer you will be able to find something else," she said. "Employers know this and are using it to their advantage. They are cutting our hours, cutting our already low wages, and if we say something they say 'Go ahead and leave, there's lot of people who are waiting in line for this job.' . . . Domestic workers take care of our families here and in our home countries. . . . If we lose our job, it will mean no food, no rent, not just for us, but for our families."

But Pena sees this crisis as an opportunity for reform. "This crisis gives [legislators] the opportunity to help restructure the economy for the better—to make it more fair," she said.

Gill-Campbell described a campaign in New York State that is trying to do just that with a Domestic Workers Bill of Rights. It would ensure domestic workers receive notice, severance pay, an annual wage increase, paid vacation, sickness benefits, personal days, and protection from discrimination. She said the legislation might "serve as a model for the type of innovative policy we can develop to protect the most vulnerable and support sustainability for all of the workers in this country."

Wanda Solomon of Mothers on the Move and Right to the City described her community in the South Bronx "one of the poorest congressional districts in the nation with 42 percent of our residents living below the poverty line." The economic collapse "has only deepened a crisis that we have always faced." Her community—like other low-income communities and communities of color—also is disproportionately burdened with hazardous waste and pollution and consequent ailments like childhood asthma.

Solomon said that the stimulus package and federal investment in a green economy gives rise to the hope that it will be used for economic development. "However, low-income people of color are not being consulted about where they think this money should be spent," she said. Her coalition wants to see resources used "to address the unjust distribution of pollution and the associated health concerns within our neighborhoods."

"We believe in a growing green economy that is based on equity and will create meaningful jobs and healthier and safer communities." Solomon said. "We look forward to sitting at the decision-making table."

Tammy Bang Luu of Grassroots Global Justice also articulated some key challenges faced by lower-income communities across the nation—primarily the need for affordable, reliable public transit.

"Public transit systems throughout the country are falling apart at the seams with dwindling operating funds, resulting in cuts in service and fare increases," she said, and creating huge barriers to opportunities for employment, housing, and education. She said public transit investment is also needed in response to the climate crisis. She noted that the Highway Bill expiring in September invests 80 percent in roads and 20 percent in public transportation. To support healthier communities and new opportunities "this formula must be turned on its head— 80% for public transportation, 20% for highway maintenance," she said.

Luu also spoke of "reversing the trend" of exploitation of tribal lands through federal investment in Native-owned and -operated renewable energy facilities, particularly in wind and solar energy.

Jacinta Gonzalez of the National Day Labor Organizing Network spoke of the exploitation of day laborers which—as with domestic workers—has only grown more extreme with the economic crisis.

"For most of the day laborer and low-wage immigrant population in the US, their undocumented status is like a huge sign that says no labor laws need apply," Gonzalez said. "As the economy falls into a true crisis and unemployment rises, workers, desperate for any job that will allow them to provide for their families, find that more and more contractors only hire them in order to steal their labor."

Gonzales described three cases in New Orleans where companies with multimillion-dollar state and federal contracts to build affordable housing "robbed the workers of thousands of dollars in clear violation of federal worker protection laws. . . . Simply put, as jobs decline, wage theft is on the rise and no one but the most vulnerable workers themselves is doing anything to stop it."

She said laws against wage theft need to be strengthened and enforced, and that currently local authorities and the Department of Labor both fail to respond. Also, until comprehensive immigration reform is enacted, undocumented workers will continue to be exploited through the threat of deportation.

"The current political economy takes for granted thousands of day laborers that as a disenfranchised population are excluded from labor law," Gonzales said.

All of the speakers from the Inter-Alliance Dialogue spoke of their experiences not only to illustrate their constituents' immediate needs but also to point to a broader agenda. To that end, the Alliance is currently working on a Recovery Package for Democracy. This agenda will address structural racism in education, housing, transportation and employment; workplace democracy, including organizing and collective bargaining rights; urban communities' participation in state and local decision-making; and a green, global economy that respects and invests in historically exploited communities.

After the hearing, the coalition met at the White House with Jared Bernstein, Economic Policy Adviser to Vice President Joseph Biden.

"It was a great meeting," said Sarita Gupta, Executive Director of Jobs with Justice. "We were able to meet Jared Bernstein and introduce him to all of our networks, which is important given that we have not always had access to the White House. Mr. Bernstein gave us a good overview of the Vice President's Middle Class Task Force. We explored where our interests overlap and he gave us valuable feedback on ways in which we could keep communication going between us. . . . We look forward to reconnecting with him and others on the Task Force when we've completed our comprehensive proposal."

The fresh thinking of the Inter-Alliance Dialogue offers a powerful alternative to the status quo.

---

# Resisting Foreclosures
## *September 12, 2009*

In Georgia, the ease with which someone can lose a home is staggering. A foreclosure-eviction can occur without judicial review in just thirty-five days, and at 10 a.m. on the first Tuesday of every month, the state's159 counties hold a sheriff's auction of foreclosed homes.

That translated to 1,500 homes for sale in Atlanta on Sept. 1. Rev. Jesse Jackson and the Rainbow PUSH Coalition—including 125 ministers from throughout the South—were in town to try to stop the auction.

They appealed to both Citibank and Wells Fargo to withdraw homes from the sale. Citi pulled thirty of its forty properties and will restructure those mortgages. Wells Fargo is still considering its response. Jackson commended Citi for taking "courageous action" but also noted that there is a need for a "massive restructuring" to truly stem the tide of foreclosures.

"The systematic hemorrhaging of foreclosures is outdistancing by far the loan modifications," Jackson said in a recent interview. "We've given a massive blood transfusion to the banks, but it's not linked to stopping the hemorrhaging at the bottom. We're taking care of a head wound . . . but the aorta is gushing."

Indeed, as of June 30, 1.5 million homes had gone into foreclosure and 2.4 million are expected to foreclose by the end of the year. Thirteen million foreclosures are projected over the next five years. The crisis has also spread to prime loans—they now represent 27 percent of foreclosed loans, "up from 17 percent during the comparable 2008 period," according to McClatchy Newspapers. Nationwide, 23 percent of homeowners are now "under water"—owing more on their mortgages than their homes are worth. Meanwhile, only about 10 percent of homeowners eligible for relief under the Obama administration's anti-foreclosure plan have received help.

"That leaves 90 percent to the bankers without an incentive to restructure loans rather than repossess homes," Jackson said. "Right now, the government is going house by house by house by house—like dipping a spoon in the ocean. There's a structural abnormality . . . that will not work. It's like if you're going for the right to vote—going city by city by city by city . . . or do you have a federal restructuring of the right to vote? Period." Jackson is outraged that the banks—even subprime lenders, some of whom engaged in "redlining and targeting, steering and clustering"—received a bailout, and are now profiting, with "no linkage to use the bailout to modify loans."

"Banks are sending out press releases saying they are recovering, but they are being stimulated to recover," he said. "Meantime, we're still losing jobs, and houses, and student loans . . . and the same banks that are getting 0 percent interest on loans are unwilling to reduce the homeowner rate. They're getting 0 percent money and charging students 16 percent. . . . They're taking a stimulus and getting a fee for free money."

Rainbow PUSH has embarked on an ambitious and focused campaign—to restructure people's loans en masse—to stem the tide of foreclosures. It involves calling on the Federal Reserve Bank to institute an across-the-board interest rate reduction on all residential mortgages (Jackson proposes a 6 percent cap); Congress to give bankruptcy judges the power to modify mortgages (the House passed such legislation but it failed in the Senate); the Department of Justice to enforce fair lending and civil rights laws and prosecute those involved in predatory and discriminatory lending practices; and banks and the private sector to participate in the Obama administration's anti-foreclosure programs in order to modify 75 percent of troubled home mortgages.

The campaign plans foreclosure actions this month in Los Angeles, Antioch, California, the Federal Reserve in San Francisco, and again in Atlanta. Meetings will be held between key staff of Rainbow PUSH and the Federal Reserve, FDIC, Senate Banking Committee Chairman Chris Dodd, and House Financial Services Committee Chairman Barney Frank.

"We're taking our case to the streets, directly to the people," Jackson said. "An aroused people can make things begin to happen."

The need for these actions at both the local and national level is clear. The foreclosures impact not only the people being thrown out of their homes, but also their neighbors. The Center for Responsible Lending projects that in 2009 alone nearby houses will suffer a $502 billion decline in property values. That means an even greater hit to state and city budgets already devastated by the recession.

"When you lose the homes to foreclosure your neighbors' homes lose value," Jackson said. "You shrink the tax base, then money for education, police, teachers, firemen and libraries goes right down the river."

Jackson believes taking on the foreclosure crisis is only part of the equation.

"I really can't separate jobs—the need for stimulation, incentives to reinvest in the infrastructure, reinvest in America—and housing and healthcare and education," he said. "People with jobs can better afford health premiums, and house premiums, and school premiums. We need a targeted stimulus at job creation and we cannot [ignore] the need for revisiting our trade policy. . . . Trade must be fair to be free. And organized labor can't compete with slave labor. . . . When you are dismissive of human rights—workers', women's and children's rights—you're dismissive of [our] capacity to compete and to grow. I know the trade thing is a harder and higher mountain to climb, but it's a mountain that has to be climbed."

Jackson is right. There is indeed a clear connection between these basic struggles for jobs, homes, health, and education, and a need to address it as a whole. But it's also true that taking on the foreclosure crisis alone will require a herculean effort—the kind of inside-outside strategy we've seen (win or lose) in the healthcare debate. Jackson and other progressives who understand the power of organizing, mobilizing and agitating have a vision for how to take on the status quo.

"Begin to resist these auctions en masse and publicly. Make resistance an issue, not just the auction an issue," Jackson said. "Demand bankruptcy reform laws. Fight for a structural change in the mortgage rates. Target a given bank in your area—which may involve civil disobedience, or litigation, or a demonstration—but it does require action. That's what we have to do. Activists cannot be silent in their protest. Our silence betrays our quest for justice."

This article was co-authored by *Nation* reporter/researcher Greg Kaufmann.

# The Deficit Hawks' Road to Ruin
## *March 2, 2010*

In the face of this Great Recession, the Senate's recently passed $15 billion jobs bill is more like a sick joke than a serious legislative initiative.

We have lost more than 8.4 million jobs since December 2007. One out of five Americans is now unemployed or underemployed. More than six people are seeking jobs for every one that's available. In low-income communities, the jobless rates are not those of a recession but of another depression, and the Economic Policy Institute (EPI) estimates that child poverty will rise to 27 percent overall, and to over 50 percent for African American children, in the next year or two.

As economist Lawrence Mishel, president of EPI, told me, "In the midst of the worst jobs crisis in over 70 years, passing a $15 billion bill—comprising mostly of a tax credit of questionable efficacy—is like trying to extinguish a 10-alarm fire with a leaky garden hose."

In contrast, bold plans that match the scale of the crisis aren't getting enough attention. For example, EPI calls for: a one-year extension of unemployment compensation and COBRA health benefits; fiscal relief for states that will otherwise lay off more teachers, firefighters, police officers and other workers; a New Deal–like public service employment program; investments in transportation and school modernization; and a carefully crafted job-creation tax credit. It would cost $400 billion in the first year to create 4.6 million jobs, and the entire cost could be recouped within ten years by enacting a financial transactions tax. Also, in a recent cover story in *The Nation*, economist Robert Pollin laid out an ambitious yet realistic plan to create 18 million jobs over the next three years through leveraging private-public partnerships.

But don't expect any of this to have an easy time in Congress, where the deficit hysteria now sweeping the political and pundit class constrains the possibility for bold public policy. A recent *New York Times* headline screams, "Huge Deficits May Alter U.S. Politics and Global Power." The *Wall Street Journal* offers this grim warning: "Deficit Balloons into National-Security Threat." The *Washington Post* describes "a budget hole that is driving accumulated debt to dangerous levels."

Behind these sorts of warnings are many of the people who were so fixated on deficits that they missed the housing and credit bubble—not to mention the Wall Street chicanery that made them possible. Now they are peddling the idea that we risk a major debt crisis if government spending continues to fill the gap left by the decline of private-sector demand and investment.

The deficit hawks are unable to distinguish bad deficits from good ones. Bad deficits result from collapsing revenue—whether due to wasteful tax cuts or sluggish economic activity—or unnecessary wars of occupation and other wasteful military spending. Good ones stem from spending to create jobs and spur growth through investments in infrastructure, science and technology, new energy sources, education and worker training.

Instead of giving into the deficit hype with discretionary domestic spending freezes and bipartisan deficit-reduction commissions, President Obama would be wise to directly challenge the conservative narrative that a responsible government cannot drive economic activity.

The president could note that the federal debt held by the public is well within our historical experience. As of the end of 2009, it was 53 percent of GDP—a level that is only slightly higher than in 1993. By 2019, the Congressional Budget Office projects the debt will increase to 68 percent of GDP, still below the level of debt in the 1940s, which reached a peak of about

121 percent in 1946. And even with massive deficits, debt-servicing burdens are projected to remain low, according to an analysis from the New America Foundation.

The president could explain that by virtue of the dollar's role as the world's principal reserve currency, America can accumulate more debt than other economies. Without dollar-denominated debt, the world economy would come to a screeching halt. And that the reality isn't likely to change in the short or medium term, given the problems with the euro and the yen and China's resistance to financial liberalization.

And Obama could argue that, as our experience after World War II amply demonstrates, by investing in a productive economy, we can comfortably reduce our debt while expanding the shared prosperity of the American people.

The Democrats should give Americans a clear choice. Push for a bold jobs bill—let Republicans stand up and filibuster it, just as Democrats forced Kentucky Sen. Jim Bunning (R) to do in his indefensible effort to block an extension of unemployment benefits. Then, come November, take a pro-jobs record to the American people, having exposed the GOP for the obstructionist party that it is.

---

# If Only Financial Reform Really Were Funny
## *March 9, 2010*

In a hilarious video plug for the proposed Consumer Financial Protection Agency, the popular comedy website funnyordie.com gathers *Saturday Night Live*'s famed presidential impersonators—from Chevy Chase to Will Farrell—to advise a slumbering Barack Obama (Fred Armisen). Dana Carvey, reprising

Daddy Bush, tersely sums up the whole shebang about financial reform:

> What you gotta understand is that we got a regulatory issue here. We gotta regulate that or we're gonna get more bubbles. Gonna get bigger, larger, then pop, money goes to the weasels.

Got that right. After the worst financial collapse since the Great Depression, financial reform isn't a luxury. And it shouldn't be a partisan issue. Everyone from the Tea Partiers to Volvo-driving liberals has a stake in shutting down the casino and getting the big banks under control.

Of possible reforms, creating an independent agency to protect consumers from financial abuse should be one of the easier lifts. The problems are obvious. Consumers are battered routinely by predatory mortgage brokers, shifty credit card companies and rapacious payday lenders with exorbitant fees. We've seen that these practices can bring down the global economy, not just the vulnerable consumer. And the utter failure of the Federal Reserve and other regulators to use their powers to police the banks has amply demonstrated the need for an independent cop on the beat. As Elizabeth Warren, chairman of the Congressional panel bird-dogging the bank bailout, likes to note, the government does a better job monitoring the safety of toasters than the safety of mortgages that can bankrupt families.

Meanwhile, the fixes to these problems enjoy overwhelming popular support.

Polling by the Pew Research Center shows that nearly 60 percent of Americans favor tougher regulation of banks. And, as pollster Celinda Lake notes in a survey for the liberal political group Accountable America, the tougher—"round up and throw in jail"—the more popular. As Warren said at a conference on financial reform in New York this month: "This is a dispute between families and banks, not between conservatives and liberals."

So there is no better measure of how craven and corrupt our politics have become than the news that the proposal for the Consumer Financial Protection Agency is about to be abandoned in the Senate. Republicans opposed it from the start, while shamelessly peddling themselves to Wall Street's deep pockets. In the House, not one Republican voted in favor of the diluted reform bill that includes an independent CFPA. And in the Senate, Republicans announced that the price of bipartisan agreement was to shelve any notion of an independent agency. Instead, they're pushing for a new presidentially appointed watchdog to be put inside the Federal Reserve—with rule-making subject to objections by the very same regulators who failed so consistently and ignominiously to protect consumers in the past. Senate Banking Committee Chairman Chris Dodd is trying to get Democrats to sign on to an only slightly toothier version of this compromise. Barney Frank, Dodd's counterpart in the House, had the better reaction: "I thought it was a joke at first, to be honest."

In this debate, the president has been largely absent without leave. Mired in the interminable healthcare debate, he has been unable or unwilling to provide Americans with a clear explanation of what needs to be done to dig our way out of the hole we're in. Without a White House willing to fight hard for reform, Republicans and corporate Democrats pay little price for catering to the bank lobby.

"I have been most struck by how invisible the issue has been as part of the public debate," Bill McInturff, a Republican pollster, told the *New York Times*. If voters don't "understand what it is and why it matters," he added, "it's unlikely to have much consequence in the campaign."

With the *Post*, the *Times* and *60 Minutes* all assuring us that White House Chief of Staff Rahm Emanuel is a political genius, this White House failure is truly befuddling. Surely, nothing is more vital to the economy's future, or to the Democrats' political fortunes, than to take on the banks, get them under control, provide consumers with some protection and make banking a boring profession once again.

The sad thing is that an independent CFPA, as important as it would be to American families, would not even begin to address the hard stuff. Goldman Sachs would still be able to peddle the derivatives that have brought down polities from Greece to Jefferson County, Alabama. The banking sector would be as concentrated and "too big to fail" as ever. The deformed executive-compensation schemes that give bankers multimillion-dollar personal incentives to take untoward risks would remain in place. And federal regulators would continue to stand by.

In the funnyordie.com video, Carvey playing Bush I advises Obama that he should risk his popularity to get the CFPA passed. But this isn't about popularity; it's about challenging the power of the banking lobby. Armisen's Obama asks why he has to "clean up this mess that you all created. Take on the banks and all their trillions of dollars." Well, says Jim Carrey's Ronald Reagan, "As George Washington once said to John Adams, 'Tag, you're it.'" We should all hope that, before it's too late, the real president wakes to realize that.

---

# The Senate's Attempt at Goldman-like Fraud
*April 20, 2010*

Fraud, a crime in finance, is often merely an insult in politics. But there are disturbing parallels between the securities fraud charges outlined in the Securities and Exchange Commission's civil lawsuit against Goldman Sachs and Senate Minority Leader Mitch McConnell's fraudulent case against financial reform. Only, in one case the apparent victims were sophisticated investors, and in the other the designated saps are American voters.

Goldman stands accused of creating and marketing an investment tied to subprime mortgages without disclosing that the underlying securities had been selected by a billionaire investor, John Paulson, who was betting on their failure. The Wall Street powerhouse may have been alone in this particular ugliness—Bear Stearns, hardly a paragon of virtue, apparently turned down a similarly structured deal with Paulson. But it's clear that fraud was pervasive in the lead-up to the financial debacle. Last week, Senate hearings exposed the fraudulent mortgage practices that were central to Washington Mutual's business plan. The Lehman Brothers bankruptcy report revealed the use of accounting gimmicks to hide debt—a tactic that the *Wall Street Journal* suggests remains widespread in the industry. We saw how Goldman arranged complicated currency swaps that enabled politicians in Greece to mask the level of that country's debt while marketing its bonds, practices that were apparently widespread with US municipalities as well. And ProPublica, the Pulitzer Prize–winning investigative organization, exposed how several banks helped the hedge fund Magnetar market similar securities that Magnetar was betting on to fail.

The activities among these that are illegal should be prosecuted; the scams that are not yet illegal should be banned. In particular, complex financial innovations should be outlawed or forced into open exchanges, with banks required to put their own money at risk in any complex security they market. We also need an independent and aggressive Consumer Financial Protection Agency that will police everything from payday lenders to credit card companies that have thrived by gouging their customers. We need to alter the compensation schemes that give bankers million-dollar incentives to cut corners. And we need to radically simplify the financial system, with banks that are too big to fail broken into more manageable entities. The bill now before the US Senate does not go far enough, though some senators are trying to move it in the right direction. Among them are Democrats Sherrod Brown (Ohio), who will offer an amendment to limit the size of banks, and Blanche Lincoln (Ark.), who has surprised critics by proposing legislation to crack down on derivatives trading. Still, with the bank lobby spending millions and employing more than 125 former legislators and aides to delay, dilute and disembowel reform, these efforts must survive a nasty political debate marked by its own form of fraud.

Just before the SEC charges against Goldman were released, McConnell—who has been promoting his party to Wall Street political donors as the banks' last line of defense—issued a letter signed by all forty-one Republican senators in opposition to the financial reform bill. But Republicans are aware that appearing to be in the pocket of the big banks could be dangerous to their political health. So McConnell followed the playbook, virtually word for word, of cynical Republican pollster Frank Luntz, who urged Republicans to trumpet their desire for reform while smearing any Democratic plan as leading to more taxpayer-funded Wall Street bailouts. McConnell criticized Democrats for rushing the bill out of committee on a party-line vote, when it was Republicans on the committee who pushed to pass the bill, putting off amendments and debate until it got to the Senate floor. McConnell then topped off this farce by accusing President Obama of "trying to politicize" this issue.

When testifying before the Financial Crisis Inquiry Commission, Goldman chief executive Lloyd Blankfein defended the practice of marketing securities without telling buyers that it was betting against them, arguing that sophisticated investors could make their own choices. McConnell might argue that his deceptive rhetoric is aimed at voters who are sophisticated enough to make their own judgments about the truth. Let's hope that's right.

---

# Where's the Will to Get Americans Back to Work?
## *May 18, 2010*

Why isn't our government doing more to put people back to work?

Mass unemployment is a human and national calamity. It destroys families, crushes hopes. The longer it lasts, the more it cripples economic recovery and undermines democracy. Nearly 27 million Americans are unemployed or can't find more than part-time work. Yet legislators are reacting to this reality somewhat like the proverbial deer in the headlights—frozen, hoping not to get run over.

Maybe there's a sense that they've already taken care of the problem. Indeed, in a speech in economically beleaguered Buffalo last week, President Obama came close to declaring victory. Beyond giving a perfunctory nod to Americans who are still hurting ("I won't stand here and pretend that we've climbed all the way out of the hole") and talking a bit about small business loans, Obama wanted to celebrate: "We can say beyond a shadow of a doubt, today we are headed in the right direction. . . . All those tough steps we took, they're working. Despite all the naysayers who were predicting failure a year ago, our economy is growing again. Last month we had the strongest job growth that we'd seen in years. . . . Next month is going to be stronger than this month. And next year is going to be better than this year."

It's true that the president's recovery plan successfully stopped the economic free fall he inherited. The economy has started to grow again, and that growth is beginning to produce some jobs, with more added last month than expected. But the hole is deep. At the current rate, it would take five years to return to pre-recession rates of employment. And there's real doubt as to whether the current growth will continue. The Recovery Act and the extraordinary intervention of the Federal Reserve have given the economy its greatest lift. Yet Recovery Act spending peaks this fall, and brutal cuts at the state and local levels are already negating its effects. Meanwhile, the Fed is slowly beginning to unravel its emergency subsidies, but zombie banks still aren't doing much lending. And, of course, no one knows how far the economic turmoil in Europe will spread.

It would seem that new action by Congress to create jobs is more than justified. Yet there wasn't much in the president's Buffalo speech that would make a compelling argument for acting now on jobs.

Also standing in the way of government action is the increasingly loud conversation about the coming debt crisis. The president's bipartisan deficit commission, stacked with deficit hawks, has prematurely launched a debate about US austerity.

It doesn't help that some voters, especially independents, are starting to tell pollsters that they're concerned about deficits and suspicious of spending.

But deficits, for all the scare stories, are not an immediate emergency. We still need to put people to work. And we should be prepared to see deficits increase in the short term in the interest of creating jobs that will sustain the economy in the long term.

Yet without a strong argument from the White House, and with a consensus building around the idea that deficit and spending cuts should be the priority, too little is happening on jobs. Last December, the House passed a $150 billion jobs bill.

It can't get a hearing in the Senate. This year, Rep. George Miller (D-Calif.) introduced a $100 billion bill for state, local and public-service hiring. It hasn't gotten a vote in the House. Even an extension of unemployment insurance and healthcare protection through the end of the year faces conservative obstruction. Republicans tend to line up against any new jobs agenda. And when Blue Dog Democrats, worried about deficits, join them, there's not much hope. In fact, what is needed is something far bolder. The AFL-CIO has detailed a $400 billion plan that would put people to work. This would have a negligible effect on long-term debt projections, which primarily reflect soaring healthcare costs. And a jobs agenda could be paid for once the economy got going. The AFL-CIO suggests passing a financial-speculation tax and a tax on banks that kicks in a couple years from now. That at least would send the bill for the crisis to those who caused it.

Compare Obama's words with the straight talk of Rich Trumka, the president of the AFL-CIO: "When it comes to creating jobs, some in Washington say: 'Go slow, take half steps, don't spend real money.' Those voices are harming millions of unemployed Americans and their families—and they are jeopardizing our economic recovery. It is responsible to have a plan for paying for job creation over time. But it is bad economics and suicidal politics not to aggressively address the job crisis at a time of stubbornly high unemployment."

Bad economics and suicidal politics. He got that right. Unemployed workers can't help the economy grow. And while economists may chatter about recovery, voters won't believe the economy is on the mend until people are back at work, and the outcome of the November elections will hinge on that perception. It would be smart economics and smart politics to summon the will to take action on jobs. A nation that ignores the calamity of joblessness is a nation at risk.

# A Vote for Tax Sanity
## June 2, 2010

Teachers, firefighters and cops are being laid off. Social services slashed. Subsidies to help the unemployed buy health insurance were deep-sixed in the latest tepid jobs bill passed by the House. At a moment when new revenues are desperately needed for a serious public investment agenda, job creation and continued economic recovery, Congress is sounding alarms about the need to shrink the deficit and find cuts, cuts and more cuts. It's insane, inane and exactly what we don't need right now.

Instead, what we do need is a national discussion—front and center—about reforming a tax code that has been rigged via high-priced lobbyists to favor the wealthy at the expense of a struggling middle class.

Despite the major shortcomings in its jobs bill last week, the House did take one significant step in the right direction on taxes. It voted to close one of the most obscene and inequitable loopholes benefiting the richest of the rich—the so-called "carried interest" loophole that taxes hedge fund and private equity managers at a 15 percent capital gains rate rather than an ordinary income tax rate of 35 percent.

That's right, these mega-billionaires pay a lower rate on the bulk of their income than their administrative assistants—not to mention those same cops, firefighters and teachers now facing layoffs. This is morally and economically reprehensible—especially since the corporate tax base has already been severely eroded due to offshoring, tax havens and other quasi-legal tax plans devised by high-end legal and accounting firms. A 2008 GAO report found that two-thirds of US corporations paid zero federal income taxes from 1998 to 2005. Twenty-five percent of the largest US corporations had $1.1 trillion in gross sales in

2005 but paid no federal income taxes. Where is the debate on corporate tax rates and loopholes?

While Wall Street lobbyists were successful in delaying the start date of the House-approved tax reform to January 1, 2011, and only 75 percent of carried interest will be taxed as ordinary income while 25 percent will still be treated as capital gains, the House deserves credit for showing some moxie. Industry lobbyists and their benefactors used all of their usual tricks of the trade, including fear-mongering—warning that closing this loophole would kill jobs, hurt minorities and slow any recovery in the real estate market.

"This is not a time to raise taxes on investments in business. That's a sure way to kill jobs," said Republican Congressman Lee Perry of Nebraska. But the measure passed and will raise approximately $17 billion in urgently needed revenues over the next decade. It now must survive the Senate, where most progressive legislation in these last eighteen months has gone to die.

In fact, efforts to close the carried interest loophole have been defeated in the Senate for three years running. Already, Democratic opponents to reform are resisting—and these aren't your usual Lieberman-Nelson-Baucus suspects, either—Senators Maria Cantwell, Robert Menendez and John Kerry are just a few voicing objections. Further compromises are already in the works, such as taxing only 60 percent of this income at the normal rate, with 40 percent continuing to be treated as capital gains.

"I think there are some distinctions that ought to be drawn, personally," said Kerry. "There's a distinction between long-term, patient, capital formation, with risk, and things that are sort of masquerading as an investment that are fees."

But John Irons, research and policy director of the Economic Policy Institute, has it right when it comes to these so-called "distinctions." He told me: "Work is work. It doesn't matter if you are a plumber, a firefighter, or a venture capitalist. We should not be giving preferential treatment through the tax code to venture capitalists and hedge fund managers just because they found a way to game the system and 'pay' themselves through capital gains rather than ordinary income." Then-candidate Barack Obama supported closing the loophole all the way back in July 2007. He should show some leadership when the Senate returns from recess and takes up the House bill. After all, this is yet another opportunity for the Democratic Party to show that they stand with working people on an issue of fairness that also happens to be a no-brainer politically.

At a time when economic hardship is so widespread and we have Gilded Age–like income inequality, how is it that that Congress would even think twice about asking the wealthiest and most powerful Americans to start paying their fair share of taxes? That's just for starters. The long-term goal must be to overhaul our tax system so that it supports, not subverts, fairness—whether it's unlimited deferred compensation for CEOs, tax deductibility of exorbitant CEO pay packages or closing the carried interest loophole. Without deep tax reform, working people in this country will always get shafted.

## Tough Reforms, but Not Tough Enough
### June 29, 2010

This week, assuming the now-routine Republican filibuster can be overcome, Congress will pass what President Obama hails as "the toughest financial reform since . . . the aftermath of the Great Depression."

The president is right. The reform legislation is far stronger than many Congress-watchers expected. Public fury at the Wall

Street bailout and continued scandals stiffened Congressional spines. Popular mobilization ensured that backsliding would be exposed. And as a result, there are some good things in this bill. It provides consumers with protection from various forms of abusive and predatory lending (except from auto dealers, who managed to exempt themselves from the reach of the new consumer-protection bureau).

It gives regulators a mandate to monitor the biggest financial institutions and clear authority to shut down failing institutions. It promises that the multitrillion-dollar market in over-the-counter derivatives, the risky exotica that exacerbated the financial collapse, will be better regulated through open exchanges. And it gives regulators the authority to impose high capital requirements, forcing banks to hold more equity and thus assume less risk. The bill even taxes the larger banks to pay for its costs. These are significant changes and, as illustrated in last weekend's meetings of the G-20 nations, are far ahead of reforms in other nations.

But are these changes adequate? That depends largely on how you see the problem. If you believe, as Treasury Secretary Tim Geithner presumably does, that the current banking system is basically sound, then the bill—which largely tracks the administration's reform proposals—has much to offer. But if you believe—as do former International Monetary Fund chief economist Simon Johnson, Nobel Prize–winning economist Joseph Stiglitz and other economists, thinkers and activists—that the big banks are simply too big and engaged in exotic gambling with great risk and little societal return, then the reforms are merely a decent first step.

Obama has said that we can't go back to an economy where the banks make 40 percent of all corporate profits. But the big banks are emerging from the crisis more concentrated than ever, and financial sector profits are already up to nearly 30 percent of total corporate profits. The reform bill does nothing to break up the big banks or to change their basic way of doing business. The legislation also gives immense discretion to obscure regulators who will make up the rules. These days, given the catastrophe wrought by misplaced faith in self-regulating markets, a revived Securities and Exchange Commission, a beleaguered FDIC and even the bankers' bank, the Federal Reserve, are showing some muscle. But the bank lobby is still extremely effective. Many political appointees are products of Wall Street. And regulators, charged with ensuring the soundness of banks, are attentive to arguments against costly regulation.

And there's the rub. The current banking structure and practices virtually ensure repeated financial crises. Take that from uberbanker Jamie Dimon, CEO of JPMorgan Chase. In his testimony before the Financial Crisis Commission, Dimon said, "It's not a surprise that we know we have crises every five or ten years. My daughter called me from school one day and said, 'Dad, what's a financial crisis?' And without trying to be funny, I said, 'It's the type of thing that happens every five to seven years.' And she said: 'Why is everyone so surprised?' So we shouldn't be surprised."

But Dimon's insouciance about recurrent financial crises is misleading and dangerous. First, it applies only to recent history. After the New Deal reforms, as Harvard Law professor Elizabeth Warren has noted, America went nearly fifty years without a major banking crisis. The New Deal regulations closed down the financial casino and turned banking into a safe and boring occupation. It is only since those regulations were shredded that we've seen recurrent and increasingly costly financial crises.

Second, Dimon implies we should just relax about financial crackups. This ignores how costly they are to society. This most recent collapse has cost millions of people their jobs, their homes and their retirement savings. It has endangered pensions, forced ruinous cuts of public services and doubled the national debt as a percentage of gross domestic product in the resulting recession. Having been bailed out by taxpayers, Dimon may feel serene about a financial crisis every five years; the rest of us can't afford to be.

We've seen the stakes at risk, the forces arrayed, the leaders involved. We've witnessed the first skirmishes. But the fight to create a system in which the financial masters of the universe serve the real economy has only just begun.

# Making the Economy More Just
## *July 21, 2010*

Congress has passed the Wall Street Reform and Consumer Protection Act, but the task of transforming our economy into one of shared and sustainable prosperity has only just begun. Structural reform will come not through the sweep of a single piece of legislation but with new, innovative economic models that better reflect the democratic values of this country.

The good news is that some of these transformative ideas are already taking root. Here are five ways to build a more just economy that Americans are experimenting with across the country.

### *The answer is "B"*

Corporations are compelled to pursue a single objective: maximize profit. In fact, a company can be sued for following goals that veer from that statutory obligation.

That's why Maryland State Sen. Jamie Raskin sponsored the Benefit Corporation legislation that was signed into law this spring. It gives businesses the option to register as a "B corporation," an entity legally obligated to maximize both shareholder value and advance a common public purpose such as cleaner air, open space or affordable housing. The B corporation's stated public goal is vigorously monitored by independent, third-party groups. It's a new business model with social consciousness in its DNA.

B corporation legislation has also been passed in Vermont, and it is being considered in New York, Pennsylvania, New Jersey, Oregon, Washington and Colorado.

### Banks for the people

Hundreds of billions of public dollars have flowed to bail out Wall Street banks, which, in turn, have rewarded us by resuming the practice of giving obscene salaries and bonuses while failing to get credit flowing again. One bank that didn't need to be bailed out, though, was the state-owned Bank of North Dakota. The bank, which was created in 1919, avoided the subprime and derivatives debacle and has $4 billion under management to meet its customers' credit needs.

The state-bank model looks increasingly appealing to states and residents who are tired of giving their money to giant multinationals that fail to reinvest in their communities. Proposals for state-owned banks are being considered by Massachusetts, Virginia, Washington, Illinois, Michigan, Hawaii, Vermont and New Mexico, and they were championed by gubernatorial candidates in Oregon and Michigan.

### Move your big money

Arianna Huffington's Move Your Money campaign handed consumers a creative tool with which to hit the big banks. It encourages them to divest their money from those banks and open accounts at smaller community banks and credit unions. Last week in New York City, the most powerful local union presidents and city Comptroller John Liu took another step when they let Wall Street banks know their response to the mortgage crisis is unacceptable.

The threat made implicitly in a letter—and explicitly by some of the union leaders—is that these institutional investors will move their pensions to more responsive financial institutions if the banks don't improve mortgage-modification efforts immediately.

These unions represent over 500,000 working families, and New York City has a few bucks at its disposal too. Civic and labor leaders can use this model to let banks know that if they don't behave as good corporate citizens, they will move their big money to institutions that do.

### Taxing the casino

The high-speed wheelers and dealers of stocks, derivatives and currencies in the Wall Street casino were major players in bringing our economy to its knees. That kind of short-term trading serves no useful purpose, and a financial speculation tax is one way to rein it in.

A tax of 0.25 percent or less on each trade would be negligible for regular investors but significant to those looking for the quick score. It would also generate significant revenue at a time when resources are slim; an Institute for Policy Studies report points out that such a tax could bring in an estimated $180 billion annually—more than any other revenue-raiser on the table.

There is also global support for the reform. Britain imposes a 0.5 percent stock "stamp tax" on each trade on the London stock exchange. Also in favor of the tax are French President Nicolas Sarkozy—who will chair the Group of 20 in 2011—and German Chancellor Angela Merkel.

## Worker is boss

The *Post* reports that non-financial companies are "hoarding" $1.8 trillion in cash while they continue to "hold back on hiring." Not so the Evergreen Cooperatives of Cleveland—community-based, worker-owned operations supported by a mix of private and public funds. The Evergreen Cooperative Laundry and Ohio Cooperative Solar are already up and running, and ten other such enterprises are slated to open in the city this year.

Workers buy equity in the co-ops through payroll deductions and earn a living wage working at green jobs. The businesses focus on the local market—meeting the procurement needs of "anchor institutions" such as large hospitals and universities in the area. Each co-op pays 10 percent of its pretax profits back to the umbrella organization to help seed new enterprises.

Other cities considering this model include Atlanta, Baltimore, Pittsburgh and Detroit. And other towns around Ohio are considering it as well. At a time when so many jobs are being slashed or outsourced, the Cleveland cooperatives show us how we can create local jobs and reinvest in our communities.

Those who believe the financial sector should serve rather than dominate the economy will welcome these reforms. They are radical and achievable. But they will demand determined idealism and tough organizing in the years ahead.

# America Has a Financial Watchdog. Now It Should Fight to Keep It

*October 12, 2010*

Even before Elizabeth Warren and the Consumer Financial Protection Bureau take on the most deceptive, exploitative consumer rip-offs in the financial services industry, Republicans are maneuvering to make the mission extremely difficult—if not downright impossible.

Witness House Republican efforts to deny funding to the Treasury Department and Warren during the period when they are tasked with getting the bureau up and running. And Sen. Richard Shelby, the ranking Republican on the Senate Banking Committee, said he'd want to "revisit"—meaning emasculate— the financial reform bill if the GOP regains the majority in Congress in November. "The consumer agency bothers me the most," Shelby said. "I thought the creation of it and the way it was created was a mistake."

That's why the remarkable coalition that took on the financial titans during the reform debate, and then successfully waged a campaign for Warren's appointment to build the bureau, now needs to reinvigorate its effort to create a truly strong and independent agency.

At the height of the fight, the financial industry mobilized an army of 2,603 lobbyists, including seventy-three former members of Congress, and it was spending $1.4 million a day to eliminate the agency.

But Americans for Financial Reform (AFR)—a broad and diverse coalition that included the AARP, the AFL-CIO, the Economic Policy Institute, USAction, the National Urban League and Public Citizen, among others—worked with Congressional allies and organized constituent pressure to ensure a much tougher bill than corporate lobbyists bargained for. And the intent is that the new consumer bureau will work to end credit card rip-offs and debt-relief scams, police the troubled mortgage market and predatory lending, and resolve consumer complaints. The bureau won't actually have the chance to enforce rules on behalf of consumers until July 2011. Yet as Warren and her colleagues begin to formulate new rules, and as the reality of financial reform begins to take shape, they will face a blitz by Wall Street lobbyists and their Congressional enablers.

"The congressional attacks are likely to be attempts to carve out or restrict power, or attempts to get rid of the whole bureau," predicts AFR Executive Director Lisa Donner. "And they can distract people from the job of putting the agency together and getting down to work. Many specific special interests could also wage battles that would take lots of time and energy to defeat."

It will be critical to keep people outside of Washington informed and engaged so that the bureau's fate isn't determined by an "inside game" of lobbyists and their patrons. Warren can lead in that regard, using her bully pulpit to bring attention to industry abuses and making sure the promise of reform is sustained in the staffing of the new agency. (She's off to a promising start in bringing on such tested consumer protectors as Raj Date, the former executive director of the Cambridge Winter Center for Financial Institutions Policy.)

But it will be up to the coalition that fought for Warren's appointment to make lawmakers realize that they cater to special-interest lobbyists at their political peril. Skillful media advocacy will be needed to counter the backroom handshakes and well-funded ad campaigns.

Warren is in place to stand up to the industry—and President Obama appears to be standing firmly behind her. But even so, Donner argues, "they won't be able to do their jobs unless there is outside pressure pushing back against what will be huge pressure from the financial industry, on the shape of the whole bureau and on every rule that they start to look at. It's our job on the outside to make sure our voices are heard loud and clear." The fight to create a powerful financial watchdog for consumers is not a right-vs.-left fight but a wrong-vs.-right fight. Or as Warren puts it: "This is a dispute of families versus banks. It's not conservatives versus liberals." It was inside-outside organizing that carried reform this far, and it is inside-outside organizing that Warren needs at her back now to win this next fight and beyond.

---

## Among the Wealthy, a New Voice for Fiscal Sacrifice
### *November 30, 2010*

President Obama's discussion Tuesday with leaders of both parties about the expiring Bush tax cuts comes at a time when a growing chorus of progressives and other reasonable-minded Americans have been ramping up pressure on the White House to allow the cuts for millionaires to end—as intended—at the end of the year. Last week that chorus was joined by a group of unlikely, albeit welcome, new singers: the millionaires themselves.

In a November letter to President Obama, a group calling itself Patriotic Millionaires for Fiscal Strength argued that the wealthiest Americans do not need, and should not be given, an extension on tax cuts that have done next to nothing to improve broad economic prosperity. "We are writing to urge you to stand firm against those who would put politics ahead of their country," the letter's authors write. "Now, during our nation's moment of need, we are eager to do our fair share."

Signers include a number of early Google executives as well as leaders of companies such as Ben and Jerry's, Men's Wearhouse and Princeton Review. They aren't the first group of ultra-wealthy people to signal discomfort with senseless fiscal policy designed to benefit the top 2 percent. A group of 700 business leaders and individuals known as Responsible Wealth have called the Bush tax cuts "irresponsible" and "downright inexcusable." Bill Gates Sr. and Warren Buffett, of course, have also called for a change in priorities.

For the most part, these are not the kinds of proclamations we have come to expect from America's rich. More often than not their views are distilled through megaphones such as the Chamber of Commerce, which wields outsized influence and uses both foreign and national dollars to further the causes of the relative few. We have come to expect America's wealthy to stand behind the Republican Party—a party itself composed largely of millionaires in Congress—and to demand new income tax cuts, or corporate loopholes, or the end of the estate tax, even while they peddle faux concern about the federal government's long-term debt position.

It's worth remembering, however, that it wasn't always this way.

There was a time when the concept of patriotism—the idea of putting country above self—extended beyond our foreign policy. There was a time when economic patriotism was very much a part of the business community's mind-set, even embedded in the worldview of the kinds of Northeast Republicans who are now all but extinct. Robert Johnson, for example, one of the founders of Johnson & Johnson, urged his business colleagues in a 1947 speech never to ignore the plight of the working class. Doing so, he said, "is as foolish as it would be to ignore public health, crime, and the need for education."

During the golden era of the 1950s, a Republican president, along with Republican members of Congress, accepted a top marginal tax rate for millionaires that was 91 percent. "The only way to make more tax cuts now is to have bigger and bigger deficits and to borrow more and more money," President Eisenhower argued. "This is one kind of chicken that always comes home to roost. An unwise tax cutter, my fellow citizens, is no real friend of the taxpayer."

That sentiment would be unimaginable coming out of the mouth of a modern Republican. Ideology has trumped that kind of frankness and logic. Instead, the business community and the wealthy, and the Republican Party they prop up, have abandoned principle and policy—as well as any sense of a social compact—in exchange for a totally distorted view of reality.

After all, any honest look at our economic plight suggests that we must change our posture if we're to confront these challenges successfully. There may have been a time, during the boom of the '90s perhaps, when the business community and the wealthy would have had great incentive to focus their efforts on reducing their tax rates and lobbying for lax regulations that they could argue might otherwise stifle their profits. But that kind of selfishly narrow worldview, that kind of chipping-away-at-the-margins attitude has no place in this time of deep and painful economic hardship.

It isn't regulations and tax rates that are stifling business. It's a lack of demand, spurred by a lack of investment by business, caused by an economic crisis that was, in turn, the result of the kind of reckless deregulation these same individuals and businesses spent the last several decades fighting for.

Millionaires aren't better off over the long run with the continuation of the Bush tax cuts. They'd be better off if the $700 billion it will take to pay for those cuts was instead put into new stimulative efforts—the kind of efforts that would spur real economic growth. Those initiatives would create jobs and new prosperity not just for the wealthy, but for everyone. They would drive demand.

When business is doing well, millionaires will be doing well too. In the meantime, their selfishness hurts everyone, including themselves. Will they ever snap out of it and see the new reality as it presents itself in front of them? Only time—and perhaps the negotiations that began today—will tell. In the meantime, this group of Patriotic Millionaires gives us hope. They give us reason to believe that not everyone at the top believes that it's only the top that matters.

# Banking for the People
## *February 7, 2011*

When you read the Financial Crisis Inquiry Commission report released last week, it's hard to believe that not so long ago banks were downright boring. Citigroups, JPMorgans, Bank of Americas, and Morgan Stanleys weren't peddling worthless mortgage-backed securities so that Masters of the Universe could collect obscene bonuses. Instead—in response to the Great Depression and some common sense regulations—banks were mostly local, single outlets that collected deposits and made sensible loans.

But beginning in the 1970s, bipartisan public policy ushered in a new era of deregulation and consolidation. The argument was that behemoth banks would be safer, more sophisticated and efficient, and would save consumers money and support economic growth.

For the most damning evidence of just how wrong that argument is, check out the lost wealth and wrecked lives of this Great Recession. The statistics on the size and wealth of today's banks are also very revealing: in 1995, small and mid-sized banks with assets up to $10 billion held 61 percent of all US deposits; today they hold only one-third. The Giant Banks—with over $100 billion in assets—had just 7 percent of US deposits in 1995, but today hold 44 percent. And despite the fact that small and mid-sized banks possess just 22 percent of all bank assets today, they nevertheless make a dramatic 54 percent of all small business loans. (In contrast, the largest twenty banks average $380 billion in assets and yet do just 28 percent of small-business lending.)

This concentration of financial power is not only dangerous, it also fails to serve the needs of the real economy. Stacy Mitchell, senior researcher with the New Rules Project, says that examining the balance sheets of local and giant banks reveals "two entirely different types of businesses." Local banks are still largely engaged in taking deposits and moving money into the community through the likes of mortgages and small business loans, while giant banks take deposits and engage in speculative trading that privatizes profits, socializes costs, and exacerbates economic inequality.

"We're fortunate that the small banks are still out there, because if it weren't for them, a lot of the basic economic activity in our communities—the real source of jobs in our communities—would not have the financing that it needs," says Mitchell.

Indeed, there are still about 8,000 credit unions and more than 7,600 community banks in the nation. The pressing question is: How do we support and grow these institutions, and return to a people-centered banking system that makes credit readily available and invests in our communities?

One possible answer is the State Bank movement.

The Bank of North Dakota was established in 1919. All state revenues are required by law to be deposited in the bank, and technically all assets of the state are also assets of the bank.

"That means it's got a huge deposit base and a huge capital base," says Ellen Brown, author of *The Web of Debt.*

According to Brown, North Dakota has a huge surplus, the lowest default and unemployment rates in the country, and the most local banks per capita.

"The North Dakota State Bank has actually helped the local banks because they partner with them and provide capital," says Brown. "Local banks elsewhere in the country got sucked into the mortgage-backed securities situation where they would sell off their loans in order to have the capital to make more loans. That doesn't happen in North Dakota because the state bank stepped in and helped with capital needs."

State banks might also be helpful in confronting the budget crises faced by state and local governments. According to Brown, when President Obama proposed that the Fed help states just as it helped Wall Street when it made $12 trillion available through short-term loans and the purchase of toxic assets, the Fed said it wouldn't happen because that kind of activity is not part of the Federal Reserve Act.

But a state with its own bank could easily undertake such action, refinancing the deficit at 0 percent interest (just as banks are loaning to one another for virtually nothing, while states are currently borrowing at an average rate of 4.7 percent!).

There are currently three states with bills pending to create state banks—Washington, Illinois and Oregon. Legislation to begin state bank feasibility studies is being considered in Hawaii, Virginia and Massachusetts.

There's transpartisan support for the state bank movement. Barbara Dudley, co-chair of Oregon Working Families Party, says that allies on the Oregon state bank bill include small business associations, farmers, and Republicans. (In fact, a strong state bank bill is being introduced by a Republican from eastern Oregon.)

"We need to get out of our stuck places in terms of thinking who it is that might be willing to think about these ideas and put them forward," says Dudley.

Jared Gardner, co-chair of Oregonians for a State Bank, also spends a good deal of his time listening to bankers and small business advocates, hardly your usual suspects in progressive fights. He says there is broad agreement on the need to reinvest in communities through these kinds of efforts.

"We have an economic leakage happening in our communities. Working people work really hard, and then we pay all of this interest out of our state," says Gardner. "If we can support a vibrant community banking system, then we will have more small business jobs, more jobs, and a healthier economy that responds to local needs."

Of course, achieving this will require constraining the size and limiting the power of big financial institutions. *The Nation*'s national affairs correspondent William Greider notes that small banks typically don't want to disturb their relationships with the big banks "because in a pinch they can go to them for help through a tough moment . . . that's their life blood." On the other hand, Greider says this issue "goes to all of those institutions in the economy that either didn't know, and now know, or have been sulking for years about the advantages that the government hands out to certain institutions and not to others, and they are now on the table and visible. This politics is going to get stronger, I predict."

Indeed, this will be a tough and long fight to say the least. But the more people see the relationships between the US banking system and their concerns about jobs and the economy, their children's futures and the state budget crises, the more people may be willing to organize and fight for this kind of systemic change.

# It's the Economic Debate, Not the US, That's Bankrupt

*April 12, 2011*

The government is open, but hope has lost its audacity.

After negotiations in which Republicans ended up gaining more cuts than they originally sought, President Obama chose to celebrate "the largest annual spending cut in history." Lest we forget, these cuts total $78 billion from the president's own budget, with programs for working and poor families taking the biggest hit. Any more triumphs like this and Obama will become a new American synonym for pyrrhic victory.

Lost in the coverage of the juvenile, perils-of-Pauline, last-hour rescue from a government closure is the substance of the deal. The great con of the Boehner–Tea Party good-cop, bad-cop negotiating pose is that it focuses attention on intra-party melodramas. The real deal gets lost in the noise.

The cuts—"79 percent of what we wanted" in House Budget Chairman Paul Ryan's words—will be exacted immediately, despite an economy still struggling to recover from the worst downturn since the Great Depression. A Congress packed with millionaires seems more attuned to the rising stock market and record corporate profits. But 25 million people are still in need of full-time work; home values are sinking; gas and food prices are rising and wages are not.

The most sensible American economists warn against cutting back spending and laying off workers now. Even fiscal hawks like the co-chairs of the president's deficit commission, Erskine Bowles and Alan Simpson, opposed cuts in spending in the current fiscal year. Similarly, Fed chairman Ben Bernanke, the conservative appointee of George W. Bush, warned against cutting spending or raising taxes in December, arguing that the economy still was struggling to get going.

That's all forgotten now. "So be it" was Speaker Boehner's infamous response when asked if the House budget assault would cost federal jobs. Goldman Sachs and Moody's projected the original Republican plan would cost 700,000 jobs over the next year; now we'll lose only three-fourths of that number. Some triumph.

The priorities in the deal also offend. Originally, all of the Republican cuts would have been taken from domestic programs, with deep reductions in education spending on everything from Head Start to Pell grants for lower-income college students. Obama succeeded in limiting the damage by spreading the cuts out more. The defense budget will rise by $5 billion (less than the $7 billion Republicans wanted). But the toughest cuts will come from the departments of Education, Labor, and Health and Human Services. Our costly infrastructure investment gap will rise. A $1 billion across-the-board cut in domestic spending sets the precedent for future—and senseless—across-the-board cuts.

Although the media seldom mention it, the cuts aren't really a "down payment" on deficit reduction. They simply are a partial payment for the $700 billion, ten-year cost of the extension of the Bush top-end tax cuts that Republicans insisted on in December.

Now Washington plunges immediately into the battle over the fiscal year 2012 budget. Tea Party tribunes—led by Rep. Michele Bachmann—are vowing to block the pro forma vote on raising the debt ceiling unless there are structural changes to the budget. Having played chicken with shutting down the government, they are now raising the stakes by threatening to shut down the world economy.

Republicans have doubled down on their reverse Robin Hood agenda. The plan put forth by House Budget Committee

Chairman Paul Ryan calls for the wealthy to launch another of-fensive in the class war they've been winning. It would slash an-other 20 percent from domestic programs, end Medicare as we know it, cut a trillion from Medicaid, repeal protections for consumers and the environment. It would do this not to reduce the deficit—the Congressional Budget Office estimates that the Ryan plan would increase the deficit over ten years—but to pay for extending the Bush tax cuts and further lowering tax rates on the rich and corporations.

According to aides, Obama has decided to don the mantle of deficit hawk, offering a more measured alternative to Ryan's ruinous plan. Unlike Ryan, Obama will repeal the top-end Bush tax cuts, get reductions from the Pentagon and retain the savings from healthcare reform. He plans to offer up cuts in Medicare and Medicaid, and possibly put Social Security on the table, something Ryan had the good sense to avoid.

Lost in this discussion is what the country needs: a clear strategy to build the economy and revive the middle class. That requires making the investments vital to our future and figuring out how to pay for them. It requires taxing what we have too much of (financial speculation and extreme concentration of income and wealth) and investing in what we have too little of (education programs such as pre-K, 21st-century infrastructure and renewable energy). And it would address the real—and sole—source of our long-term debt crisis: not Social Security and Medicare, not "entitlements," but a broken healthcare sys-tem, dominated by powerful drug, insurance and hospital lob-bies, that costs about twice as much per capita as the health systems of other industrial countries and ensures that while other systems may have bad results, ours has worse.

Contrary to what the Tea Party says, America isn't broke. The Washington establishment is bankrupt intellectually, not fi-nancially. The last bastions of middle-class security—Social Security, Medicare and Medicaid—are at risk in the class war that the right is waging for the rich. If the president offers not a defense but a parlay, citizens will have to mobilize to make it clear to Washington that it has not yet gotten the message.

# Find True Centrism in the People's Budget
## *May 5, 2011*

The Congressional Progressive Caucus (CPC) People's Budget— the strongest rebuke to the Robin Hood in reverse "Ryan Budget" that was passed by the best Republican House *Citizens United* can buy—is receiving some well-deserved national attention as the budget debate now moves to the Senate.

*The Nation* immediately recognized the sense and sanity of the progressive plan to create a budget surplus in ten years— through tax fairness, bringing troops home and investing in job creation—and others are now praising its strengths too.

"The Courageous Progressive Caucus Budget," writes *The Economist*. "Mr. Ryan has been fulsomely praised for his courage. The Progressive Caucus has not. I'm not really sure what 'courage' is supposed to mean here, but this seems precisely backwards."

*New York Times* columnist Paul Krugman describes the People's Budget as "the only major budget proposal out there offering a plausible path to balancing the budget . . . unlike the Ryan plan, which was just right-wing orthodoxy with an added dose of magical thinking—[it] is genuinely courageous because it calls for shared sacrifice."

While a Democratic Senate won't pass this budget, with some savvy and organized pressure from the grassroots and outside groups, it could push its principles during the upcoming debate on the budget and debt ceiling, and an expected deficit reduction package from the "Gang of Six."

For example, closing tax loopholes that encourage companies to ship jobs overseas, eliminating oil and gas subsidies, ending our wars abroad, taxing the mega-rich—these are true centrist policies, reflecting mainstream views. While embracing these good ideas might do damage to some Senators' corporate campaign contributions, it could pay off at the polls (and strengthen our democracy, which ideally would be more than a peripheral consideration for our legislators).

"The public wants job creation, tax fairness, strong retirement protections and deficit reduction—none of that is in dispute," Rep. Raúl Grijalva, co-chair of the CPC, told me. "The People's Budget has been embraced by the public and the economic community. All the Senate has to do now is lead by following. Anyone who takes a serious look around the country sees the need for a fair budget that lifts us all up together. The People's Budget fits the bill and needs to be considered."

An April 17 *Washington Post*/ABC poll found 72 percent support raising taxes on Americans with incomes over $250,000 per year as the best way to eliminate the national debt. The People's Budget does just that—rescinding the upper-income tax cuts in December's tax deal and creating higher-income tax brackets for millionaires and billionaires as proposed in Congresswoman Jan Schakowsky's Fairness in Taxation Act.

A March 31 Gallup Poll indicates the top two preferences for improving the economy are to "stop sending jobs overseas" and "create more infrastructure work." The People's Budget accomplishes both goals, including an investment of $1.45 trillion in job creation, education, clean energy, broadband infrastructure, housing and R&D, and finally creating a long-proposed national infrastructure investment bank to support loans and grants on projects that are vital to US economic competitiveness. It would also tax the earnings of US-controlled foreign subsidiary corporations as earned income, rather than promoting offshoring by deferring those taxes until earnings are repatriated to the United States.

The budget debate will play out in the Senate and the media for the next several weeks, and it can indeed be moved in the direction of a People's Budget—if Senators hear from constituents and begin to speak out in support of these principles. They need to know that these are the issues you will be voting on—a budget that makes the wealthy pay their fair share, that ends the wars and brings the troops home, that invests in infrastructure and job creation. They need to know that there is a blueprint out there that accomplishes this and it deserves their attention and support—the Congressional Progressive Caucus People's Budget.

This effort will continue into the summer, when the CPC participates in a twelve-city nationwide "People's Tour." No matter your issue—peace, the environment, education, poverty and economic inequality—all issues will be impacted by these vital budget choices we make. Get involved in the People's fight now.

# Why Aren't the Powers That Be Tackling the Jobs Crisis?
*May 10, 2011*

Washington is the only city in America where housing values are going up. That may help explain why the political class is so divorced from the nation's agonies. Sure, the entire nation celebrated the dispatch of Osama bin Laden, but when it comes to the economy, the Beltway is a world unto itself.

Two years from the official beginning of the "recovery," America continues to suffer a deep and punishing jobs crisis. One in six Americans of working age is unemployed or underemployed. College students, laden with record levels of debt, are graduating into the worst jobs market since the Great Depression. Long-term unemployment is at unprecedented levels. At current rates of job growth, we won't return to pre-recession employment levels until 2016. And the jobs that are being created—largely in the service industry—tend to have lower pay and benefits than the jobs that were lost.

Republicans won big in 2010 elections with now–House Speaker John Boehner bellowing coast to coast, "Where are the jobs?" But since coming to Washington, the Tea Party–dominated House has focused on everything but jobs—moving to repeal healthcare reform, cripple financial reform, assail the Environmental Protection Agency, defund Planned Parenthood and NPR, and enact savage cuts in domestic spending.

Perhaps the reason is that the party is bereft of ideas on how to create jobs. Last week, Senate Republicans chose freshman Sen. Rob Portman (R-Ohio) to roll out a seven-point "Senate Republican Jobs Plan." Portman, the Office of Management and Budget director under George W. Bush, was a curious choice, since he contributed to the administration that ran up record deficits and produced zero job growth and declining incomes while driving the economy off the cliff.

Turns out this wasn't an accident, since much of the new Republican agenda is the old Bush agenda. The argument remains the same: the way to recover from the Great Recession is to go back to the policies that drove us into it—more top-end and corporate tax cuts, more deregulation, more corporate trade accords. Now those who brought us disaster would add deep and immediate spending cuts, including "entitlement reform" (read cutting Social Security and ending Medicare and Medicaid as we know them). And then they would lard on the hot-button conservative fixations du jour—repeal healthcare reform, stop "card check" for unions, stop the EPA from regulating greenhouse gases, subsidizing nuclear power and "drill, baby, drill."

Hard to take any of this seriously. Tax cuts would add to the cash that companies are sitting on while they wait for customers to show up. Cuts in spending would add to government layoffs. Pushing deregulation two years after Wall Street excesses blew up the economy takes chutzpah, not common sense. The three Bush trade accords—Panama, Colombia and South Korea—will not make a measurable difference for jobs one way or another. Even Portman didn't seem to be paying much attention; he rolled out the plan in front of an Ohio manufacturing plant that has been subsidized by the stimulus plan and alternative-energy subsidies that Republicans are committed to ending.

The next day, House Democrats unveiled their more ambitious "Make It in America" plan. This recognizes that the country can't keep shipping jobs abroad while borrowing $2 billion a day from abroad to pay for what we import. The package contains its share of political malarkey—the Braley Bill to ensure that all American flags are made in America, for example—but at its center is a serious strategy for revitalizing the country, one that deserves far more attention and debate than it's getting. It tasks the president with creating a manufacturing strategy for the country. It would establish an infrastructure bank and invest in rebuilding America's decrepit roads and bridges. A range of incentives are proposed for capturing a lead in the green industrial revolution that will sweep the world. The plan also would legislate buy-America procurement policies to help create markets at home while setting up a mechanism to challenge Chinese currency manipulation.

Yet even this plan slights present dangers of mass unemployment—failing to call for federal aid to the states and cities to avoid layoffs of police officers and teachers, and failing to provide public jobs for the young who are unable to find work under current conditions.

As Ezra Klein of the *Washington Post* noted, it is a measure of Washington's remove from the country that the two plans were unveiled by the two bodies with the least power to make anything happen—the minority House Democrats and the minority Senate Republicans. Those who do have the power—the White House, the House Republican majority and the Senate Democratic majority—remain silent about jobs. Instead, they are locked in a macabre dance to the death on deficits—oblivious to the human casualties caused by mass unemployment.

This might be diversionary, at best, were America not in such dire straits. Home values are falling again. Wages aren't keeping up with prices. States and cities are laying off more employees. The trade deficit is rising, despite the lower dollar. Masked by the statistic of 9 percent unemployment are 25 million people in need of full-time work. Mass unemployment, particularly in a society like ours with such a limited safety net, is a tale of misery, one that resounds across the country and goes virtually unheard in our capital. Americans think Washington isn't listening—and they are right.

*Part III*

# HERDING ELEPHANTS

# The Folly of Palin's High-Priced "Populism"
*February 9, 2010*

Speaking to the Tea Party convention in Tennessee, Sarah Palin roused the upscale crowd with a dose of white-hot populism: "While people on Main Street look for jobs, people on Wall Street, they're collecting billions and billions in your bailout bonuses." She suggested that top bankers should be fired or prosecuted. "Everyday Americans are wondering," she declaimed, "Where are the consequences for helping to get us into this worst economic situation since the Great Depression?"

But Palin's populist formula hasn't caught on with Congressional Republicans. Instead of trying to stir outrage on Main Street, they're focused on trying to rustle up cash and allegiances on Wall Street. The pitch: Wall Street should be experiencing "buyer's remorse" about Obama now that he's trying to tax and break up the big banks. And if you're ticked off by Obama's (mild) reforms and (albeit, occasional) upbraiding of "fat cat" bankers, then you should buy Republican. The *Wall Street Journal* reports that House Minority Leader John Boehner scurried to meet with JPMorgan chief executive James Dimon, a major Obama donor, stressing that Republicans opposed the president's moves to control executive pay and impose new banking regulations. Meanwhile, John Cornyn, the head of the committee in charge of raising dough for Republican Senate candidates, has been making regular trips to New York. "I just don't know how long you can expect people to contribute money to a political party whose main plank of their platform is to punish you," Cornyn told the *New York Times*.

It's clear that a financial-industry overhaul—regulating and shrinking the big banks so that they don't go back to making risky bets with the confidence that taxpayers will cover their losses—is necessary. But not one House Republican voted for financial reform in December. And bipartisan Senate negotiations on reform just broke apart over Republican opposition to creating a Consumer Financial Protection Agency, or any quasi-independent agency with the power to protect consumers from the abuses, predatory lending and frauds of the financial community. Not surprisingly, Sen. Richard Shelby, ranking Republican of the Banking Committee, has been raking in Wall Street contributions.

Republicans are demonstrating they'll go for the money—national interest, be damned. And that attitude extends beyond financial reform. Take the Republican response to Obama's proposed overhaul of federal student loans. The president wants to move from subsidized private loans that the government guarantees anyway to direct lending—a switch that could save an estimated $80 billion over ten years. The savings from ending this classic special-interest rip-off could, in turn, be used to expand the number of Pell Grants to help poor students go to college and for tax credits to help working families pay for tuition. It is, as the president says, a "no-brainer." But there's enough lobbying money up against student-loan reform—Sallie Mae spent $3.48 million on lobbying in 2009—that it apparently made Republicans think twice. When the House version of the bill went up for a vote last fall, all of six Republicans supported it.

Of course, courtship rituals between politicians and big money aren't new to Washington. And Republicans aren't the only ones playing the game. In fact, the banks' high-powered Democratic lobbyists are on the hunt for Democratic senators who will help kill student-loan reform altogether.

The natural impulse for too many Democrats heading into a tough election year will be to compete for Wall Street money by diluting financial, student-loan and healthcare reforms. That's why progressives need to move on three fronts. Expose how

Wall Street interests and bipartisan lobbyists block reforms. Redouble efforts to pass the Fair Elections Now Act, so small-"d" democratic public financing counters special-interest money. And challenge the Supreme Court's recent *Citizens United* ruling with a constitutional amendment strategy.

Democrats should also give Republicans plenty of room to do themselves in. By openly declaring themselves for sale to Wall Street, Republicans are displaying the kind of crony capitalism that drives Americans to form Tea Parties.

Ironically, this doesn't seem to bother Sarah Palin. Faced with a choice between subsidizing the banks and poor kids, she went with the banks, warning the Tea Party activists that the Obama administration is "taking over" everything, including "healthcare, student loans." With views like that, she won't have any trouble getting speaking gigs at $100,000 a shot.

# Eric Cantor's Cant
## *July 19, 2009*

Virginia Congressman Eric Cantor may be a GOP rising star, but he sure is a hypocrite. How else to describe someone who's a leading critic of President Obama's Recovery Act and joins his Congressional colleagues to urge Virginia's Department of Transportation to apply for stimulus money for high-speed rail? If that isn't two-faced, what is?

He's also a demagogue: "Millions of jobs will be crushed by the Administration's policies." Say what? The stimulus may have been too small and overemphasized tax cuts, but it's helped states, including his own, with longer unemployment benefits, expanded food stamps and subsidies for people who've lost jobs to extend their health insurance. It's also kept teachers in the classroom, cops on the street and got workers rehired. Hours after Cantor delivered the GOP's weekly radio address blasting the stimulus, Vice President Biden announced that $1.5 million of the bill's money would go to the Richmond Police Department to retain officers. And $20 million is going to Chesterfield County, a suburb of Richmond, to help 275 teachers from being fired. Virginia's working men and women should remember that Cantor fought hard to cut a provision in the stimulus bill that was designed to help low-income workers.

As Obama marks his sixth month in office, his presidency will be judged by its laser-like focus on creating jobs—good jobs, and many of them. Double-digit unemployment is a ticking time bomb, and his economic team needs to work quickly to defuse it. But Cantor and crew don't care about creating jobs. They want to spin the debate about the economy so their party, which has absolutely nothing to offer working people, games the 2010 midterm elections.

It may be, as some argue, that the politics of getting a second stimulus through a Congress filled with GOP obstructionists and conservative Democrats is too tough at this time—especially with the battle for healthcare reform in full gear. If that's the case, what's needed instead is a simple and comprehensive package that focuses on job creation. In their must-read *Nation* article, "A Jobless Recovery" (July 13), Leo Hindery Jr. and Leo Gerard lay out a set of common-sense proposals for a job-led recovery: "We can either focus our economic recovery efforts on creating full employment for the 150 million workers who are not part of the top 0.2 percent and on rebuilding the country's manufacturing base. Or, as we have been doing for nearly three decades, we can concentrate on policies that mostly just benefit the incomes of the wealthiest 300,000."

The economic spin battle underway—disconnected from the real economy and working Americans' lives—is filled with demagogic and alarmist rhetoric about out-of-control government spending and federal debt. But in the absence of consumer spending and with banks failing to lend—even while they report record profits and hand out huge bonuses—government is the last resort. It must spend in order to avert a deeper recession. But Eric Cantor and his crew just don't get it. Instead of laying out job creation policies, they whine. And they whine. The question is, why are we still listening to people who broke the back of the middle class, engineered the largest redistribution of wealth upward to the very rich and now dare to attack fairly modest government-led efforts to help working families weather this economic crisis?

# The Right-wing Witch Hunt Against ACORN
## *March 8, 2010*

After eighteen months of screaming headlines and attacks vilifying the anti-poverty group ACORN—attacks reminiscent of a New McCarthyism that threatened the group's very existence—it's clear now that this was a right-wing witch hunt which, sadly, too many Democrats and the mainstream media failed to factcheck.

In December, the Congressional Research Service cleared ACORN of allegations of improper use of federal funding and voter registration fraud. The latest to weigh in on the controversy is Brooklyn District Attorney Charles Hynes. After a four-month investigation, Hynes declared "no criminality has been found" with regard to the conduct of three ACORN employees in the infamous and—turns out—misnamed "pimp-prostitute" video.

In fact, a law enforcement source told the *New York Daily News* that the unedited version of the video which caused all the outrage "was not as clear."

"They edited the tape to meet their agenda," said the official.

Conservative operative James O'Keefe—who was later arrested after an alleged attempt to bug Democratic Senator Mary Landrieu's office in New Orleans—was in reality wearing a white shirt and khakis in the ACORN office and posing as a law school student trying to protect his girlfriend from an abusive pimp. The outrageous pimp outfit was shot later and used to promote the video.

"O'Keefe and the Fox attack machine targeted ACORN because of our successful work to empower hundreds of thousands of low and moderate families as voters and active citizens," said ACORN spokesman Kevin Whelan. "Hopefully [the DA's] announcement, and similar results from independent reviews, will make politicians and media examine the facts more carefully the next time a valuable community organization is attacked."

The damage already done to ACORN includes severely curtailing its work helping low-income people with tax preparation and obtaining the Earned Income Tax Credit, fighting foreclosures, and investigating wage and hour exploitation of workers. The hysteria has also driven away private funding, and there is "defund ACORN" language in the recently signed Omnibus bill that ACORN and the Center for Constitutional Rights are fighting in court.

As a result of the funding struggle, local chapters of ACORN are now reconstituting themselves as separate, stand-alone organizations with their own names. Seventeen state groups have either done that or will do that by the end of the month.

Fox and tabloids like the *New York Post* did a hatchet job on ACORN that too many in the mainstream media were eager to run with. It seems to me those outlets have a special obligation to now step up and tell the full story.

## Time to Revise the Conservative Gospel
### *June 1, 2010*

Louisiana Gov. Bobby Jindal, last seen haplessly offering up conservative nostrums in response to the president's 2009 State of the Union address, is now begging for the federal government to act. "BP is the responsible party, but we need the federal government to make sure they are held accountable and that they are indeed responsible," Jindal said after surveying the oil spill impact on the Louisiana coastline last week.

Jindal raised eyebrows by departing from the old Republican text in this way. But actually, what's surprising is that after the worst financial collapse since the Great Depression, the worst mining disaster in thirty years, and what is now the worst environmental disaster in the nation's history, more conservatives aren't revising the gospel about the blessings of deregulation and the horrors of government. Despite what should be obvious failings, deregulation, smaller government and privatization remain central to the dominant Republican message.

Case in point is Newt Gingrich. The former Republican House speaker seems to be pushing the notion that rather than renovate their ideas, conservatives should become more shrill. His new book, *To Save America*, is a screed against President Obama's "secular socialist machine," which poses a "mortal threat" to America as we know it. And he retreads the entire conservative mantra—smaller government, lower taxes, less regulation, strong dollar, free trade, privatization, even the ownership society—as if we hadn't just pursued those policies over the cliff.

There's also Rand Paul. The Senate candidate suggested that in the context of the oil spill, the administration was "really un-American" in its "criticism of business" and that "this sort of blame-game" is unnecessary because "sometimes accidents happen."

Paul's position, of course, is tied to Tea Party anger at Big Government and the mission to rein in Washington. And there's a part of this faux populist critique that's spot on: Washington is indeed corrupted by money.

But what the Tea Partyers miss is that this corruption is in part the product of too little government involvement—and the success of the conservative agenda over the past thirty years. President Reagan, preaching that government was the problem, not the solution, gleefully set about rolling back regulatory authority and budgets, cutting staff while packing agencies with political appointees from the very companies they were supposed to regulate.

President Clinton believed in effective government, but his New Democrat administration accommodated itself to conservative themes, privatizing and outsourcing government, celebrating reductions in the size of government, touting the benefits of market-based regulation. Then came George W. Bush, who revived Reagan's course, denigrating government employees and appointing regulators opposed to regulation, while corruption and cronyism ran amok.

And so the Securities and Exchange Commission failed to rouse itself to respond to repeated warnings about Bernard Madoff's Ponzi scheme. The Federal Reserve stood idly by as the housing bubble inflated and the banks made ever wilder bets with more exotic instruments. And regulators of the Minerals Management Service were literally in bed with the oil companies they regulated, trading sex, drugs and parties for cursory oversight.

We learned once more, at a very high price, that markets need laws and limits. Self-regulating markets are a myth, voluntary regulation a cover for corruption.

Cleaning up the Washington mess was, back in the day, a central part of Obama's attraction as a force of change. That's why the deals cut in the healthcare legislation, so patently part of the old way of doing things, were dismaying. That's why bailing out the banks without vigorously reorganizing them has been so corrosive. And that's why the president's halting, at times inarticulate, response to the catastrophe in the gulf has been painful to witness.

What we really need is a citizen's movement focused on cleaning out Washington, curbing the flood of money in politics, boarding up the revolving door and putting serious cops on the corporate and financial beats. That movement would push to overturn *Citizens United*, the wrong-headed Supreme Court decision that opened the floodgates to corporate money in politics, and move to ensure publicly financed "clean" elections. It would expose politicians who vote the interests of their donors over the interests of their voters. It would insist on rules that would prohibit legislators from using service in public office as a stepping-stone to making a personal fortune in lobbying.

This movement is a progressive burden. Conservatives have little to offer here. With rare exceptions, such as Bobby Jindal, they are determined to continue to denigrate government and gleefully dismantle its capacity. It is up to progressives to make the case that government can work for the common good.

# Enough with the Partisan Posturing

*September 15, 2010*

Will the 2010 election campaign provide us with a debate worthy of a great nation in trouble? The early harbingers aren't good. The pundit herd has already declared the election over, with only the scope of the Democratic reverses yet in question. The two parties are gearing up for a fierce debate on whether to extend the Bush tax cuts to everyone including the wealthiest 2 percent or merely to everyone except the very rich.

We can't afford this partisan posturing. Fifteen million Americans are unemployed. Poverty is up. One in four homes is under water, worth less than what is owed on it. Voters deserve a serious debate about what is to be done. And what are the choices that the two parties present?

Rep. John Boehner (R-Ohio), the perpetually tanned Republican leader, has laid out the Republican plan: keep tax rates where they are and cut $100 billion in spending next year. This can only add rubble to the ruins.

Beyond that, Republicans have no common plan other than obstruction. Their default position is defined by the special interests that have long dominated Washington. As former Bush speech writer David Frum noted, "Republicans have done insufficient serious policy work over the past half-dozen years. The legacy of this inactivity is a party on the brink of power, lacking an intellectual framework for the use of that power."

Boehner, the country club denizen who first came to national attention handing out checks from the tobacco lobby on the floor of the Congress, personifies that posture. When Congress took up regulation of the big banks, Boehner rallied bank lobbyists to oppose it. Not surprisingly, when he started a Boehner for Speaker fund, among the first big checks was one from Citigroup. What is the Democratic alternative? The president recently found his voice in speeches in Milwaukee, Cleveland and in last week's White House news conference. He powerfully summarized Republican adherence to the failed ideas that drove us into the ditch, contrasting the "governing philosophy" between the two parties. He scored Republicans for holding extension of middle-class tax cuts "hostage" to sustaining tax breaks for millionaires and argued for a government that stands on the side of working people.

When it came to what needed to be done for the economy, the president sensibly offered an appetizer of $50 billion for rebuilding roads, rails and runways, and developing an infrastructure investment bank that could leverage private investment as well. But his main course was a bouillabaisse of business tax cuts. Some of the tax proposals were threadbare Democratic campaign staples—ending the tax breaks for companies that ship jobs abroad. Some were routine—making the research-and-development tax cut permanent. Some were simply lame—the 100 percent depreciation for corporate investment in 2011, which will waste billions subsidizing investments that companies would have made anyway. All were designed for electoral positioning.

But even if passed, these proposals aren't anywhere near what needs to be done to reshape the economy and put people to work. Obama has been eloquent on this in the past. In his Georgetown University "Sermon on the Mount" speech last year, he argued that we can't recover to the old economy that was built on debt and bubbles—and should not want to. We have to build a "new foundation" for the economy with investment in world-class education, in research and development, in a 21st-century infrastructure. Transition to new sources of energy will help secure a lead in the green industrial revolution. Curbing financial speculation and balancing our trade, so we make things in America once more, are essential. To enact this project, Washington will have to free itself from the destructive grip of powerful corporate lobbies.

This agenda is both good policy and a powerful political message. It provides a context for what Obama has done to date—from the recovery plan to financial reform—and the case for staying the course.

The current toxic political environment, the 24/7 attack media and expensive modern campaign tactics, all favor gotcha politics, not a serious debate on the country's direction. Not surprisingly, both parties now vie to make the election a referendum on the other: Republicans on the "failed Obama economy," Democrats on the "failed Republican ideas that got us into this ditch."

Given their idea vacuum, such a referendum may be a good strategy for Republicans, but it is counterproductive for Democrats. While the president's emergency measures staved off collapse, they haven't created the jobs or the renewed economy we need. He needs to put forth a compelling argument about what we've learned from the halting growth experienced thus far, and what we need to do now. If the Democratic call is stay the course, it would be helpful for voters to be clear about just what that course is.

# Predator's Ball
## *October 20, 2010*

"Après nous, le déluge." Surely the reactionary gang of five on the Supreme Court should have cited Louis XV in their *Citizens United* decision overturning precedent to open the floodgates to corporate campaign spending. For all the fixation on Tea Partyers, what is most notable about this election is the rising tide of money that is lifting many Republican candidates—and how it ultimately contradicts the message that GOP contenders are delivering to voters.

Only two months ago, Democratic Party operatives were boasting that the war chests of Democratic incumbents would repel Republican challengers. That was then. In the last quarter, Republican challengers surpassed Democratic incumbents in fundraising.

More important, the campaigns have been aided by an unprecedented wave of independent expenditures—over $150 million and rising, the vast bulk spent on attack ads against besieged Democrats. Many of these contributions are anonymous, made to nonprofit institutions that don't have to reveal their donors. Karl Rove, infamous as George Bush's political "brain," has essentially displaced the Republican National Committee with his American Crossroads and Crossroads GPS organizations, claiming that they will dispense over $50 million into the elections.

This flood of conservative money isn't an accident. As a clarifying article by Eric Lichtblau in the *New York Times* detailed, conservatives—led by Senate Minority leader Mitch McConnell, the "Darth Vader of campaign finance"—have systematically sought to dismantle the post-Watergate efforts to limit the impact of money in politics and to curb secret donations.

They've linked legislative obstruction with litigation, placed conservative zealots on regulatory agencies to block enforcement of the laws, and propagated the ideological distortion that money is speech. Aided by the reactionary majority on the Supreme Court, the conservative drive has effectively shredded much of the financial arms control of the post-Watergate period. As Lichtblau reported, conservatives acknowledge their purpose: the more money in politics, the better the party of the monied class—the Republicans—is likely to fare.

The barrage of attack ads, however, comes not simply from the absence of legal restraint, but from the decision of conservative corporate wealth to open fire. Some of this surely is ideological, the financial side of Tea Party revolt against Democrats in power. But much of it isn't about ideology; it's about interest. Faced with the cumulative calamities besetting this nation, President Obama had little choice but to challenge entrenched corporate interests. He sought to cut subsidies to Big Oil and King Coal. He pushed healthcare reform to the dismay of the insurance companies. Financial reform, however limited, angered Wall Street's barons. He even had the gall to suggest that private equity billionaires should pay income taxes like the rest of us.

The response, as the *Post* reported, has been a corporate-financed "frenzy fueled in part by a relatively small number of rich donors—oil and gas industry chief executives, construction magnates and other tycoons."

That reality mocks the Republican pieties about being born-again conservatives. The money flooding into Republican coffers isn't for small government or balanced budgets. It's for retaining profitable subsidies, rolling back consumer or worker protections, sustaining anti-trust exemptions, reopening the financial casino, thwarting efforts to tax the wealthy. The respected economist Jamie Galbraith described this as the "predator state," where powerful corporate interests profit by creating and defending lavish government benefits. The Tea Party protest has been sparked in part by the widespread sense that government serves the powerful, not the middle class—that it bailed out Wall Street, not Main Street. But the Republican campaign is bankrolled in no small measure by money from those intent on maintaining their government privileges and subsidies.

This tidal wave of corporate cash—which could run up a $5 billion price tag on the most expensive midterm election in history—is "the dagger directed at the heart of democracy," as Bill Moyers said in a speech at Common Cause's 40th anniversary gala. It is increasingly possible, he added, for "oligarchs and plutocrats to secretly buy our elections and consolidate their hold on the corporate state."

This, in the end, is the current front of a historic struggle. Who governs America—the powerful few or the many, money or citizens?

---

## Americans Aren't Buying the GOP Agenda
### *November 10, 2010*

In the wake of the election, conservatives are full of advice for President Obama. The "unmistakable message" of the election, says presumptive House Speaker John Boehner, is "change course," and that begins by cutting spending and lowering taxes. The election, writes a dyspeptic George F. Will, was "nationwide recoil against Barack Obama's idea of unlimited government." A rational and alarmed American majority, says Will, believed that "government commands and controls" were "superseding and suffocating the creativity of a market society's spontaneous order."

Were voters really unleashing their hidden Friedrich Hayek and Ayn Rand?

It's true that conservatives, aroused in part by the Tea Party and its opposition to Obama, came out in large numbers—making up more than 40 percent of the electorate last week. The Obama base, probably exhausted—as Velma Hall famously told the president in an October town hall meeting, "of defending you, defending your administration"—turned out in smaller numbers.

But the whiter, older, more conservative electorate last Tuesday remained skeptical of the conservative agenda. On spending, these voters were of mixed minds. Asked in exit polls what the first priority of Congress should be, as many said spending to create jobs (37 percent) as said reducing the deficit (39 percent). On taxes, the conservative position was taken by a distinct minority of Tuesday's voters, with 39 percent saying Congress should extend the Bush tax cuts to all, while more than half the voters supported extending them only to those with incomes under $250,000 (37 percent) or not extending them all (15 percent).

An election-eve poll done by Greenberg Associates for the Campaign for America's Future (CAF) and Democracy Corps asked voters to choose between a jobs agenda including rebuilding infrastructure, extending middle-class tax cuts and investing in science and technology versus a program modeled on the Republican pledge of cutting spending, extending all tax cuts and providing small businesses with a tax cut. The electorate that voted in Republicans preferred the investment agenda by 51 to 43 percent.

Gore Vidal once described America as "the United States of Amnesia." Yet it would be bizarre if Americans were pining for the "market society's spontaneous order" while they were still struggling to dig out of the deregulated market's catastrophic collapse. Many yearn for a simpler time, for a return to the era when America was prosperous and the middle class was growing—as in the post–World War II years, when the top tax rate was 90 percent, a conservative Republican president was building the interstate highway system, capital and currencies were tightly regulated, labor unions represented 30 percent of the workforce and wages were rising.

But even the voters who rebuked Democrats for failing to fix the economy aren't yearning for George Will's dystopian, unregulated markets. In the CAF-Democracy poll, voters were asked whether they favored or opposed a plan to "launch a five-year strategy to revive manufacturing in America," including "providing companies with incentives to make it in America, ending tax breaks that reward moving jobs abroad, enforcing 'buy America' provisions on government spending, countering unfair trade and currency practices by China and others, investing in research and technology to foster new products and markets."

It is hard to imagine a greater conservative nightmare: an industrial strategy with five-year plans, buy American, spending, trade wars. Yet 80 percent of conservative voters yearning for the "creativity of the market society's spontaneous order" approved of the plan, over half strongly, as opposed to 9 percent opposed.

So suffer George Will his Adam Smith tie pin, but ignore his advice. Let Boehner maintain his perpetual tan. If Democrats want to listen to voters, they'd be well advised to push hard on a bolder program to rebuild America and put people back to work.

# The GOP: Gobbling Up Our Blessings
*November 23, 2010*

Thanksgiving may be a time to give thanks for our blessings, but in Washington, the resurgent Republican conservatives want needy Americans to have fewer of them. The new Republicans have the same old leaders—and their passion hasn't changed. It isn't about offering a hand up to the afflicted—it's about handouts to the connected.

In the lame-duck session now convened until the end of the year, Republicans have continued their strategy of obstruction—opposing the New START treaty, opposing repeal of "don't ask, don't tell," opposing consideration of immigration reform, opposing even passage of appropriations for the current year. Their passion is focused on getting one thing done. They will run through the wall to extend the extra tax cuts enjoyed by those, largely millionaires, earning more than $250,000 a year. Forget about deficit reduction. According to Republicans, these tax cuts—costing an estimated $700 billion over the next decade—need not be balanced by spending cuts or "paid for" in the Washington parlance.

At the same time, Republicans are willing to filibuster to block extension of unemployment benefits to the long-term unemployed. They won't sign on, they say, unless there are cuts in domestic spending to offset the extension. The basic support of the families of more than 3 million workers will begin to expire at the end of this month. So much for holiday cheer.

The extra tax cuts for the rich (they collect the same tax cuts as everyone else on their first $250,000 of income) will cost about $68 billion next year alone. Extending unemployment insurance for the long-term unemployed will cost about $65 billion.

The top 1 percent of Americans captured a staggering 66 percent of all income gains over the past decade. America's inequality is now at record extremes. And, as the independent Congressional Budget Office and John McCain's economic adviser, Mark Zandi, agree, providing tax cuts for the rich is the least effective way to boost the economy. The beneficiaries tend to save the money, invest it in growing markets abroad or, worse, throw more into the financial casino now reopened on Wall Street, fueling the computerized hyper-speculation that has nothing to do with productive investment.

At the same time, the human toll caused by the economic recession continues to rise. There were 2.9 million job openings in September, but the total number of unemployed workers was 14.8 million, with half of these workers jobless for twenty-one weeks or more. Long-term unemployment insurance is keeping millions of workers and their families out of poverty. It is, without question, one of the most effective ways of boosting the economy, as the unemployed spend that money to buy food, pay rent or make car payments while looking for work.

Congress has never cut back on these benefits when unemployment was more than 7.2 percent. Today, official unemployment is at 9.6 percent, with rates reaching more than 16 percent in African American communities. With six workers for every one job opening, this is a human calamity.

Voters have more decency than today's conservative leaders. In a new national survey on unemployment benefits by the National Employment Law Project and Half in Ten, an organization whose goal is to cut poverty in half in ten years, 67 percent of all voters believe Congress should continue to provide unemployment benefits until unemployment comes down substantially.

Why go to the wall for the wealthy while abandoning those who have lost their jobs through no fault of their own? This isn't hard to fathom. Secret donors spent more than $138 million in the last election, with 80 percent of the money going to Republicans. NBC News reports that a goodly proportion of the secret funds raised by Karl Rove's Crossroads GPS operation came from wealthy hedge fund managers furious at Democratic efforts to repeal the outrageous "carried interest" loophole that allows them to pay a lower rate of taxes than their chauffeurs.

The Chamber of Commerce, Bloomberg reports, pocketed more than $86 million in secret contributions from the healthcare industry last year—40 percent of the chamber's spending. This year, the chamber spent nearly $33 million in secret donations on the elections, virtually all for Republican candidates vowing to repeal healthcare reform.

The chamber's priorities—lowering taxes on the wealthy and corporations, repealing healthcare, rolling back Wall Street reform—reflect those of its contributors. They are also totally divorced from the priorities of the American people, who are overwhelmingly focused on jobs and the economy.

It should not surprise anyone that the priorities announced by Mitch McConnell and John Boehner, the Republican Congressional leaders, reflect those of the Chamber and not citizens. McConnell promises to vote again and again on repeal of health reform. Republican committee chairs have promised to roll back bank regulations and to weaken environmental and consumer protections. And they have pledged to cut $100 billion from domestic programs, largely those directed at the vulnerable. Not surprisingly, they are likely to filibuster to block a vote on the Disclose Act, which would shed light on the identity of the secret campaign donors.

"Where are the jobs?" That was House speaker-presumptive John Boehner's mantra during the election campaign. But jobs are as AWOL in the Republican priorities as is compassion for the unemployed.

# Paul Ryan's State of the Union Response
## January 25, 2011

Republicans have chosen Rep. Paul Ryan, the new chairman of the House Budget Committee, to respond to the president's State of the Union address tonight. In the civility intermission that has followed the assassination attempt against Rep. Gabby Giffords just outside Tucson, Ryan will no doubt be respectful, and sorrowful that he must dissent from the president's course. Don't be fooled.

Ryan is an Ayn Rand–quoting zealot, one of the Republican Party's self-styled "Young Guns." He's spent his adult life inside the Beltway, on the political right, with no experience in the world of business, labor, the executive branch or the private sector. Incubated in a right-wing think tank, writing speeches for Jack Kemp and William Bennett, he was elected to Congress at age 28. Ryan became the most loyal of loyal foot soldiers in the Congress presided over by Tom DeLay and Denny Hastert, a fact Ryan now glosses over as he describes those Congresses as "corrupt."

Ryan has been dubbed a Republican "thinker" by national reporters desperate to find someone they can praise in a party that was extreme before the Tea Partyers came to town. But, in fact, his rhetoric is a barely varnished echo of the ravings of Glenn Beck. He accuses Obama of a "treacherous plan," saying that Democrats have a "hardcore-left agenda," and claims that Democrats are steering the country "very far left, very fast"—a direction he describes as "completely antithetical to what this country is about."

This sort of rhetoric, once scorned as sophomoric at best, is now common currency on the Republican right. While Ryan will be careful to avoid such language in the GOP response to the State of the Union, he'll reveal his ideological zealotry in the policies he will propose.

Most of those policies will come from Ryan's "Roadmap for America's Future," a budget manifesto published last year that the *Post*'s Ezra Klein aptly described as "nothing short of violent."

In a nation where the top 1 percent already captures 25 percent of the nation's income and possesses more wealth than the bottom 90 percent, the roadmap would give the richest households a new round of staggering tax cuts. It would reduce tax rates, eliminate taxes on capital gains, dividends and interest, and abolish the corporate tax, the estate tax and the alternative minimum tax.

The respected Center for Budget and Policy Priorities, drawing on estimates of the nonpartisan Tax Policy Center, concluded that the average tax cut for the top 1 percent of the population (with incomes over $633,000) would be $280,000. The richest one-tenth of 1 percent, who had incomes over $2.9 million in 2009, would pocket a handsome $1.7 million a year in tax breaks. Some of this revenue would be replaced by a value-added tax that would raise the cost of every good Americans buy, ensuring that middle-income people would pay far more in taxes than they do now. Some would be made up by drastic cuts in healthcare spending. Ryan's giveaway to the rich would also drive up federal deficits and debt.

Understanding the purpose of the "roadmap" is key to understanding Ryan. When he speaks of "fiscal responsibility," what he really means is that middle-class and working Americans will shoulder the responsibility of tackling debts and deficits, while multinational corporations and financial institutions will reap the benefits of favorable government policies and taxpayer-funded bailouts.

His plan would unravel employer-based health care by ending the tax exclusion for employer-sponsored health insurance. It would eliminate traditional Medicare, eviscerate Medicaid and terminate the Children's Health Insurance Program. These would be replaced by a voucher system designed to lose value over time. Ryan would also use "price indexing" to slash average Social Security benefits by 16 percent for those retiring in 2050 and 28 percent in 2080.

As head of the House Budget Committee—accorded what House Speaker John Boehner calls "stunning and unprecedented" power to shape the budget—Ryan is leading the GOP's charge to cut $100 billion out of "non-security discretionary spending" this year—requiring cuts of 20 percent in everything from the FBI to cancer research, Pell grants for students, Head Start and grants to public school districts. This is a recipe, given the country's faltering growth, for increasing unemployment and misery.

Ryan, of course, refuses to identify which programs would be cut or how deep the damage would be. "I'm a budgeteer," Ryan says. "I just bring down the cap"—an utterly irresponsible description of budgeting, which is entirely a question of choosing priorities.

As a career politician steeped in the art of "framing" a poll-tested, focus-grouped message to make it palatable, Ryan will no doubt sound reasonable, invoking basic American values, promising that jobs, growth and opportunity will result if only we adopt his priorities. But don't just listen to State of the Union platitudes. Consider the record and the proposed policies. Beneath that shock of unruly hair is an ideologue with extreme notions that, if adopted, would endanger our future and leave most Americans far worse off.

# Are Conservatives Endangering the High Court?
*February 15, 2011*

Less than a month after President Obama signed the healthcare reform into law, Justice Stephen Breyer predicted that the legislation would one day make it to the High Court. Now that four federal judges have ruled on the matter, it appears that Breyer was right, and he may be weighing in, along with his colleagues, sooner than expected. What's at stake is not just the law itself or the fate of the tens of millions who wait for its benefits, but the very legitimacy of the Court.

At issue is to what extent Congress has the authority to use an individual mandate to regulate health insurance—a question that few, until recently, expected to be controversial. Jurists across the political spectrum, including Charles Fried, President Reagan's solicitor general, have argued that the mandate is unquestionably constitutional. Harvard Law professor Laurence Tribe said it would require "illusory" formulations to find otherwise.

Yet in Florida and Virginia, two federal judges appointed by George W. Bush disagree. One, Henry Hudson, ruled the individual mandate unconstitutional, and the other, Roger Vinson, voided the legislation in its entirety. Both decisions have an unmistakably political tone. Vinson's in particular reads like a Tea Party manifesto.

I hope that the Supreme Court, when finally confronted with the issue, will hold itself to a higher standard. But right now, the signs are not very encouraging. If the Court's conservatives choose to overturn the legislation on clearly political grounds, it would call into question the legitimacy of the Court. It would show, once and for all, that certain justices are governed by ideology rather than precedent. That would appear especially true when considered against the backdrop of recent events.

Clarence Thomas, for example, has recently come under fire for defying perfectly reasonable financial disclosure requirements, refusing to include key information about his wife's employment and income on twenty years' worth of documents. In doing so, he has shown a disregard for the law unbecoming a judge at any level. This failure is made worse by the fact that Virginia Thomas was the founder of Liberty Central, a Tea Party organization that has received corporate contributions not subject to any legal limit (only made possible by her husband's vote in the *Citizens United* case) and has lobbied for the repeal of the "unconstitutional" healthcare legislation.

Might Thomas rule again in a way that aligns with the objectives of those political elements? That is the worry of, so far, seventy-four House Democrats, who sent a letter to Justice Thomas insisting that he recuse himself from any healthcare case. "Your spouse is advertising herself as a lobbyist who has 'experience and connections' and appeals to clients who want a particular decision," said the letter. "They want to overturn health-care reform."

Justice Antonin Scalia, too, has been the subject of recent controversy. Scalia and Thomas have also come under fire for appearing at political retreats hosted by Tea Party financier Charles Koch before the *Citizens United* case came before the court. Even if the case was not pending, the justices showed poor judgment in attending an event that raised a troubling perception of conflict of interest. Common Cause recently filed a petition asking the Justice Department to investigate whether the justices should have recused themselves and whether the decision can be vacated in response.

In this highly politicized context, it is the public's confidence in the Court that is most at risk. That confidence, as described by Justice Stephen Breyer in his impassioned dissent in *Bush v. Gore*, "is a public treasure. It has been built slowly over many years" and is a "vitally necessary ingredient of any successful effort to protect basic liberty and, indeed, the rule of law itself."

According to Jeff Shesol, author of *Supreme Power*, an increasingly relevant history of Franklin Roosevelt's battle with the Supreme Court, "What's at risk is not just a loss of faith in particular justices or even the Supreme Court as a whole, but a broader loss of public faith in the rule of law and the fairness of the judicial system. When the Supreme Court is simply politics by other means," he said, "there is corrosion that seeps into the rest of the system."

Of course, we're well past the point of imagining that justices are free of political views or policy preferences. That kind of willful naiveté ended in the 1930s, when the Court went to war against the New Deal (and, in the end, surrendered). Even so, we need to believe the justices are working hard to retain an open mind.

That is not possible to believe when justices—in opinions and in public forums and interviews—expound an inflexible set of beliefs and are perceived to warp and disfigure the law to fit those preferences in each case. When justices use cases to score ideological points, to advance a broad and sustained argument against governmental action, the law becomes little more than an instrument applied bluntly in pursuit of an agenda. It is not that we expect justices to completely disassociate themselves from the world, but we cannot accept their flagrant and excessive involvement in matters that are before—or will soon come before—the Court. Their behavior makes impartiality an impossibility.

Is it too much to ask of our Supreme Court justices that they exercise a basic level of restraint, especially in such a hyperpolarized environment? Do Justices Thomas and Scalia and Chief Justice John Roberts really understand what's at stake—and what the damage their actions can do to the institution they have an obligation to protect?

## Conservative Zealotry vs. Economic Reality
### March 15, 2011

One thing about the current generation of conservatives: getting mugged by reality hasn't changed the way they look at the world. We've just come through a calamitous financial collapse—caused by reckless Wall Street gambling and toothless watchdogs—that triggered a Great Recession and doubled the US national debt. The collapse is the greatest cause of large deficits, but conservatives act as if the deficits caused the collapse.

A recent stop in London revealed that this isn't just a Tea Party phenomenon. There, the new Tory-dominated coalition led by David Cameron looks and sounds like a sprightlier off-shoot of House Speaker John Boehner's troops. Cameron has set out on a forced march for fiscal retrenchment, imposing deep and immediate spending cuts (and tax increases) to bring deficits down in Britain. This plan is sold with a jaunty recital of conservative gospel: the economy has begun to recover, and action on deficit reduction will boost the confidence of business and consumers. The resulting revival, it is argued, will generate more than enough private-sector jobs to make up for those lost in the public sector.

Yet the 2010 fourth-quarter economic numbers revealed that the British economy was declining, not growing. The government went from adding jobs to shedding them. And consumer confidence has collapsed since Cameron and his troops started chanting that the country "was broke." Cameron dismissed the results, declared "war on the enemies of enterprise" and insisted that he would carry on. The magic of what Paul Krugman calls the "confidence fairy" and private-sector growth would overcome all.

In Washington, Boehner's caucus exhibits the same zealotry. "The American people want us to cut spending," the GOP speaker repeats, ignoring the vast majority of polls that show Americans care far more about jobs and the economy. We will "cut and grow" is the new conservative message. Get government out of the way and the economy will blossom.

Yet Goldman Sachs projected this month that the deep cuts in domestic programs in the 2010 budget passed by the House could cut our growth rate in half. John McCain's former economic adviser, Mark Zandi, projected a loss of 700,000 jobs. If the budget cuts cost federal jobs, said Boehner, sounding like a latter-day Marie Antoinette, "so be it." He believes the private sector will more than make up for the loss of such jobs.

Remarkably, President Obama has once more been absent without leave. In his State of the Union address, he hailed the recovery and turned to deficit reduction. A few weeks later, he said it was time to "live within our means." He hasn't drawn a line against short-term cuts, choosing instead to argue for cutting less.

In the run-up to the 2010 elections, the administration assumed that job growth was picking up (remember "Recovery Summer"). The Election Day "shellacking" stemmed largely from the fact that voters didn't see the jobs and didn't think the White House had a clear view on how to create them.

The president and Republicans seem to believe that the "confidence" that comes from immediate spending cuts will offset the jobs lost from those cuts as well as offset declining household disposable income, plummeting housing prices and massive household indebtedness.

In Britain and the United States, it is bizarre to hear the same cruel conservative ideas and arguments defining policy while both countries are still struggling to recover from the human catastrophe they caused. And in both, economic reality doesn't interfere with conservative faith.

In the United States, 25 million people are in need of full-time employment. Housing prices are headed back down; trade deficits are going back up. State and local governments have largely exhausted rainy-day funds and are laying off workers. Businesses are sitting on trillions in cash while waiting for consumer demand to pick up. At last Thursday's "Summit on Jobs and America's Future," sponsored by the Campaign for America's Future, economists showed that at current rates, it would take eight years for the United States merely to return to pre-recession levels of employment.

For the unemployed, time isn't measured in hours or months. It is measured by savings exhausted, homes lost, dreams crushed, children uneducated, marriages broken. Eight years is a calamity. But the White House and Republicans are arguing only about how much and what to cut, assuming that business needs only confidence, not consumers, to start hiring again.

You have to admire conservative gall. Financial collapse and global economic calamity changes not a word of their mantras. At the depth of the crisis, former Federal Reserve chairman Alan Greenspan, the Ayn Rand devotee and toothless watchdog whose willful lassitude did as much as anyone to allow Wall Street to blow up the economy, admitted to "a flaw" in his worldview. But last week, Greenspan was newly unrepentant, charging that Obama's governmental "activism" was standing in the way of recovery.

Greenspan didn't mention that the pre-crisis decade featured declining wages and benefits for most American families, Gilded Age inequality, the hemorrhaging of manufacturing jobs, unsustainable trade deficits and ruinous financial speculation. But neither Greenspan nor conservatives, nor, tragically, Obama, are about to let reality get in the way of ideology.

# Are There No Standards for Punditry?
## *March 29, 2011*

Last Sunday, ABC'S *This Week* turned to none other than Donald Rumsfeld, the former Bush administration defense secretary, to get his informed judgment of the mission in Libya. Last month, the journal *International Finance* featured former Federal Reserve chairman Alan Greenspan commenting on what is "hampering" the economic recovery.

Fox News trumped even that, trotting out retired Marine Col. Oliver North, the former Reagan security staffer who orchestrated the secret war in Nicaragua, to indict President Obama for—you can't make this stuff up—failing to get a Congressional resolution in support of the mission in Libya.

Next we'll see a cable talk show inviting the former head of BP to tell us what it takes to do offshore drilling safely. Are there no standards whatsoever for punditry? Do high government or corporate officials suffer no consequence for leading us into calamity? Public officials who have failed spectacularly in office should have the common decency to retire in disgrace. But even if modern-day officials know no shame, why in the world would opinion pages, network talk shows and reputable journals give them a forum to offer their opinions, when they have shown that their advice isn't worth the air it disturbs?

On ABC, Rumsfeld criticized Obama for "confusion" in the Libyan mission, noting that the coalition "is the smallest in modern history."

As Bush's defense secretary, Rumsfeld played a lead role in perhaps the worst foreign policy calamity since the British burned down the White House in the War of 1812. He helped cook the books that justified the war of choice in Iraq, costing thousands of Americans their lives and limbs and the government a projected $3 trillion. His war squandered the global goodwill in the wake of Sept. 11, 2001, left millions of Iraqis dead or displaced, and strengthened our adversaries in Iraq and the terrorists of Al Qaeda.

Rumsfeld personally approved the torture techniques that despoiled the nation's reputation when they were revealed at Abu Ghraib prison. He is now hawking his unrepentant and disingenuous memoir, which concludes that the Bush administration "got it right" on the big things in Iraq and elsewhere. Why would any rational news show invite his opinion on anything except maybe how to live with yourself after screwing up big-time?

Greenspan, the ex-Maestro chairman of the Federal Reserve, argues that "the current government activism is hampering what should be a broad-based, robust economic recovery, driven in significant part by the positive wealth effect of a buoyant U.S. and global stock market."

But Greenspan hasn't got a clue. His ruinous policies at the Federal Reserve helped drive the economy into the worst downturn since the Great Depression. He cheered on the housing bubble while denying its existence, touted the benefits of subprime mortgages, turned a blind eye to reports of pervasive fraud and abuse in mortgage markets and opposed the regulation of derivatives that, he claimed, were making the system more stable.

Greenspan admitted he was "shocked" that his worldview had a "flaw." An apology, penance, self-reflection and even a memoir describing what he did wrong are in order. Surely we can be spared Mr. Greenspan's opinion of what impedes recovery from the Great Recession that his own blind market fundamentalism did so much to produce.

And do we really need Oliver North's views on the Constitution and the law? "[I]t's unparalleled in my entire experience in the military going all the way back to the 1960s," North said. "Every president has gone to the Congress to get a resolution to support whatever it is he wanted to do."

This from the White House operative who ran a secret war not only without Congressional authorization, but also despite a Congressional prohibition—a folly that ended in his indictment and nearly in the impeachment of his president.

There is a striking double standard operating in America. We hear much about enforcing "accountability" from the powers that be. Teachers, students and schools are judged in high-stakes tests. Minority students particularly are subjected to "no excuses" school punishments. Punitive "three strikes and you're out" prison sentencing disproportionately snares those caught for drug possession or other nonviolent offenses.

At the top of society, bankers, CEOs and hedge funders enjoy increased license, prestige and lavish rewards. Yet when their excesses, lawlessness, ideological blindness or simple incompetence result in calamity, there seems to be no consequence. When Charles Ferguson received an Oscar for his riveting documentary *Inside Job*, he reminded the audience that "not a single financial executive has gone to jail, and that's wrong." Wall Street bankers haven't been prosecuted.

Rumsfeld and the neocons still enjoy plush chairs in think tanks as well as high visibility and high speaking fees. Greenspan is allowed to pose as the Maestro, even after his reputation has been completely shredded.

In Japan, high officials who failed so spectacularly would be contemplating seppuku. In Britain, they'd resign, repair to drink and end up in the House of Lords. In America, they become pundits and are offered a stage to argue the same ideas that earlier brought the nation to near-ruin, rewriting history to fit their theory.

As Talleyrand said of the restored French monarchy under Louis XVIII, they have "learned nothing and forgotten nothing." It is a pity that these discredited pundits are offered a stage to project their inanity on the rest of us.

## Emperor Trump Has No Clothes
*April 22, 2011*

For a media that loves infotainment, the horse race and spectacle—and has trouble tackling real policy issues and digging deep—Donald Trump is the gift that keeps on giving: all spectacle, all the time.

Now he's out there on his ugly birther trip, riding it to the top of the polls amidst a GOP presidential field in disarray. And other than a few notable exceptions, the media is largely playing the role of cheering spectator for Trump's latest self-aggrandizing parade—none more so than Fox, which has treated his birtherism-based candidacy as a cause célèbre. Media Matters notes thirteen Trump appearances on the network since March 20.

But the more significant issue raised by the media coverage is this: if Trump is going to portray himself as a presidential contender, and the media is going to give him mega-time to do that, then let's take a hard look at his record and his views—particularly on "fiscal responsibility," which Congressman Paul Ryan and the GOP say is the issue of our time.

"I haven't seen anybody do anything for a long time that's really tough coverage on Donald," says David Cay Johnston, the Pulitzer Prize–winning reporter formerly with the *New York Times* who has written extensively about Trump's net worth as well as his business dealings in the gambling industry in his book *Temples of Chance*. "He's done exceptionally well at getting the media to treat him on the grounds that he wants—which is he doesn't mind if you poke fun at him as long as you're writing about him and making him sound important."

In a recent column, Johnston points out that in examining four years of tax returns, he discovered that Trump paid no taxes in two of them.

"He pays little to no income tax because he does these real estate deals that allow him to take—as a professional real estate developer—unlimited paper losses like depreciation against income he gets from NBC for his show," says Johnston.

He's also had more business bankruptcies than wives, and Johnston says Trump's bravado about his wealth and business acumen contradicts his real record. According to Johnston, Trump typically does two kinds of deals: he borrows more than 100 percent of the purchase price for real estate and takes a fee off the top; or he's paid a fee to put his name on a building. Johnston suggests that Trump's fortune relied on government favors and stiffing his creditors.

"Ordinary casino workers who got into debt had their licenses yanked or in one case their wages garnished, but Donald was not held to that standard," says Johnston.

As Johnston describes in *Temples of Chance*, in 1990 one of Trump's advisers told the New Jersey Casino Control Commission that Trump was one day away from uncontrolled bankruptcy. The commission then approved a privately negotiated deal that relieved Trump of millions in debts. Why did the bankers go along?

"Government rescued Trump by taking his side against the banks," Johnston says, "telling them that if they foreclosed they would own three seaside hotels that lacked casino licenses."

Trump's celebrated wealth is also likely not what Trump would have the public believe. In 1990 Johnston obtained Trump's personal net worth statement that his bankers had prepared for him. At the time, Trump was claiming it was as high as $1.4 billion. Yet the statement revealed a negative net worth of $600 million—he owed $600 million more than the value of his assets. Johnston wrote a column with the lede, "You are probably worth more than Donald Trump."

"Donald is one of many people in public life who whatever they say at the moment is their version of the truth, and empirical reality may not support what they say," says Johnston. "He never produced any documented evidence indicating a net worth anywhere in the range of a billion dollars or more, he only claimed it. It doesn't take that much of an income to appear to be fabulously wealthy. I don't think he can sue anybody for making that observation."

Indeed, Trump has proven litigious with those who dare question his version of the truth. He filed a $5 billion defamation lawsuit against Timothy O'Brien for estimating his net worth at between $150 million and $250 million. It was dismissed, but NBC investigative reporter Michael Isikoff reports that Trump recently showed up at a Jersey City courtroom, where he was "slipping notes" to his attorneys who are appealing the ruling. And former *Newsweek* senior editor Jonathan Alter recalls appearing in a documentary and saying that Trump was a "media hound" and that his claim of being "the greatest real estate developer in the world not only isn't true—he's not even the greatest real estate developer in New York." Alter says he then promptly received a letter from a Trump attorney threatening him with a lawsuit.

Contrast Johnston's hardnosed reporting with *New York Times* columnist David Brooks' fawning over Trump in a recent op-ed, "Why Trump Soars": "Donald Trump is the living, walking personification of the Gospel of Success. . . . He labors under the belief—unacceptable in polite society—that two is better than one and that four is better than two. . . . In private jets, lavish is better than dull. In skyscrapers, brass is better than brick, and gold is better than brass."

In fact, Johnston even has a word to say about that jet: "See how much a 727 three-engine jet that hasn't been made in over 25 years goes for," says Johnston. "If he were really rich he'd have upgraded to a G-5 or a Boeing business jet."

Like so many corporate oligarchs, Trump has done well with the help of his armada of lawyers and accountants to avoid taxes and intimidate those who contradict him. He's a single entity that has a lot in common with the Big Banks—reckless, highly leveraged, and a look at the books reveals he's not what he appears: Emperor Don has no clothes.

Fire him.

# Keep Your Hands Off My Medicare!

*May 3, 2011*

It's been a common refrain of politicians in Washington for as long as the capitol has been unpopular: "It's good to get outside the Beltway, good to go get back to the real America." But in recent days that cliché might feel a bit stale for Republican House members, who voted last month for Representative Paul Ryan's budget proposal. Inside the Beltway, Ryan is called "courageous," a "visionary," a "serious man" for having the bravery to put forth a budget that pays for tax cuts for the wealthy by ending Medicare as we know it. Back home in his district, he's becoming known as the leader of the most serious assault on seniors since President Bush's attempt to privatize Social Security.

In April, Ryan was greeted not with the outsized praise of *New York Times* columnist David Brooks at his town hall in Milton, Wisconsin, but instead with sustained boos. On Friday, according to *Politico*, he asked police to remove a man from his town hall because the man refused to stop yelling about the impact the Ryan budget would have on Medicare.

He's not alone. In New Hampshire, the first six questions posed to Rep. Charlie Bass (R-NH) were about his vote in favor of Ryan's budget. "I'm not surprised it's controversial," said Bass of his vote. But for a man who won his seat during the 2010 Republican wave by a little more than 3,000 votes, it's an open question as to whether his career can afford such controversy.

In addition to Ryan and Bass, at least six other GOPers have faced pointed questions and outright protest at town halls, reminiscent of the Tea Party anger seen at Democratic town halls in 2009. Rep. Daniel Webster (R-Fl.) arrived at his town hall greeted with signs that said "Hands Off Medicare." The meeting rated from God and are in need of his forgiveness. Then trust only in Christ to save you from the consequences of your sins. Believe that Jesus died for your sins on the cross and was raised from the dead in order to conquer death, bridging the gap between you and God caused by sin. Turn from (repent of) your sins, and accept Jesus' offer to come into your life as your Savior.

If you sincerely desire to have hope in Christ, tell God in words like these:

*"Dear God, I admit that I am a sinner and need your forgiveness. Thank you for sending Jesus to suffer the punishment that I deserve for my sins. Please help me every day to turn from my sin and live a life that pleases you. Thank you for your gift of eternal life and for the hope I now have in you. Amen."*

Scripture references: [1]John 10:10, [2]Romans 3:23, [3]Isaiah 59:2, [4]Romans 6:23a, [5]1 Corinthians 15:3-4, [6]Romans 6:23b, John 3:36, [7]Romans 8:35,38-39

To read the Bible, learn about Jesus, or find a church in your area, visit **Crossway.org/LearnMore**.

www.goodnewstracts.org

ISBN 978-1-6821-6115-9

# HOPE

## FOR HARD TIMES

became so contentious that police officers intervened to quiet the crowd. The *New York Times* described one such town hall as approaching "near chaos." The *Orlando Sentinel* described another as reaching the level of "bedlam."

Already, some members are backing away from their votes. By the end of Charlie Bass's town hall, he already seemed to be wavering. "If there are certain facets of the budget that are manifestly unpopular, I think that should be taken into consideration . . . this is the beginning of a long conversation." How manifestly unpopular is Ryan's plan for Medicare? A recent *Washington Post*/ABC News poll showed that more than 80 percent of all Americans disapprove of cuts to the program. A whopping 70 percent of Republicans opposed them as well, making it one of the most unpopular positions supported by a national party in modern memory.

Even Speaker Boehner himself ducked away from the budget. He told ABC News, "It's Paul's idea. Now other people have other ideas. I'm not wedded to one single idea." Last week, *Washington Post* reporter Greg Sargent, writing about yet another town hall uproar, asked if we could "call this a national phenomenon yet?"

In the words of President Obama, yes, yes we can.

Democrats and progressive allies are already getting started, working to mobilize voters to attend future town hall meetings. A campaign called "Don't Make Us Work 'Til We Die" organized two days of action in thirty-five cities across the country in April. MoveOn.org is encouraging its members to attend town halls as well. The Congressional Progressive Caucus is planning a whistle stop "people's agenda" tour in seventeen cities—as a follow up to their "People's Budget." Other groups are planning large mobilizations in August to coincide with the month-long summer recess.

SEIU, for example, plans to organize massive nationwide protests around "national flash points," including during August recess. "We felt like we were called in this moment to roll the dice and to think about how to use our members' resources for the greatest hope for changing members' lives," SEIU President Mary Kay Henry says. "I hope what people will see is more of what we all witnessed in Madison . . . more people in the streets making demands about what kind of America we want to see."

As *The Nation*'s John Nichols reports, the goal of this campaign, called "Fight for a Fair Economy," is to begin shifting the character of the national debate from one defined by right-wing talking points and ginned up by Tea Party "populism" to one that reflects the aspirations of the poor and middle class.

And with the recent announcement that Harry Reid will hold a vote for the Ryan budget in the Senate, it's clear that the issue of ending Medicare won't just be the House's albatross.

Democrats see a lot of short-term political opportunity here. Seniors have been the least receptive of any demographic group to President Obama and Democrats in Congress. Even a modest swing in their vote could upend the political landscape. Steve Israel, chairman of the DCCC, has said he believes the Ryan budget, which all but four Republicans voted for, will cost the Republicans control of the House come 2012. And it may remake the dynamic in the Senate, where conventional wisdom has suggested that Democrats are especially vulnerable to losing control of the chamber.

There's no question that the issue allows progressives to draw clear distinctions between Republicans and themselves, and with such overwhelming opposition to the Ryan plan, it's likely that the GOP will be on the defensive for months, if not years, to come.

But there is also a broader, and perhaps more important opportunity for progressives: the opportunity to reset the terms of the debate and make an aggressive case for what the president called "the basic social compact in America." The 2009 town hall protests were characterized by misinformation. The now infamous protest sign that read, "Take your government hands off my Medicare" was emblematic of a decades-long campaign to denigrate government, leaving the American people with a deeply false impression of its role in their lives.

Indeed, a 2010 study by Cornell political scientist Suzanne Mettler found that when Medicare beneficiaries were asked if they had ever benefited from a government social program, 40 percent said no. Forty-four percent of Social Security beneficiaries said the same thing, as did more than a quarter of food stamp users and 43 percent of unemployment insurance receivers.

But unlike the 2009 protests, the 2011 protests represent a genuine opportunity to cast government not as something to be "drowned in the bathtub," as Grover Norquist once described it, but instead, as a crucial lifeline, not just for the working class, but for every American. With Medicare as a shining example, this new national conversation has the potential to redefine government not as a guttural negative, but as a vital partner in American life.

Republicans have been caught flat-footed in this debate. What has been most astonishing thus far hasn't been the national reaction to the budget, but Republicans' surprise at it. They are apparently so disconnected from the lived experiences of most Americans that they genuinely believed ending Medicare would have broad appeal. Now they're learning the hard way, and yearning for a swift return back to the warm embrace of Washington.

# On Food Stamps, Gingrich Hasn't a Clue
## May 18, 2011

When Newt Gingrich derided President Obama as "the food stamp president," he was using the same old GOP race-baiting tactics that brought us Cadillac-driving "welfare queens" and Willy Horton.

But he also revealed something unintentional about his already imploding candidacy: Gingrich is absolutely clueless when it comes to the economic reality of 44 million Americans who feed their families with the help of the nation's most important anti-hunger program, food stamps (or SNAP, the Supplemental Nutrition Assistance Program).

Two years into a so-called "recovery," a record number of Americans—one in seven—receives food stamps. That's because the program is designed to respond to economic downturns and increased hardship. And that's exactly what it's done. It's one of the last remaining (and relatively strong) threads in our tattered and torn safety net—the same net which Republicans would gladly put through the shredder.

As the Center on Budget and Policy Priorities (CBPP) notes, between December 2007 and December 2009, the number of unemployed workers doubled, and the number of workers out of a job for more than six months but still looking nearly quadrupled. SNAP caseloads rightly increased by 45 percent. (In contrast, TANF cash assistance caseloads increased just 13 percent, since it's subject to the whims of states' restrictive eligibility requirements, thanks to Gingrich-Clinton welfare reform.)

Part of the reason SNAP is so effective is that its federal eligibility rules are largely uniform across the nation so benefits are available to most households with low incomes. So who does Gingrich think those families turning to SNAP to stave off hunger are exactly? Here's a cheat sheet—perhaps he can make use of it as he attempts to save his flailing campaign:

More than 75 percent of SNAP participants are in families with children, and nearly one-third are in households with elderly people or people with disabilities. Over 34 percent of household heads are white, 21 percent African American, and less than 10 percent Hispanic. And the people receiving the benefits are exactly the people who really need them—over 90 percent have incomes below the poverty line, and 40 percent have incomes below half the poverty line (or "deep poverty," just $9,155 for a family of three.) Finally, nearly three times as many SNAP households worked as relied solely on welfare benefits for their income.

And just how effective is SNAP as an anti-poverty tool?

In 2009, SNAP lifted 4.6 million Americans above the poverty line, including over 2 million children and 200,000 seniors. For an average of $4.46 per day per household member, it is as effective an anti-poverty measure as the Earned Income Tax Credit and the most effective program when it comes to lifting families out of deep poverty.

In short, SNAP has been doing the job it was designed to do—until now, with bipartisan support.

"No one Administration deserves credit for helping to strengthen SNAP," says Stacy Dean, vice president for food assistance policy at CBPP. "Work started at the end of the Clinton Administration to ensure that eligible people in need of food assistance were able to access the program. The Bush Administration worked very hard with states to improve program access. Caseloads really started to rise in 2000 as a result of the economic downturn and the work to improve access. President Obama inherited rising caseloads that were driven primarily by the recession."

But Gingrich took a whack at food stamps back when he was speaker in 1995, attempting to convert the program into a block grant, and now his House Republican descendants want to do the same.

Under the House-passed Ryan budget, SNAP would be cut by almost 20 percent based "on the false claim that the program is experiencing 'relentless and unsustainable growth,'" according to the CBPP. The fact is the program responded to the economic hardship of the recession and increase in poverty, and enrollment will decline as the economy recovers and need declines. But if we block grant it, the very responsiveness that is key to SNAP's success will be lost as eligibility and benefit standards vary by state. Also, its ability to act as a stimulus by putting money in the hands of people most likely to spend it would be limited.

"Aside from the obvious fact that SNAP saves lives, SNAP is rapid and provides effective assistance to families and individuals who are struggling," says Rabbi Steve Gutow, president of the Jewish Council for Public Affairs. "We should be strengthening it, not diminishing it and not attacking it on what appears to be mainly ideological grounds."

It is ugly and inhumane—but par for the course—that Gingrich and the GOP would spin SNAP's success to push a case for gutting it.

"There still are unprecedented numbers of Americans who are struggling with no wages or low wages," says Jim Weill, president of the Food Research and Action Center. "We have the resources, even in these difficult times, to eliminate hunger in this country. The consequences of not doing this are far too severe, and the moral cost is even greater."

# The Michele Bachmann I Know
*June 14, 2011*

Last night at the Republican debate in New Hampshire, Michele Bachmann announced that she'd formally filed her papers to run for president. Even more surprisingly, the post-debate punditry concluded that she'd won (or tied Mitt Romney) for the win in a debate peppered with inane questions about whether or not the candidates preferred Coke or Pepsi, Elvis or Johnny Cash. Bachmann got in her usual anti-Obama one-liners, but she also repeatedly mentioned that she's a mother to twenty-three foster children and a tax litigation attorney. It worked for some; a lot of critics seemed to think a less overblown, more credible candidate Bachmann emerged last night.

It's times like this that make me want to turn off the TV, but I know I have to take a walk around the room and remember how Bachmann first emerged on the national political scene. I was there—in a studio one October evening at 30 Rock, on the set of Chris Matthews' *Hardball*.

I figured it was just another pre-election 2008 segment, but suddenly this Congresswoman from Minnesota I really hadn't heard much about is on the screen, by remote from DC. My spine stiffened as I heard Bachmann say, "I'm very concerned that he [Obama] may have anti-American views."

My retro-red-baiting antenna perked up. Here was this Congresswoman from the good state of Minnesota speaking about a man who was about to become president.

Bachmann then called on the media to "take a great look at the views of the people in Congress and find out—are they pro-America or anti-America?"

At that moment, all that I had learned about McCarthy and the deforming "-ism" he brought to our national politics came to mind. I also had a tough time believing I was hearing this language in October 2011. But neo-McCarthyism was roaming the land, stewarded by Sarah Palin and her passel.

So, when Matthews turned to me for a response, I did my best to stay collected.

I told him then what still holds true when I think of Bachmann today: "This is a politics, at a moment of extreme economic pain in this country, that is incendiary, that is so debased. I think it's very scary, because this is a country I love."

Turns out in October 2008, plenty of people (though not quite enough people) felt the same way I did. As money poured in to support until-then largely unknown Democratic-Farmer-Labor candidate Elwyn Tinklenberg, the National Republican Congressional Committee pulled its resources out of the race. In the end, however, Bachmann defeated Tinklenberg by less than three points in her ruby-red district.

It's been a while since that encounter, but Bachmann has gone into overdrive, continuing to push her politics of fear and loathing and demonization, though usually in a less raw, more insidious way. We saw this last night in her response to questions about abortion, when Bachmann, who is "100 percent pro-life," said that "all of the firepower" and the "real battle" is on the "issue of taking an innocent human life."

Michele Bachmann's rhetoric has an ugly history—here and elsewhere—one that emerges in times of deep economic anxiety as we are experiencing now. It's a politics that channels the basest, meanest instincts of our political culture.

Just a few weeks ago, in fact, Bachmann sent out an e-mail saying that she is "prayerfully considering" a presidential run and asking for donations to her "Make Barack Obama a One-Term President Money Bomb." She lunges forward to assert that "Obamacare is bringing socialism to our doorstep" and "we must protect our traditional values." The e-mail links to a video in which she again appeals for donations to "lead an all-out assault on his socialist policies. That's why we're launching a money bomb today."

Fearmongering and division—alive and well, courtesy of Bachmann.

She is no fool. Deft and adept at the noncommittal smear, she has used the "non-answer" to further her agenda, as she did in an interview with George Stephanopoulos back in February, when she repeatedly refused to say whether Obama is a Christian and a US citizen.

At other moments, she will still go full throttle and overt, as in this interview with the *Financial Times*. "People are beginning to realize that Obama is a socialist," she said. "And that is not the way America is."

In May, Bachmann's neo-McCarthyism won praise from fellow witch-hunter Glenn Beck, who said on his radio show, "The country is in trouble. Michele Bachmann will admit that there are enemies within."

Bachmann assured Beck that the admiration (and the ignorance) was mutual. "You've named names, you've named organizations," she said. "That's empowered people. The infamous Glenn Beck chalkboard—that's where the American people have been learning the truth."

Bachmann is now the vanguard of the right-wing populist movement—particularly with the more genial Mike Huckabee out of the race and her sister-nemesis Sarah Palin not yet in it—she will be the voice of this strand of social conservatism in the campaign.

While her followers portray Bachmann as a "modern woman," never forget that what she really represents is a retro throwback to a kind of American that is intolerant, bigoted and out of step with the best instincts and possibilities of this country.

*Part IV*

TOWARD A NEW NATIONAL SECURITY

# Needed: New National Security Thinking
## November 30, 2009

Tonight President Obama will announce his new Afghanistan policy. By all accounts it will be one of military escalation. This is a tragic moment—both for the nation and his presidency—and it is one I had hoped the president would avoid by courageously leading us in a wiser direction, one that views 21st-century challenges anew, in fresh and necessary ways.

It is true that Obama would have needed real political courage to extricate himself from his predecessor's war. He would have faced toxic blowback from a military and media establishment poised to attack. But in a war-weary nation, amidst great economic trouble, he could have used his great oratorical and political skills to marshal people of all kinds to his side.

Instead, with this escalation, we see the continuing grip of the National Security State—whose premises have been shared by the conservative and liberal hawks for close to sixty years and which essentially remain unchallenged among the establishment and the mainstream media. Obama will now be held hostage to this mindset as a war bequeathed to him by a reckless and destructive administration becomes his own war.

This retro thinking and failure to explore real alternatives to military escalation reveal a deeper structural problem—the fact that there are too few countervailing voices or centers of power and authority to challenge the liberal hawks and interventionists, and very few if any are allowed to enter the halls of power. The political establishment works from its narrow consensus; meanwhile, the media fails to offer a full range of views.

Our challenge now as progressives is to begin to lay the groundwork so that the failed National Security States' premises are exposed as ones no longer suited to addressing central challenges and threats of our time—from global pandemics and economic inequality and instability, to nuclear proliferation and, yes, decentralized networks of terrorists. We need structural reform if we're to have a rich and deserved contest of ideas and views in our politics and society.

As James Carroll argues in a *Boston Globe* op-ed, "The time when 'new thinking' is most needed is before war starts," and we must "put in place the structures of new thought that will prevent its repetition."

How do we build pressure for structural reforms and the changes we believe in? How do we change the paradigm so that we expose the retro National Security State as the failure it is? The structural problem demands action on several fronts. We need a serious think/do tank on national security issues which is capable of contesting the underlying premises for specific interventions and also challenging the prevailing assumptions underlying the National Security state. It also needs to work closely with progressive organizations with ties to the grassroots in order to build a broad-based movement for change. (Raising the idea of a new think/do tank is not meant to diminish the valuable work already being done at a handful of existing places.)

If we don't look at the structural issues, we will always be fighting against the latest, newest, terrible, bad person/country that requires invading, occupying, or bombing with the latest weapon. We will also continue to lose reform-minded leaders to the powerful post–Cold War Military-Industrial-Terrorism complex. It's not hard to see how a Democratic candidate and now president like Obama—relatively unschooled in security issues—got caught up in establishment thinking. In choosing his foreign policy team, he looked to experienced advisers from the last Democratic presidency—a Clinton administration replete with establishment Democrats.

And then there's the example of Lyndon Johnson, a Southerner, a master of the Senate, who did not have political courage to face down his military and counterinsurgency best and the brightest. Listen to the tapes of his conversations with his friend and mentor, Senator Richard Russell, and you hear a man who would face down almost anyone but was terrified of his right-wing, terrified of being called "soft." So how do we change the meaning of "being tough" in the 21st century?

I believe we progressives/ethical realists/clear-minded people/citizens who believe in common sense share some blame in not building a more powerful alternative foreign policy bench to compete with these counterinsurgency experts populating DC think tanks and Congress. Structural reform must now be the work for thinkers and activists working with elected officials who are open to understanding the world and its future in new and not-ready-for-primetime ways—even as a president we had high expectations for is escalating a war that may well deplete this country of the resources needed to rebuild its promise, while doing little to nothing to make us or the region more se-cure or stable.

# Smart Defense
## *November 18, 2008*

Last month, Congressman Barney Frank called for a 25 percent cut in the defense budget—approximately $150 billion in annual spending—saying, "We don't need all these fancy new weapons. I think there needs to be additional review."

Predictably, the Republican backlash was swift. House Mi-nority Leader John Boehner called Frank "incredibly irrespon-sible." House Armed Services Personnel Subcommittee ranking member John McHugh (R-NY) labeled the proposed reduction "unconscionable." Democrats—especially those on the House Armed Services Committee—didn't exactly embrace Frank's target, either.

But Congressman Frank isn't backing down. In an e-mail to me yesterday, he wrote, "Much of the reduction will come from ending the war in Iraq and from cutting unneeded weapons systems. I believe that it's appropriate to reduce defense spending, and this is a goal I wanted to set. I don't have specific details at this point, but I will be working with my colleagues to identify weapons systems that we can reduce, and I also want to look at drawing down the number of our overseas bases."

Even a senior Pentagon advisory group—the Defense Business Board—recently concluded that the current budget is "not sustainable." And according to the *Boston Globe*, "Pentagon insiders and defense budget specialists say the Pentagon has been on a largely unchecked spending spree since 2001 that will prove politically difficult to curtail but nevertheless must be reined in."

The current budget allots over $500 billion to defense and an additional $200 billion for the wars in Iraq and Afghanistan. As a recent editorial in the *New York Times* tells us, the budget is "nearly equal to all of the rest of the world's defense budgets combined." It represents 57 percent of the total discretionary budget.

In the Unified Security Budget for the United States, FY 2009 research fellow Miriam Pemberton of the Institute for Policy Studies and former US Assistant Secretary of Defense Lawrence Korb, senior fellow at the Center for American Progress, outline not only cuts that need to be made to implement a sane defense budget, but also the shift in priorities required to confront the real security challenges of the 21st century. The Unified Security Budget (USB) pulls "together in one place US spending on all of its security tools: tools of offense (military forces), defense (homeland security) and prevention (non-military international engagement.) This tool would make it easier for Congress to consider overall security spending priorities and the best allocation of them."

In a recent *Defense News* op-ed, Pemberton and Korb write, "The balance between our spending on military forces and other security tools—like diplomacy, nonproliferation, foreign aid and homeland security—needs to change."

For example, the USB demonstrates that forgoing the scheduled increase in the troubled F-22 fighter jet for FY 2008—$800 million—would be sufficient to triple the amount spent on debt cancellation in the world's poorest countries. Or increase by 50 percent US contributions to international peacekeeping operations. Or triple the amount allocated in FY 2007 for domestic rail and transit security programs.

Along the same lines, canceling the Bush administration's initiative to build offensive space weapons could provide the $800 million needed to double the originally requested annual budget for the State Department's Office of Reconstruction and Stabilization.

The report offers $56 billion in cuts to spending on offensive weapons, and $50 billion in new expenditures on defense and prevention. It transforms the Bush administration's 9:1 ratio of spending on offense as compared to defense and prevention to 5:1. According to the report, "This budget would emphasize working with international partners to resolve conflicts and tackle looming human security problems like climate change; preventing the spread of nuclear materials by means other than regime change; and addressing the root causes of terrorism, while protecting the homeland against it."

The Institute for Policy Studies (IPS) and its Foreign Policy In Focus (FPIF) network of progressive experts also released a report last year—Just Security—which details how $213 billion could be cut from US military spending. Even with this cut, the United States would retain the largest military in the world and spend over eight times more than any of the next largest militaries.

Look for an inside-outside strategy to reframe the debate on the defense budget to emerge in the coming weeks. This week, ProgressiveCongress.org (of which I'm a board member) will coordinate a meeting between progressive thinkers like Pemberton and members of the Progressive Caucus to discuss the issue of unsustainable defense spending, alternatives to the status quo, and tactics and strategies on how to win this debate.

Progressives are under no illusions as to the obstacles to making a real and meaningful shift in the way the United States approaches the defense budget. As Winslow Wheeler, director of the Straus Military Reform Project at the Center for Defense Information, told the *Globe*, "The forces arrayed against terminating defense programs are today so powerful that if you try to do that it will be like the British Army at the Somme in World War I. You will just get mowed down by the defense industry and military services' machine guns." Or, as even the Bush administration's Secretary of Defense Robert Gates said of the scant resources devoted to the diplomatic corps as compared to military equipment, "Diplomacy simply does not have the built-in, domestic constituency of defense programs."

With increased public awareness of the misplaced priorities of the past eight years—runaway defense spending being no exception—and the growing demands and dangers of our cratering economy and broken healthcare system, now is the moment for citizens to seize and organize around an alternative vision that reflects our determined idealism and grounded realism.

# Obama Must Get Afghanistan Right
## *January 8, 2009*

President-elect Barack Obama not only had the good judgment to oppose the war in Iraq, he argued for the need "to end the mindset that took us into" that war. So it's troubling that he ramped up his rhetoric during the campaign about exiting Iraq in order to focus on what he calls the "central front in the war on terror"—Afghanistan. His plan now calls for an escalation of 20,000 to 30,000 additional American troops over the next year—nearly doubling the current 32,000.

*New York Times* columnist Tom Friedman criticized the Dems' position on Afghanistan as ill-conceived "bumper sticker politics." Too many of the leading Dems have become part of a poorly reasoned bipartisan consensus that threatens to entrap the United States in another costly occupation—a war that *New York Times* columnist Bob Herbert describes as "more than seven years old and which long ago turned into a quagmire." It currently costs the Pentagon $2 billion per month to support the US troops in Afghanistan. An escalation would drain resources that are vital to President-elect Obama's goals for an economic recovery, healthcare, and social justice at home, while impeding other critical international initiatives such as the Middle East Peace process and a regional diplomacy in South Asia.

Once again, as in the run-up to the war in Iraq, too few people in Congress and the mainstream media are asking tough questions. There are some notable exceptions—see Friedman and Herbert—and in Congress, there's Senator Russ Feingold who writes in a recent op-ed:

> Few people seem willing to ask whether the main solution that's being talked about—sending more troops to Afghanistan—will

actually work. If the devastating policies of the current administration have proved anything, it's that we need to ask tough questions before deploying our brave service members—and that we need to be suspicious of Washington 'group think.' Otherwise, we are setting ourselves up for failure.

There are strategic reasons to oppose a military escalation and occupation. On national security grounds, a US occupation would be counterproductive to the stated goal of defeating Al Qaeda. The moment for action against Al Qaeda in Afghanistan was immediately after 9/11. Now, Al Qaeda operates out of Pakistan, and the key to reining it in lies with a democratic Pakistani government. Andrew Bacevich, a retired Army colonel and a professor of history and international relations at Boston University, wrote about the "sinkhole" of Afghanistan in *Newsweek*:

> The chief effect of military operations in Afghanistan so far has been to push radical Islamists across the Pakistani border. As a result, efforts to stabilize Afghanistan are contributing to the destabilization of Pakistan, with potentially devastating implications. . . . To risk the stability of that nuclear-armed state in the vain hope of salvaging Afghanistan would be a terrible mistake.

US occupation is also exacerbating tensions in South Asia, where the Kashmir conflict and Mumbai attacks have nuclear-armed Pakistan and India at "each others' throats."

At a moment when US diplomatic leadership is needed to pursue peace, and cooperation is required to take on Al Qaeda, major groups within Pakistan's military and intelligence services are now providing support to Islamic extremists with the aim of thwarting US policy. The United States is viewed as propping up an unpopular and corrupt Karzai government that *New York Times* reporter Dexter Filkins describes as "seem[ing] to exist for little more than the enrichment of those who run it" and "contributing to the collapse of public confidence . . . and to the resurgence of the Taliban." The Karzai government also aids and abets a flourishing narcotics trade. All of these factors fuel anti-American/anti-government sentiment in Afghanistan and Pakistan. But perhaps nothing causes rage toward the United States more than mounting civilian casualties.

According to a report from the Human Rights Watch documenting air strikes and civilian deaths, the majority of deaths caused by international troops come from air strikes. Using statistics provided by the US Central Command Air Forces, the report noted that US aircraft have dropped about as many tons of bombs in June and July this year as during all of 2006. At least 321 civilians were killed in NATO or US aerial raids this year—triple the number in 2006. A UN report now estimates that up to 500 Afghan civilians are dying monthly from US cluster bombs, most of them children and teenage boys. Finally, a UN study shows that civilian deaths have not only increased Afghan resentment of foreign forces but also motivated many of the suicide bombings. As an Afghan vegetable-stand owner told the *Washington Post*, "I never heard of a suicide bomber in Afghanistan until the Americans and this government came."

The other often-cited national security objective—ensuring that Afghanistan doesn't become a haven for terrorists—doesn't call for this kind of escalation. First, it doesn't make sense to fight an unwinnable war to prevent Al Qaeda from using Afghanistan if they can operate relatively freely in Pakistan. Also, it would be difficult to find a less attractive place strategically than Afghanistan from which to direct an international terrorist network or threaten US interests or global commerce.

What is required in order to pursue peace in the region is better delivery of targeted aid and reconstruction that improves the daily lives of the Afghanistan people. In a recent statement, the international relief and development organization Oxfam

America urged a change of focus: "Unless the next American President . . . builds on the existing commitments to help lift the Afghan people out of extreme poverty and protect civilians, it will be impossible for the country to achieve lasting peace." Many argue that only increased presence of US troops will create the security needed for delivery of aid, but the Karzai government is too corrupt and too weak outside of Kabul to ensure that the aid goes to the people who need it. A negotiated settlement with elements of the Taliban would create far greater stability than we could ever hope to achieve through an escalation, arming militias and doling out Viagra to tribal leaders—as the *Washington Post* reported last month is the practice of US intelligence officials.

Some raise human rights concerns about the consequence of a US/NATO departure. In particular, some groups feel that US troops are needed to protect Afghan girls and women. But many Afghan women activists and organizations—like former Afghan Parliament member Malalai Joya and the Revolutionary Association of the Women of Afghanistan (RAWA)—have called for a withdrawal of foreign troops from Afghanistan. Here's how Joya put it: "Over 85 percent of Afghans are living below the poverty line and don't have enough to eat. While the US military spends $65,000 a minute in Afghanistan for its operations, up to 18 million people (out of a population of only 26 million) live on less than US$2 a day, according to the Food and Agriculture Organization. . . . As soon as possible, the US/NATO troops must vacate our country. We want liberation, not occupation. With the withdrawal of occupation forces, we will only have to face one enemy instead of two." We currently spend $36 billion annually on military operations in Afghanistan, which would climb with escalation. We've spent $11 billion since 2002 on non-military development. Withdrawal of troops doesn't end US aid—it allows resources to be spent more wisely, focusing on creating opportunities and rights for women, and alternatives to the narcotics trade for poor farmers. As Sonali Kolhatkar, co-director of Afghan Women's Mission said, "For this, or any other idea to work, the US occupation must end. That's the first big step to recovery."

While President-elect Obama has the possibility of re-engaging with a world repulsed by the destructive polices of the Bush administration, it is likely that escalating the war in Afghanistan will endanger that possibility. Escalation may cause a rift with European allies, whose people have turned against this war, and our ability to extricate ourselves from the quagmire will only get harder. Consider the warning of former national security adviser, Zbigniew Brzezinski: "We are running the risk of repeating the mistake the Soviet Union made. . . . Our strategy is getting in deeper and deeper." Russian military officers caution that Afghans cannot be conquered, as the Soviets attempted to do in the 1980s with nearly twice as many troops as NATO and the United States currently have in the country and with three times the number of Afghan troops that Karzai can deploy.

The best prospect for more concerted action against Al Qaeda is a planned withdrawal of US forces and for reconstruction to be taken over by a multinational coalition that has as few American fingerprints as possible. The fact that this is an American project is the principal reason why Pakistani groups support the Islamic insurgents. To be fair, President-elect Obama has spoken on the importance of development aid and resolving the opium trade, but military escalation remains the centerpiece of his plan. The point of withdrawal is not to abandon Afghanistan, but to take a different approach to targeted aid, smart diplomacy and intelligence cooperation. A regional solution will be tough—one that involves Pakistan, India, Afghanistan, China, Russia and Iran (who opposes the Taliban and also has its own fight with Afghan drug warlords on its border), as will a negotiated settlement between the Karzai government and the Taliban. But these should be the priorities of the Obama administration, rather than sending more young men and women to die in the mountains and deserts of Afghanistan and making this President Obama's war.

## Helping Afghan Women and Girls
### *February 2, 2009*

As the coalition I'm working with—Get Afghanistan Right—continues to make the case that the Obama administration would be wise to rethink its plan to escalate militarily in Afghanistan, I've tried to engage the arguments made by some feminists and human rights groups who believe that such an escalation is necessary to protect Afghani women and girls. I share their horror when I read stories like this one by *New York Times* reporter Dexter Filkins describing an acid attack against girls and women—students and their teachers—at the Mirwais School for Girls. But how will escalation or increased US troop presence improve their security or make their lives better?

I thought it would be important to speak with someone who has experience working on the ground with Afghan women's organizations, Kavita Ramdas, president and CEO of the Global Fund for Women. For fifteen years, she has worked with groups like the Afghan Institute for Learning—which serves about 350,000 women and children in their schools, healthcare centers and human rights programs.

This is what Kavita said:

> We're hearing from groups we've worked with for over a fifteen-year period now, on the ground inside Afghanistan and with Afghan women's groups and Pakistan as well.

First, I think it's remarkable that our approach to foreign policy—not just for the last eight years, but with regard to Afghanistan and Pakistan in general over the last thirty years— has been almost entirely military focused. There hasn't been any willingness to take a cold hard look at how effective or in-effective that strategy has been in whether or not it has helped stabilize the country. And there has been much less attention paid to whether this militaristic approach has done anything positive for the women of Afghanistan. It's doubtful whether America's foreign policy has ever had the welfare of Afghan women at heart. As many Afghani women have said to us, "You know, you didn't even think about us twenty-five years ago," and then all of a sudden post 9–11, we're sending troops to Afghanistan and ostensibly we're very concerned about women. But there's very little willingness to really look at the implications of a military strategy on women's security. It is very important to begin with the following question: If the strategies that we used up to this point have not succeeded in ensuring the safety and well being of women and girls, what makes us think that increased militarization with 30,000 ad-ditional US troops is somehow going to improve the situation and security of women in Afghanistan?

The second question is: What has been the role of the ex-isting troops in Afghanistan with regard to the situation and the security of women? In general, what happens when re-gions become highly militarized, and when there are "peace-keeping forces," militias, as well as foreign troops—which is NATO and the United States, primarily? In most parts of the world, highly militarized societies in almost every instance lead to bad results for women. The security of women is not improved and in many instances it actually becomes worse.

What do I mean by that? Take for example Afghanistan. In 2003, almost every woman's group I met with in Afghanistan, which was already a few years after the initial invasion, said that although they were very grateful for the fact that the Taliban was gone, the presence of foreign troops in Afghanistan in general and in Kabul in particular had highly increased the incidence of both prostitution as well as trafficking—it's not one and the same thing. Prostitution in the sense of being something "voluntary" because very poor women and girls would come down, particularly from the countryside where villages are in a state of absolute dire impoverishment . . . there's very little to eat, very little production. . . . I talked to so many women and women's organizations who've said, young girls sleep with a soldier in Kabul for $40, $50, which is more than their mothers could make as a teacher in a full month. That's the incidence of prostitution as a function of—people call it in the women's movement "survival sex"—the trading of sex for food on a survival basis.

Then there is also trafficking, which actually also increases because when there are military settlements, camps, barracks . . . criminal elements start bringing in women—forcibly or coercing them under other guises. Girls—in this case mainly from the Uzbek and Hazara tribes, as well as a number of Chinese girls in Kabul—are actually trafficked in to fill the "needs" of foreign troops. Very few Afghans can afford to actually pay for these kinds of services, so you have a situation where the main customers are the military troops.

Then you put on top of this the fact that there are all kinds of other armed militias and gangs moving around freely in the countryside because the more foreign troops there are, the more resistance there is going to be from indigenous forces—whether it's the Taliban, different kinds of mujahideen, different groups of ethnic tribal factions. Throughout history, whenever foreign troops are present, there will be resistance against those foreign troops in one way or another.

Those militias and militant groups are also armed, roaming and wandering, going randomly into villages and targeting women as they please by sexually assaulting and raping. As for the incidents that you've been hearing about—whether it was the girls who got acid splashed on their faces that you read about in the *New York Times*—these incidents have been going on for the last four or five years across the country. Girls going to school and teachers have been attacked, and under very various pretexts. Either the Taliban, mujahideen or various factions are attacking them for being "morally loose" or "promiscuous." These people are armed—and because war tends to infuse large amounts of testosterone into large groups of men, living and wandering around together— this does not create the safest of environments for girls in villages, for schoolteachers, for women of any kind—women working in the fields. And so, what we've been hearing reports of are random sexual attacks on women in villages, on girls walking to school, on teachers or other women who are working. So attacks on women have increased, for all sorts of reasons—the most common one that we hear in the West is "Oh, these Islamic fundamentalists don't want women to work or study and so they're attacking them." But there are plenty of people who don't really care whether it's about Islam or not; they're just interested in showing their power by sexually abusing women.

One has to be very clear-eyed about why we are sending 30,000 troops. Quite frankly from a US government perspective, it's because we believe that the "bad guys"—Al Qaeda— are running riot in Afghanistan and somehow that Al Qaeda, the Taliban and the extremists in Pakistan are all one and the same, and they're all collectively bad guys, so we need to go fight them.

I wish we could say to President Obama, "Yes Afghanistan needs troops—but it needs troops of doctors, troops of teachers, troops of Peace Corps volunteers, and troops of farmers to go and replant the fruit orchards. For anyone who grew up in India or Pakistan, Afghanistan was the place where you bought the best incredible dried fruit in the world. Those orchards have been completely devastated. Afghanistan was not a country that just grew poppy for opium sales. It was a country that was forced into selling opium because it had nothing else.

So we need a different kind of troop deployment in Afghanistan; we need a massive deployment of humanitarian troops. We need to invest in Afghanistan's economic infrastructure, in its agriculture. These are villages where people are literally not able to piece together anything that comes close to a subsistence living. Afghanistan is a country in which the maternal mortality rate is the second highest in the world after Sierra Leone. Why are we not sending in teams of doctors and midwives to train local women? We're not talking about a German Marshall Plan for Afghanistan. Instead, we're talking about—without a very clearly defined "enemy"—sending in 30,000 troops to look for this shadowy enemy, and we're not even clear about what that enemy represents. Afghanistan has a very long and very proud history of having thrown out every foreign invader that was ever unfortunate enough to try to subdue them. Yet every political leader suffers from this historical amnesia and seems to lack the willingness to look at the core structures within Afghanistan society. Afghanistan is a very non-centralized nation of very unique and independent small groups and clans that have never had a formally centralized government.

Returning to this argument that sending in troops is being done because "we have to save the women" is exactly what George Bush cynically did in his use of that as a kind of justification. I think the Obama administration has to be very, very careful not to fall into this trap. Yes, there is an incredible need to make a difference in Afghanistan, but more military presence is not the solution. More presence, yes. More dialogue, yes. More engagement with both Pakistan and Afghan leaders and different factions, yes. More genuine investment in the long-term economic growth and development in Afghanistan, absolutely. But none of that is what is being promised. What is being promised is 30,000 US troops and the accompanying support systems, including the Halliburton companies that will supply, feed and look after them.

This then creates another effect which is very important to remember. You then have a group of people, who are foreigners, who do not speak or understand your language or your culture, who are allegedly there fighting the bad guys, who are members of your own people. These "outsiders" feel like occupiers—they live in relative comfort with access to food—all the trappings of what looks like a luxurious life. When the vast majority of that population is living on less than $1 a day. This creates a huge amount of resentment. You walk around any of these American camps in Iraq or Afghanistan—huge areas of land which are cordoned off—and there are SUVs and guys full of body armor and machine guns. Inside it's like a little America with the PX, hamburgers and TV for the troops to watch whatever they want. Meanwhile, outside, Afghan children on the street are still playing with cluster bombs that were dropped by the American army in 2001—they risk being blown up and losing their sight, their limbs, their fingers.

I think about how this country has been systematically denuded of its core resources—both human capital and natural capital, and it makes me grieve. Kabul used to be a place with incredible trees. Everybody who lives there now will tell you all the trees have gone. What Afghanistan needs is truly a massive Marshall Plan. No one is talking about that. I don't see anyone holding this government of Hamid Karzai accountable for what is absolutely endemic corruption. You talk to any women's groups and they will tell you that in order to go to a meeting in any ministry, just to get into the door, you have to pay a bribe. To go to the first floor, you have to pay a bribe; to get into the room, you have to pay a bribe. It is at a level of corruption that is truly extraordinary. . . . Do we want a situation in which the Afghani people will actually welcome the return of the Taliban because it will finally usher in some kind of law and order?

We have to be very careful in making these assumptions. Another question I would ask is to what degree has there been any consultation with any aspects or representatives of Afghan civil society, i.e., women's rights organizations, human rights organizations on the ground in Afghanistan, or with teachers, doctors, professionals about what is needed in Afghanistan today? Or with others who have any sense of whether the presence of these additional foreign troops will simply serve to isolate someone who is already seen as a puppet of the Americans? Or will it give him any credibility? I doubt it will give him any credibility. And then what?

What would you say to those who say, "I agree with you that we need humanitarian troops—troops of doctors, troops of midwives, etc. But we can't do that until there's more security, and the only way to get more security is to send more troops"?

I actually think that is just a bogus argument. This is not to say that these places aren't dangerous or difficult—but to Third World ears it sounds like the argument of Westerners who don't want to put their own lives at risk. When I went to Kabul in 2003, India had sent doctors, nurses, buses—and it was really interesting to see the difference amongst common Afghans, how they saw where US money had gone and where they saw Indian money had gone. Indian development aid was seen in the fleet of over 150 Tata buses—Tata is a company that manufactures buses and cars in India—over 100 buses had been sent over land through Pakistan. Pakistan actually allowed safe passage of those buses. And they were the buses that actually connected cities to each other. And every day Afghans took those buses to go to work, they used them to get around. And they had a sign—[the buses] just said Tata—and everyone knew those buses were from India. Kabul hospital has about sixty or seventy Indian doctors and nurses who were sent by the Indian government and they are assigned over there. Now, is it just that "Third World" peoples' lives are less important so it doesn't matter, so we can send them into insecure situations? I bet you if you asked the Cuban government to send doctors to Afghanistan, they would. I'm not sure the American government would like to have them there, but I'm sure they would go. I think saying, "we have to wait until it's secure and we can't send anybody," it's a very weak argument. And, of course, you don't just send anyone, either troops of soldiers or troops of humanitarian workers, without asking what local people want and what their priorities are. You sit down, like in 2002, when different groups came together to write a constitution. You see what is and isn't working in Afghanistan. Bring all the warring factions together—at least ask—which hasn't even been tried!

We're just accepting that the way to get security is with the presence of more guns. If I have more guns than you, then that makes me secure. It actually doesn't. It doesn't make us more secure. Because as soon as the other person gets more guns, he's going to come and try to take you out anyway. We know this from gang warfare. This is how gangs operate in urban centers of the United States. Having more weapons and more troops doesn't necessarily make you more secure.

What makes you secure is feeling that you have some legitimacy and some credibility amongst people in the communities where you live. Right now I don't think the Americans have a shred of that credibility. The United States did have that credibility right after the fall of Taliban. Things had gotten so bad that even though people knew that the United States came out of selfish reasons post-9–11, they were still willing to give the United States the benefit of the doubt. And at that point the United States moved on to Iraq—instead of investing in the rebuilding of Afghanistan—which really it owed Afghanistan after the thirty-five years of misery that it put Afghanistan through by "fighting a proxy war against the Russians via Afghans." We didn't commit any troops in that last hot war of the Cold War era. No Americans were killed fighting the Russians in Afghanistan. But they certainly seeded a global jihad. US funds and Saudi funds supported a military dictatorship in Pakistan and put people like Osama bin Laden and others through the ISI training camps, where they learned to fight the "godless communists." Now they have turned their sights on their erstwhile funders—the United States and its allies are now the infidels.

Although it does not seem like it, I believe that there are real alternative options that could be considered by President Obama and this new administration. Given all the goodwill in the world toward Obama right now, there is a little window of opportunity, in which I believe other nations would give the new administration the benefit of the doubt. If they said, "Let's sit down with Pakistan and Afghanistan; and Iran has to be part of that conversation too, and talk about what we can do to try to improve the situation."

What are the priorities of the people of Afghanistan? What do they most need at this time?

I'm quite sure that the people of Afghanistan would not say that what we most need is 30,000 American troops eating food enough to feed each of our families ten times over.

# Reset with Russia

## *March 5, 2009*

**Update:** In their first face-to-face meeting, Presidents Obama and Medvedev agreed they were "ready to move beyond Cold War mentalities" and launch a "fresh start" in what has been an increasingly strained relationship. There was agreement to cooperate on stabilizing Afghanistan and reining in Iran's nuclear ambitions. But the most substantive part of the meeting is the decision to develop a new arms control framework to replace the one dismantled by Bush and his team (who considered virtually any treaty a subversive document). Obama and Medvedev agreed to launch negotiations to draft a new arms control treaty that could slash US-Russian strategic nuclear arsenals by a third. (In December 2010, the senate ratified the new START treaty.)

While the tone, the words and the possibilities of the young presidents' first meeting gives me cautious optimism about the resetting of this difficult relationship, I still believe some fundamental differences and difficult issues lie ahead. As I wrote last month, the folly of a destabilizing missile defense system and NATO expansion, perhaps now, wisely, put on a backburner in light of the metastasizing geoeconomic crisis, are two fundamental issues which must be confronted if we're going to see a real reset of relations. (By the way, for those who seek a better translation of "reset" than the one provided by our State Department, try "perezagruska.")

Meanwhile, I'm still befuddled by the big red box with a yellow push button, with "reset" stamped on it, which Secretary of State Clinton presented Russia's Foreign Minister as a sign of better relations. In Moscow, which I visited in mid-March, those

who remembered Stanley Kubrick's *Dr. Strangelove* thought the
box was a prop from that iconic film. That film, by the way,
should be shown in every high school in America and Russia.

»»»

For the sake of a safer world, the United States needs to rethink
its policies toward Russia—beginning with the folly of a destabilizing missile defense system based in Poland and the Czech
Republic. Despite the fact that the majority of Czech citizens oppose
hosting the system—which is never reported in the US mainstream media—the Bush administration rushed to deploy what
Ploughshares Fund president Joseph Cirincione calls "a system
that doesn't work to defeat a threat that doesn't exist," spending
$14 billion a year in the process.

The Obama administration recently signaled a smart break
with the destructive policies of that era when it said it would
"not divert resources from other national security priorities
until we are positive the technology will protect the American
public." That bodes well for ultimately scrapping missile defense, since it hasn't tested successfully against even the most
rudimentary decoys and counter-measures any enemy would
possess.

But as Stephen F. Cohen (disclosure—my husband) makes
clear in his *Nation* cover story "The New American Cold War,"
charting an alternative and smart course for US-Russian relations
demands much more than abandoning an ineffective, unneeded
technology. Of course, we need a new arms control framework—
Bush and his team dismantled decades of bipartisan cooperation
and work in this area. We must sign and ratify the Comprehensive Nuclear-Test-Ban Treaty and eventually abide by the Nuclear Non-Proliferation Treaty that mandates building down to
a nuclear-free world. There is growing momentum for total

disarmament as seen in the Global Zero movement, and President Obama is an advocate for this stance as well.

But resetting the relationship with Russia—as both President Obama and Vice President Biden have indicated a desire to do—will require more than that. It demands an end to the triumphalist thinking that has defined the US mindset since the end of the Cold War. President Obama and some on his team seem to be on the road to understanding how vital this shift is.

However, in both capitals, Moscow and Washington, this new thinking faces opponents who seize on "reset" as capitulation. Witness the recent controversy surrounding a supposedly "secret" letter from President Obama to Russian President Medvedev that reportedly extended an offer for the United States to cease deployment of missile defense in Eastern Europe in exchange for Russian help ending Iran's alleged nuclear weapons program. Both President Obama and Russian officials deny there was any such quid pro quo offer, and Obama said the letter wasn't a secret and it addressed a host of issues including nuclear proliferation.

But the New Cold Warriors—who seek, at best, "neo-containment" for the sake of continuing the folly of NATO expansion to Russia's doorstep—seized the opportunity to reassert their dangerous ideology. According to the *Washington Post*, Robert Kagan of the Carnegie Endowment for International Peace said that "Moscow will use our desire to bring the temperature down to its advantage, on issues such as Russia's desire for hegemony over the former Soviet republics on its borders." GOP leaders sent President Obama a letter saying his reaching out to Russia on these issues was "unwise and premature" and that it "undercuts our allies." Finally, an editorial revealed the Manichean lens through which the *Washington Post* editors see the world: "Perhaps the Kremlin leadership believes that 'reset' is another way of saying 'capitulate.' If so, Ms. Clinton would do well to clarify the administration's policy when she meets [Russian Foreign Minister] Lavrov" on Friday in Geneva.

Contrast that with the kind of new thinking laid out in Cohen's *Nation* article and displayed by Cirincione. "US threats will make it more difficult for Medvedev to do something he wants to do anyway: reset the US-Russian relationship," he said. "We should be saying, 'We need to cooperate to reduce our common threats.' . . . President Obama understands he has a better chance of getting what he wants through openness rather than bravado. If he threatens Russia it makes it harder for them to make concessions."

A key to this "reset" is that the United States and its allies halt NATO expansion. These are times that demand economic recovery, not expansion of a military alliance forged to combat the Soviet Union and which threatens cooperation on mutual economic and security interests. It is a moment when Central and Eastern Europe face its worst economic crisis since the collapse of their economies following the fall of the Berlin Wall. Ukraine in particular is in desperate financial shape and will need both European and Russian support. Georgia is also in economic straits. We should shelve talk of NATO expansion and work with Europe and Russia to build a more viable economic region through a new global financial architecture. Expect European protesters to articulate similar demands in April when President Obama attends a summit commemorating NATO's sixtieth anniversary. But a new tack will face fierce opposition among those invested in NATO expansion and in the belief that Russia poses a threat to our interests.

Finally, Iran looms large. As Cirincione told me, "Any successful Iran strategy has got to have the cooperation of Russia, it's as simple as that."

Russia has no desire for a nuclear-armed Iran or an Iran with long-range missiles. It doesn't want Iran increasing turmoil on its southern border. Russia also has leverage—it could end arms sales to Iran; end or suspend cooperation on the Bushehr nuclear power plant; increase diplomatic pressure through UN sanctions or resolutions. Cirincione points out that Iran doesn't want to be viewed as a pariah state, and when Russia swings against it, Iran is isolated.

"But Russia [needs] a US-Russian relationship that involves cooperation and mutual respect—not just the US telling Russia what it's going to do," Cirincione said. "And they have to know that the US intentions for Iran don't involve starting a third war in the region. Then all things are possible."

Of course, new agreements between the United States and Russia to dramatically reduce nuclear arsenals are vital for success in dealing with Iran as the major powers create the context and pressure for non-proliferation worldwide.

There will not be a fundamental change or reset of US-Russian relations—no real partnership—until there is new American thinking about Russia.

# On 9/11/09
## *September 10, 2009*

As we extricate ourselves from Iraq, and escalate in Afghanistan, it is time to think hard about lessons learned—and not learned. Why do we have a bloated war budget which could be redeployed, wisely, to fund the rebuilding of our economy and society? Why do we continue to use conventional—and now counterinsurgency—war-fighting when the lessons of history tell us terrorism is a tactic best combated through common-sense counterterrorism measures, including policing, intelligence, and tough diplomacy. How is it that after some extraordinary media reporting, and brilliant work by CCR and the ACLU, we still debate terrorism's "efficacy"? How do we reclaim our moral compass after years of militarization and degraded discourse? How do too many in our political class justify spending trillions on war, yet balk at spending $900 billion, over ten years, on reforming a dysfunctional healthcare system?

These and other questions have and will inform *The Nation*'s reporting, analysis and work. After all, as our esteemed editorial board member Eric Foner writes below, "In times of crisis, the most patriotic act of all is the unyielding defense of civil liberties, the right to dissent."

"On Tuesday morning, a piece was torn out of our world. A patch of blue sky that should not have been there opened up in the New York skyline . . . the heavens were raining human beings. Our city was changed forever. Our country was changed forever. Our world was changed forever." So wrote Jonathan Schell in the first issue of *The Nation* following September 11, 2001.

At *The Nation*'s office, in the aftermath of the attacks on the World Trade Center towers, like everyone else in America, we watched television—horrified, saddened, angry. People wept, and at the same time took notes and got on the phones. For we had an issue closing the next day. We quickly learned that our communications links to the outer world were severed—our phone lines had run under World Trade Center 7. So in those first days, we had no incoming calls and the office computer links to the Internet were down. The facts were sketchy, and causes of the attack shrouded in a pall of uncertainty thick as the smog rising from the demolished World Trade Center.

The issue that we assembled and put to bed the next day struck a tone and purpose that the magazine has striven to maintain in the past five years. Paying respect to the human reactions of anger, hurt and grief, our editorials in that first week, and in the ones that followed, have made the case for an effective and just response to the horrific terrorist acts. We argued that such a response may include discriminate use of military force, but that the most promising and effective way to halt terrorism lies in bringing those responsible to justice through non-military actions in cooperation with the global community and within a framework of domestic and international law. As Richard Falk warned in his indispensable "A Just Response," the "justice of the cause" would be "negated by the injustice of improper means and excessive ends."

As the US military response unfolded in the ensuing days, there seemed to be more questions than answers. Who is Osama bin Laden? What is the involvement of the Taliban? What are we doing in Afghanistan anyway? Did US foreign policy create historic resentments and injustices abroad that spawned the terrible attacks? What is the best way for this country to address the root causes of terrorism? What are the aims of the war on it? What are its limits? What is the potential political and human fallout? Who are our allies? What role should the United Nations play? How to limit civilian casualties and provide humanitarian relief? As autumn in New York merged into Ramadan and Afghanistan's winter, these questions only deepened. It is striking how the essential themes laid out in *The Nation* in those initial weeks, far from being outrun by events, have gained in resonance.

One of my roles as editor has been to figure out the bridge from personal to political. How do you balance individual grief and anger at the attacks with proportionality, justice and wisdom in response? How do we reconcile legitimate fear of future attacks with protection of civil liberties, and carry on a political debate that doesn't ignore concerns of economic and social justice?

To deal with those complex issues, I was fortunate in being able to call on some of the most respected figures on the progressive left. They responded with a series of thoughtful, informed and provocative essays that have appeared in our pages. Among them: the late scholar-philosopher-activist Edward Said demolishing the clash of civilizations argument; Mary Kaldor on the new wars and civil society's role in halting terrorism; Michael T. Klare on Saudi-US relations and the geopolitics of oil; Ellen Willis on homefront conformity; Chalmers Johnson on blowback and the role of US foreign policy; William Greider on war profiteering; Bill Moyers on Americans' restored faith in government; John le Carré on why this war can't be won. Our regular columnists weighed in with their independent perspectives. And peace and disarmament editor Jonathan Schell filed a weekly "Letter from Ground Zero"—lucid, illuminating, frightening, humane essays that advanced the case for sensible and moral non-military actions.

*The Nation* has a long tradition of providing a forum for a broad spectrum of left/progressive views, which sometimes erupted in spirited debates in those weeks after 9/11. Christopher Hitchens's column, "Against Rationalization," which castigated those on the left who drew a causal relationship between US foreign policy in the Middle East and the terrorist acts, provoked a heated exchange with Noam Chomsky. This exchange ran on our website and drew a raft of comments, with readers almost equally divided. Richard Falk's article "Defining a Just War" also provoked numerous letters pro and con.

As a fog of national security enveloped official Washington and the war front, and the mainstream media enlisted in the administration's war—flag logos flying—the need for an independent, critical press seemed never more urgent. The speedy passage of the repressive Patriot Act, with scarcely a murmur of dissent in Congress, the secret detentions of more than 1,000 people and the establishment of military tribunals were troubling signs that a wartime crackdown on civil liberties was under way and called for vigorous opposition. Criticizing government policy in wartime is not a path to popularity. Our independent stand on the war and criticism of what we called "policy profiteering" by conservative Republicans in Congress (who sought to use the war as a pretext to push through their own agenda) drew virulent attacks by the pundits and publications of the right, who questioned our patriotism and trotted out the old chestnut of the left's "anti-Americanism."

Such attacks are nothing new. *The Nation* has always marched to a different drummer, opposing US involvement in the Spanish-American War and World War I and the Vietnam War, while giving all-out support to the US effort in World War II. Former *Nation* managing editor Ernest Gruening of Alaska was one of only two senators to vote against the Gulf of Tonkin resolution that led to the Vietnam morass. As Eric Foner wrote in the days after the attacks, "At times of crisis the most patriotic act of all is the unyielding defense of civil liberties, the right to dissent." Also in times of crisis, the enduring concerns of this magazine and progressives take on new relevance: the dangers of American unilateralism, corrosion of civil liberties, authoritarianism in any nation, dependence on Big Oil, military quagmire and the urgent necessity of international law and institutions.

The commentary this magazine has published in the five years since the 9/11 attacks was designed to inform honest debate in this country on key questions that confront us and to enable us to ask hard questions of policy-makers and the media. It is my hope that the ideas expressed here will guide and enrich the policies that will—and must—come.

# No Defense for This Budget

*February 2, 2010*

Deficit hysteria has reached new levels, yet where is the attention to an out of control defense budget that is now the largest since World War II? While the Obama administration's three-year freeze on discretionary spending is a bad idea, it's made even worse because unprecedented Pentagon spending is exempted from it.

Who would know from all of the whining about budget deficits that military spending is the largest discretionary item in the federal government? Exempting all security-related expenditures from common-sense cuts will have serious consequences for almost everything the government does—from job creation, poverty reduction and alternative energy development, to aid for cash-strapped state and local governments. In fact, the Economic Policy Institute reports that non-security-related discretionary spending is already at near-historic lows as a share of GDP. At a time when foreclosures are still rising, and we face double-digit unemployment, this freeze will make digging out from the Great Recession more difficult.

On Monday, the Obama administration requested $708 billion for the Defense Department next year—including $549 billion for its base budget and $159 billion for the wars in Afghanistan and Iraq. This doesn't even include the $33 billion supplement the White House will request for its escalation in Afghanistan this year.

Just last week, Representative Barney Frank reissued his call for military cuts—a call he originally made nearly a year ago in a piece for *The Nation* in which he wrote, "If we do not make reductions approximating 25 percent of the military budget starting fairly soon, it will be impossible to continue to fund an adequate level of domestic activity even with a repeal of Bush's tax cuts for the very wealthy." Frank's prescient advice received little attention from the media at that time. Not surprisingly, it's once again failed to get the attention it deserves from the mainstream press.

In fact, Monday's *Washington Post* news article—not an op-ed or editorial, mind you—on Obama's budget offers the kind of skewed frame on spending that is typical of inside the Beltway thinking. The *Post* describes "a budget hole that is driving accumulated debt to dangerous levels" and "could damage the dollar and undermine the United States' international standing." A *New York Times* headline screams, "Huge Deficits May Alter U.S. Politics and Global Power"—as if we must run for the hills. "Unless miraculous growth, or miraculous political compromises, creates some unforeseen change over the next decade," the article warns, "there is virtually no room for new domestic initiatives for Mr. Obama or his successors." Finally, the *Wall Street Journal* offers this grim warning: "Deficit Balloons into National-Security Threat."

This kind of fear-mongering obliterates any distinctions between necessary investments in areas like jobs, infrastructure, education and alternative energy, and unnecessary and wasteful tax cuts or subsidies for wealthy folks, or defense spending that is rampant with cost overruns and corruption, and way out of scale with what is truly needed for our security. These same newspapers are engaged in media malpractice when they scare people with deficit hysteria but fail to take a critical look at the defense budget.

It doesn't look like the administration will resist this kind of stale thinking on defense. But if President Obama used the common sense he spoke so well about during the State of the Union, he'd expose the mistaken notion that defense spending is akin to an effective jobs program—jobs every Congressional district will fight for. It doesn't matter that economists largely "agree that military spending is one of the least efficient ways of creating jobs per dollar of government spending."

Dr. Lawrence Korb, an assistant defense secretary under Ronald Reagan and a senior fellow at the Center for American Progress, told me, "The Administration refused to take on a lot of the investment programs that really don't make a lot of sense at this particular time. For example, the F-35 Joint Strike Fighter. It's having all kinds of developmental problems. And yet, they've put almost $11 billion in it this year to buy 45 of these things. They just had to add $314 billion over the next 5 years to the previous estimates for that program! The real issue is that you're asking everybody else to freeze spending, why can't you freeze the investment part of the defense budget and force them to make some of these trade-offs?"

The unfairly maligned House Speaker Nancy Pelosi gets it when she takes a common-sense approach to the budget. She came out with this statement yesterday: "I look forward to examining the President's proposal to freeze spending and believe waste can be found in all departments and agencies—including the Defense Department—so it too must come under scrutiny. . . . Curbing military contractors' wasteful practices must be part of our efforts to restore accountability, transparency, and fiscal discipline to the federal budget."

Even House Minority Leader John Boehner said the Pentagon shouldn't be exempted, and "there's got to be wasteful spending there, unnecessary spending there."

What's usually ignored is that there are smart and effective ways to devise an alternative approach to defense spending which would allow for needed cuts and needed security. For example, the annual Unified Security Budget—a project of Foreign Policy In Focus at the Institute for Policy Studies—takes a hard look at "spending on offense (military forces), defense (homeland security) and prevention (non-military foreign engagement)" in order to consider security spending comprehensively and make recommendations on cuts and reforms. It proposes cuts of over $60 billion in weapons systems (including reducing the US nuclear arsenal to 600 warheads and 400 in reserve) and significant reforms to the Pentagon procurement system to reduce waste. Another area which needs a fresh look is spending on US bases overseas, which Anita Dancs, an analyst for Foreign Policy In Focus, puts at $250 billion annually. These bases are also anti-democratic, and there is a growing movement of citizens in host nations who oppose the US presence.

These kinds of reforms go toward a smart question raised by Matthew Yglesias today: "The problem here is that while targeting defense waste always has some support, there are few politicians willing to question the real driver of Pentagon cost—the American military's global mission." That is indeed the larger overarching issue of America's role in world—-Globocop or Republic?

We can do better on security by spending less and much more wisely on defense. There are scores of groups already working to bring sanity to our defense budget and engagement with the world. And members of the Congressional Progressive Caucus have shown some moxie in advancing the Unified Security Budget as a smart alternative. Maybe these painful cuts will galvanize more Americans to think hard about what real security means. Right now, for those who understand what's at stake with these budget priorities, it's high time to tell your legislators and the White House that if there is indeed going to be any freeze on spending, the exorbitant defense budget should be included in that.

# Gorbachev at 80
*February 25, 2011*

The end of the 20th century witnessed an apparently irreversible wave of democratization in several parts of the world. But until the recent dramatic events in Egypt, democratization seemed to have waned—even given way to a new wave of authoritarianism around the world. Except in the promotional plans of professional democratizers, the "romance" disappeared from the news and commentary pages of most American newspapers. Now it has returned, along with a good deal of historical amnesia.

Usually forgotten is that the "wave of democratization" in the late 20th century began in a place, and in a way, that few had expected—Soviet Russia, under the leadership of the head of the Soviet Communist Party, Mikhail Gorbachev. Indeed, the extent to which Gorbachev's democratic achievements during his nearly seven years in power (1985 to 1991) have been forgotten or obscured is truly remarkable.

The amnesia began almost immediately after the Soviet Union ended, in December 1991, when the US political and media establishment began attributing Russia's democratization primarily, even solely, to its first post-Soviet leader, Boris Yeltsin. According to the quickly prevailing Washington narrative, Yeltsin was the "father of Russian democracy," the leader who began Russia's "transition from totalitarianism" and under whom its "first flickerings of democratic nationhood" occurred.

Lost in this historical misrepresentation are Gorbachev's two greatest achievements. By 1991, he had led Russia closer to a real functioning democracy than it had ever been in its 1,000-year history; and the parliamentary and presidential elections he introduced from 1989 to 1991—in the then-Soviet system—remain Russia's freest and fairest to this day.

Getting this history wrong not only dishonors Gorbachev, who turns 80 Wednesday, but also deletes from our thinking how the democratization of Soviet Russia began and how the process might yet unfold in other countries. It did not begin with protesters, violence and bloodshed in the streets, or with the overthrow of the existing regime. Instead, it came from above, from inside the ruling Soviet elite and in the person of a man who had spent his entire political career inside that profoundly authoritarian bureaucracy.

It's especially important to remember this history now, when there is renewed talk in Washington about "democracy promotion" and the need to "shepherd" countries along the presumed democratic path opened by events in Cairo. Gorbachev's evolutionary democratization reminds us that whatever the merits of various US pro-democracy programs aimed Russia, they played no role in the onset or unfolding of democratization in Moscow. Indeed, later, in the post-Soviet 1990s, they might have inadvertently contributed to democracy's undoing.

Consider the process and achievements of what Gorbachev described at the time as a transformation "revolutionary in content but evolutionary in methods and form." His approach represented a sharp break with Russia's long tradition of transformations imposed from above—in which some scholars put Yeltsin's "shock therapy" of the 1990s. When Russians say their country had more democracy under Gorbachev than later, they point out that Yeltsin's popular election as president of the Soviet Union's Russian Republic in June 1991 was the first and last time in Russian, Soviet, or post-Soviet history that the Kremlin has ever allowed executive power to pass to an opposition candidate.

Glasnost, or the ending of seven decades of Soviet censorship, was Gorbachev's other signature democratic reform. Having worked for a few months at the leading glasnost newspaper, *Moscow News*, I still remember vividly how, step by step, from 1985 to 1991, the mechanisms and taboos of censorship were dismantled.

Here, too, the result was astonishing—virtual freedom of the press, both print and broadcast, at least in the national media. Russian journalists I have known since those times still compare their freedom under Gorbachev more favorably than with what followed under both Yeltsin and his successor, Vladimir Putin—oligarchical control and corruption of the media, a resurgence of state interference in their work and the killing of journalists. (Though the killing of journalists is usually associated with the Putin era, of the seventy-six killed since 1992, forty-one were murdered during the Yeltsin years.)

Indeed, the conventional US view that Russia's democratization began after Putin became president in 2000 is contested by many Russian commentators and historians, and a few American specialists. They argue that it began under Yeltsin—particularly when the Russian president used tanks in October 1993 to disband and destroy Russia's most freely elected parliament. Since that fateful event, the Russian Duma has increasingly become a "puppet" parliament, unlike those opposition-filled, raucous legislatures elected under Gorbachev.

Whether or not one views Soviet democratization under Gorbachev as Russia's lost opportunity, as some historians do, the former leader remains a poorly appreciated, perhaps tragic, but nonetheless essential figure in the modern history of democratization. As he turns 80, having outlived the historic breakthroughs he introduced by twenty years, and having watched many of his democratic achievements squandered, Gorbachev, always an optimist during the twenty years I have known him, says he is no longer sure if Russia's democracy glass is half full or half empty.

It may be that actuarial realities have made him melancholy or even despairing, or he may be discouraged by developments in Russia. In a recent interview in *Novaya Gazeta*, the country's leading democratic opposition newspaper, of which he is part-owner, Gorbachev spoke out more bluntly than ever against the Putin-Medvedev leadership for undermining the free media and elections he introduced two decades ago. Gorbachev even warned that Russia's growing authoritarianism might result in an Egypt-style uprising: "We have democratic institutions but . . . they're used to cover arbitrary rule and abuse," he said.

Only history will determine Gorbachev's ultimate reputation. In his own country, he is still reviled by a majority of Russians, who blame him (along with Yeltsin) for destroying the Soviet Union and for the economic and social misery that followed. Other Russians, however, view him, as I do, as a leader of extraordinary vision and courage. If democracy eventually returns to Russia, Gorbachev will be remembered as the greatest reformer in that nation's tormented history.

# The Cost of Libyan Intervention
## March 22, 2011

It will be seventeen years next month since the West made the decision not to intervene in the Rwandan genocide, allowing more than 800,000 people to be slaughtered in just 100 days. Seventeen years later, President Obama has ordered military action in concert with the United Nations, to stop a new humanitarian crisis, this time in Libya, after the urging of a handful of aides. Among them were Samantha Power, who won a Pulitzer Prize for her book on the Rwandan genocide, and UN Ambassador Susan Rice, who was part of the team that failed to act in 1994. According to reports, they advocated intervention to prevent massacres ordered by Moammar Gaddafi in the city of Benghazi and elsewhere. The threat of massacre, by all accounts, appeared to be imminent.

Rwanda's upcoming anniversary, though, is not the central one that comes to mind. In a grim coincidence of history, President Obama ordered "Operation Odyssey Dawn," establishing a no-fly zone in Libya, to begin on March 19, exactly eight years after President Bush began his shock-and-awe campaign in Iraq.

For many grappling with the potential consequences of the United States entering a third military conflict with a Muslim country, it may be difficult to decide which historical analogy is more apt—that of our long quagmire in Iraq or the humanitarian crisis we failed to avert in Rwanda.

But to my mind, there are two important lessons to be learned from the debacle in Iraq that very clearly override the Rwanda analogy.

The first of those lessons involves a matter of principle. I opposed the war in Iraq because it violated international law, and despite the fig leaf of an international coalition the Bush administration tried to wrap it in, the war was essentially an unjustified, unilateral campaign to militarily eliminate Saddam Hussein's regime. We paid a heavy price for our blatant violation of international law and disregard for global opinion. Indeed, President Obama was elected in 2008, in part, to restore America's moral standing in the world. Toward that end, I believe the president was right to resist the initial calls for unilateral US involvement in Libya.

The president did what George W. Bush refused to do in 2003: He made UN Security Council approval and active regional support pre-conditions for US military action. He also took steps to try to limit America's military footprint, letting France and Britain take the lead and ruling out sending ground troops into Libya.

The administration was also careful to negotiate a UN Security Council resolution that states its goal as the protection of civilians rather than regime change. As a matter of principle, the administration's decision to seek UN Security Council action is an important step toward a multipolar world that operates according to multilaterally determined global law and in the interest of the global community.

But while the administration consulted the United Nations, it failed to seek Congressional authorization. As with the Iraq War, the war in Libya is a war of choice. The president is undertaking this action without Congressional authorization. This is a continuation of a dangerous—and unconstitutional—precedent, one that President Obama himself opposed as a senator.

"The president does not have power under the Constitution to unilaterally authorize a military attack in a situation that does not involve stopping an actual or imminent threat to the nation," said Obama in December 2007. Since Libya does not present such a threat to the United States, one wonders how Obama squares his previous understanding of the Constitution with this military undertaking.

There is also a second set of lessons from the Iraq War relating to the costs and benefits of military action that should raise serious concerns about the White House's decision.

As we learned or should have learned from the Iraq War, the use of military force can have all kinds of unintended consequences, especially in places we do not understand. The international coalition says it is going to war to prevent civilian casualties. But even with the most prudential use of military force, it's not clear that we will be able to avoid civilian casualties by our own hands, as we see from our drone strikes within Pakistan.

And as civilian casualties mount, we may see this turn into a story of American overreach. Already we see the limits of the Arab League's support, as it condemned the widespread bombing that came in the first day or two of the intervention. Until now, the democratic awakening has opened up the Arab world's future because it has been undertaken by Arab peoples, who now believe they have control over their own destiny. The Libyan intervention risks changing that narrative.

Then there is the question of where this will all end. If anything, mission creep seems to be an inevitable feature of this kind of American military action. While the language of the UN resolution forbids "foreign occupation," what will we do when chaos and small-scale humanitarian crises begin to occur across Libya?

Indeed, there is a troubling dimension to this intervention in that it reflects a mindset that associates US foreign policy, whether alone or part of an allied, multilateral force, with heroic crusades to bring down the bad guys. It is that mindset that has done so much damage in the Middle East over the years and that has saddled us with the costly burdens of two ongoing wars.

The democratic awakening in the Arab world has presented the United States with an opportunity to put its past support for autocratic governments and repressive military and security apparatuses behind it. It offers this country a chance to align our interests with democratic change and economic progress. It would be a tragedy if the United States allowed the intervention in Libya to distract us from these difficult and important challenges. The most productive role for America in the Middle East—especially over the long term—should be primarily diplomatic and economic, rather than military.

# Why Afghanistan Could Upend Obama's Reelection Strategy

*April 26, 2011*

The outlines of President Obama's reelection strategy are becoming more distinct. He'll bet that the faltering recovery has enough momentum to sell, particularly to college-educated suburban independents. He'll find a way to cut a deal with Republicans on deficits that doesn't completely derail the recovery.

At the same time, he'll draw bright lines to defend largely social issues that appeal to both his base and to independents—ending "don't ask, don't tell," defending Planned Parenthood and family planning, protecting the environment. He'll contrast Republican promises for more tax cuts to the rich with his plan to invest in areas vital to our future—education, innovation, infrastructure.

But in addition to the economy, the disastrous war in Afghanistan threatens to upend this game plan.

Afghanistan is the "good war" that has gone bad. Obama bought into the fantasies of Gen. David Petraeus and the new generation of counterinsurgency mavens, who argued that we could fend off the Taliban, hunt the remnants of Al Qaeda and build an operating nation in Afghanistan, with a government that could provide minimum security for its people. The president added his own caution: we'd have a surge but begin to withdraw US forces in July of this year.

But it all went bad. The Karzai government was more corrupt and more incompetent than the generals admitted. The Taliban proved more resourceful, the tribal relations more indecipherable. The new generation of counterinsurgency mavens proved no wiser than the Vietnam generation. Defense Secretary Robert Gates concluded that any future Pentagon secretary who advises a president to fight wars like those in Iraq and Afghanistan "should have his head examined."

The White House started pointing to 2014 as the time when US troops would depart, quietly planning to extend what is already America's longest war. "Unless the people force this issue from the grass roots, sources in the Pentagon tell me we're looking at a token 10,000–12,000 troop withdrawal [in July 2011] with a sketchy timeline—2014 or even longer—for our continued military presence," said Matthew Hoh, a former Marine who resigned his Afghanistan post in protest and now serves as director of the Afghanistan Study Group.

Antiwar sentiment is at the heart of Obama's base—and also of his appeal to independent voters. His 2008 candidacy was defined as that of the one leader who opposed the Iraq War from the beginning and who pledged to bring it to a close. Buoyed by his election and his commitment to draw down troops from Iraq, liberals largely gave Obama a pass on the Afghanistan surge, placated by his commitment to a time certain to begin getting troops out.

Antiwar sentiment didn't disappear, however; it just went mainstream. As the Great Recession exposed the breadth of America's problems and the war continued to waste lives and resources, support eroded steadily. A January Gallup poll reported that 72 percent of American voters want to "speed up" the withdrawal of troops from the 2014 date. Eighty-six percent of Democrats, 72 percent of independents and 61 percent of Republicans favored a more rapid withdrawal.

And liberal patience is exhausted. Sen. Barbara Boxer—joined, remarkably, by Sen. Richard Durbin, the second-ranking Democrat in the Senate and the closest personally to President Obama—has introduced a resolution demanding that the president lay out a plan for withdrawal with a "date certain" for the end. The Democratic National Committee, whose members are gearing up for the president's reelection campaign, passed a resolution introduced by Rep. Barbara Lee that demands a "swift withdrawal" of troops and contractors, starting with a "significant and sizable reduction [of troops] no later than July 2011."

This argument is likely to explode as we approach the president's "beginning of withdrawal" date of July 2011. The financial costs of the war—the $10 billion a month expended on it would be sufficient to erase the debilitating debts of all of the states combined this year—are increasingly indefensible. The human costs—with some 12,000 US dead and wounded, hundreds of thousands of Afghan casualties, millions displaced—are mounting. The military is pushing the president to stay the course, to minimize any force reduction until the situation stabilizes.

One can sympathize with the dilemma Obama faces. He's already under attack from the right for being weak in Libya. He is urged by Sen. John McCain and others to soldier on despite wasting billions on corruption in Afghanistan, with no clear indication of how the war provides for US security. Making the case to allies and jingoists that we should no longer play the role of "indispensable nation" isn't easy.

But clearly it is time for the president to declare victory and get out of Afghanistan. Al Qaeda has been reduced to remnants. We can't and shouldn't afford the human, moral or fiscal costs of continued occupation in Afghanistan, and the people who live there will have to decide what kind of nation they build, if any. We can support smart diplomacy to bring a political resolution to this civil war.

Defending Planned Parenthood, the EPA, Medicare and Social Security puts the administration on the side of the vast majority of Americans. The Tea Party Republican extremists are helping to reenergize the president's base, but this president has said that "the nation that I'm most interested in building is our own." He is about to find out just how seriously his own supporters take that pledge.

---

# A Chance to End the "War"
## *May 3, 2011*

"On Tuesday morning, a piece was torn out of our world. A patch of blue sky that should not have been there opened up in the New York skyline . . . the heavens were raining human beings. Our city was changed forever. Our country was changed forever. Our world was changed forever." So wrote Jonathan Schell in the first issue of *The Nation* after Sept. 11, 2001.

»»»

Nearly ten years later, in a dramatic yet sober Sunday evening address, President Obama announced that Osama bin Laden, perpetrator of the Sept. 11 attacks, was dead, the result of a US military action. He reminded us of how, in those grim days after Sept. 11, "we reaffirmed our unity as one American family . . . and our resolve to bring those who committed this vicious attack to justice."

He described the capture and killing of bin Laden as the "most significant effort to date in our efforts to defeat al-Qaeda." And he reaffirmed that this country will never wage a war against Islam. For that reason, Obama rightly said that bin Laden's "demise should be welcomed by all those who believe in peace and human dignity."

Now, with bin Laden buried at sea, it is time to end the "global war on terror" we have lived with for a decade. It is time to stop defining the post–Sept. 11 struggle against stateless terrorists as "war." Framing the fight against terror as a war was a conscious decision made by President Bush, Karl Rove and others in those first days after Sept. 11—a decision that destroyed the unity President Obama reminded us of in his address.

The "war" metaphor—as retired American ambassador Ronald Spiers wrote in 2004—"is neither accurate nor innocuous, implying as it does that there is an end point of either victory or defeat. . . . A 'war on terrorism' is a war without an end in sight, without an exit strategy, with enemies specified not by their aims but by their tactics."

The Bush administration used the "war" as justification for undermining the best of America's principles. We have witnessed the abuse of international human rights standards, the unlawful detention of thousands of women and men, and the condoning of torture.

And though President Obama has wisely refused to refer to our actions against terrorist cells as a "war on terror," he too has used the "war" as justification for the expansion of his executive authority, whether through the use of military tribunals or the embrace of indefinite detention.

Today it is time not only to end the use of the term "war on terror," but to end the war itself.

It is time to bring our troops home.

The success in eliminating bin Laden should provide courage and political space to the Obama administration to bring the Afghan War to an expeditious end by reducing US forces in Afghanistan and accelerating regionally supported peace talks among the many factions there.

As *The Nation*'s Robert Dreyfuss notes, "the war in Afghanistan, which long ago lost any sane rationale, no longer has even a pretext: Even if the Taliban take over—a highly unlikely prospect, even were the United States to pack up and leave—there simply won't be any al Qaeda to provide shelter to."

Indeed, Al Qaeda has largely been destroyed. It is highly fragmented, with membership only in the hundreds, hardly the centralized threat that justifies the deployment of hundreds of thousands of US troops. With the death of its leader, it may never find a central figure to rally around again.

President Obama and his team have a unique opportunity to reset the terms of the national security debate; the end of bin Laden has given the administration more credibility—and political capital—on national security issues.

Yes, we all live in the shadow of Sept. 11—a crime of monumental magnitude. And yes, it would be naïve to deny that terrorist cells with lethal capacity are scattered around the world. But terrorism is not an enemy that threatens the existence of our nation. Nor can it be successfully countered by the large-scale use of force or by occupying other countries or by eliminating all the places terrorists can hide. Rather, it is by the wise use of intelligence, police work and homeland security that we can keep our nation safe. Our response to terrorism cannot risk undermining the very values that define America in our eyes and in the eyes of the world.

Bin Laden and the core group of Al Qaeda who planned and executed the Sept. 11 attacks have largely been destroyed, but at an unnecessarily high price: two ongoing land wars; more than 50,000 soldiers killed or wounded; hundreds of thousands of innocent Iraqis, Afghans and Pakistanis killed; trillions of US dollars spent and the loss of American standing in the world that has yet to be fully restored.

This past decade has been a crucible for the nation, and through it we have learned that a hyper-militarized war without end does not strengthen a democracy; it strangles it.

Though he has continued far too many Bush-era national security policies, President Obama appears to understand how wars threaten to undo reform presidencies and undermine the best values of the country. If we as citizens challenge the "war" framing, if we demand that our representatives stop couching virtually all foreign policy discussion in terms of terrorism, we have a chance to build a new and more effective national security template.

*Part V*

# RECONSTRUCTING
# THE SOCIAL CONTRACT

# The Most Patriotic Act of All
## July 3, 2007

*The Nation* has always marched to a different drummer, opposing US involvement in the Spanish-American War and World War I and the Vietnam War. Former *Nation* editor Ernest Gruening of Alaska was one of only two senators to vote against the Gulf of Tonkin resolution that led to the Vietnam debacle.

As a result, we've been called—among other things—un-American and unpatriotic throughout the 142 years *The Nation* has been around and publishing. After all, going back to our founding by abolitionists, through the movement for labor rights in the '20s and '30s, and the movement for civil rights in the '60s, those who fought to achieve the American dream of equal rights for all were often scorned, ridiculed and deemed disloyal.

Our definition of patriotism is fighting to make sure your country lives up to its highest ideals—which is one reason the magazine published a special issue on patriotism for its 125th anniversary in July 1991. It came during the aftermath of the First Gulf War, when many of that war's opponents were being slapped with the "unpatriotic" label. The anniversary issue was a reflection of our love of country, and it gave voice to the rich and diverse panoply of ideas about what patriotism means, has meant and will mean.

In the lead editorial, the eminent political thinker John Schaar described the issue and its contributors:

> This patriotism is rooted in the love of one's own land and people, love too of the best ideals of one's own culture and tradition. . . . This patriotism too has deep roots and long continuity in our history. Its voice is often temporarily shouted

down . . . but it has never been stilled. . . . We should not be surprised if this voice is often heard lamenting or rebuking the country's failures to live up to its own best ideals, which have always been the ideals of the fullest possible freedom and the most nearly equal justice for all. . . . There are about as many kinds of patriots and patriotism [in this issue] as there are writers. And that is exactly as it should be. For the chief worry about the thing called patriotism is that one or another group is always trying to grab the term, put a parochial meaning on it and impose that meaning as the only legitimate one, silencing and excluding others, denying them a place at the table.

Here are some creative and keen insights on patriotism from other contributors in that issue:

William Sloane Coffin: "But if uncritical lovers of their country are the most dangerous of patriots, loveless critics are hardly the best. If you love the good you have to hate evil, else you're sentimental; but if you hate evil more than you love the good, you're a good hater. Surely the best patriots are those who carry on not a grudge fight but a lover's quarrel with their country. . . . Beyond saluting the flag, let us pledge allegiance 'to the earth, and to the flora, fauna and human life that it supports; one planet indivisible, with clean air, soil and water, liberty, justice and peace for all.'"

Molly Ivins: "I believe patriotism is best expressed in our works, not our parades. We are the heirs of the most magnificent political legacy any people has ever been given. 'We hold these truths to be self-evident. . . .' It is the constant struggle to protect and enlarge that legacy, to make sure that it applies to all citizens, that patriotism lies. . . . Vote, write, speak, work, march, sue, organize, fight, struggle—whatever it takes to secure the blessings of liberty to ourselves and our posterity. Ran across one of our good [legislators] at the end of the last session. . . . He said he felt like a country dog in the city. 'If I run they bite my ass, if I hold still, they fuck me.' Calling all country dogs: It's a helluva fight."

Jesse Jackson: "Those who have fought for the highest and best principles of our country, the true patriots, have been vilified and crucified. The true patriots invariably disturb the comfortable and comfort the disturbed, and are persecuted in their lifetimes even as their accomplishments are applauded after their deaths."

Mario Cuomo: "The term 'patriotism' seems to be raised most often in the context of military action and at times has been used as a test of support for our country's military activities. But I understand it to include a respect for contrasting viewpoints, an acceptance of dissent, a tolerance—and even a welcoming—of the clashing diversity of voices that is uniquely American. . . . A proper patriotism would recognize that there are no absolutes when it comes to solving our social and international problems, except the standard by which we must judge all goals—our willingness to help one another, and to help others."

Natalie Merchant: "Patriotism asks that we embrace a unified America, yet no simple vision of America can accommodate its diversity. . . . The heritage we retain and the characteristics of the one we adopt intermingle; we are defining and becoming American. . . . There is one tradition in America I am proud to inherit. It is our first freedom and the truest expression of our Americanism: the ability to dissent without fear. It is our right to utter the words, 'I disagree.' We must feel at liberty to speak those words to our neighbors, our clergy, our educators, our news media, our lawmakers and, above all, to the one among us we elect President."

Sixteen years later, on this Fourth of July, our nation is so very far from fulfilling the promise articulated by these great patriots. That's why *The Nation* continues to publish and struggle to make this a better place—to repair and renew that which has been shredded: our Bill of Rights, our Declaration of Independence, our Constitution . . . always informed by what the eminent historian Eric Foner wrote in the days after 9/11, "At times of crisis, the most patriotic act of all is the unyielding defense of civil liberties, the right to dissent and equality before the law for all Americans."

# In the Trenches and Fighting Slavery
## December 23, 2008

A delegation from the Coalition of Immokalee Workers recently took time during its "Northeast Tour for Fair Food" to visit *The Nation* offices in New York City. It was an honor to meet with them, to learn more about their work helping workers in the fields of Florida.

Last Friday—just days after CIW's visit—a Florida judge rendered his sentence on the state's most recent slavery case. CIW had helped the Department of Justice investigate what Chief Assistant US Attorney Doug Molloy described as one of Southwest Florida's "biggest, ugliest slavery cases ever." There was shockingly little coverage of this outrage—even in Florida. (The dedication of reporter Amy Bennett Williams of the *Fort Myers News-Press* is a notable exception.)

The Navarrete family had pleaded guilty to holding twelve men on their property from 2005 to 2007. They were beaten, chained and imprisoned in a truck, and forced to urinate and defecate in the corners. Two family members were sentenced to twelve years, and four were sentenced on lesser charges and will serve up to three years and ten months.

CIW worked with federal and local authorities during the prosecution and investigation as it has in seven Florida slavery cases over the past decade. Prior to escaping, the workers had listened to programming on labor rights on CIW's multilingual radio station—Radio Conciencia—which encouraged them that they would be able to find help if they escaped. Some of the workers who then did escape made their way to CIW for assistance.

While it's good to see some accountability for the practice of modern slavery, and the ongoing cooperation between CIW and prosecutors, the tolerance for slavery was all too evident in the wake of this trial. For one thing, Molloy told the *Fort Myers News-Press*, "We have a number of similar—and ongoing—investigations." He also said, "It doesn't help when people deny that [slavery] exists. That's like throwing gasoline on the fire."

But that's exactly what seems to be happening when it comes to the state government. Republican Governor Charlie Crist has remained silent on the issue of slavery and this sentencing—including not returning calls from *The Nation*—and his press secretary suggested that a reporter contact Terence McElroy, spokesman for the Florida Department of Agriculture and Consumer Services, which oversees the states' farms and labor contractors. McElroy seemed to dismiss the significance of the case and the existence of slavery, saying, "You're talking about maybe a case a year." After a public outcry—including responses from former president of Ireland Mary Robinson, Amnesty International USA, Florida ACLU and the Robert F. Kennedy Center for Justice and Human Rights—McElroy attempted to clarify his statement but only made matters worse, describing slavery as "quite a rarity when a case pops up."

First off, slavery doesn't exactly lend itself to being exposed. When chained, beaten, shot at, and pistol-whipped—as has happened to many of the 1,000 victims in seven known slavery cases prosecuted in Florida over the past eleven years—it's difficult for victims to bring those crimes to the light of day. "So this is really the tip of the iceberg," CIW staff member Greg Asbed told me.

Also, McElroy is doing exactly what Molloy warns of by minimizing the problem. As Asbed said, "You know, if this were happening in McElroy's department he wouldn't say, 'Well, it's only one case annually of workers being forced to work at gunpoint for no pay . . . or it's only one murder . . . it's a rarity.' And you wouldn't have Governor Crist refusing to comment. It would be a huge story and they would be forced to deal with it. The fact is that those who minimize this problem see two types of human beings—people who they think are like them, and then people like these workers who they view as lesser human beings."

CIW sent an open letter to Governor Crist—which I signed along with Eric Schlosser, Frances Moore Lappé and a slew of human rights and labor lawyers and organizations—calling on him to renounce the comments made by McElroy, meet with CIW and federal officials who prosecute slavery and demand that the Florida Tomato Growers Exchange (FTGE) allow the implementation of pay raises for workers that tomato buyers have already agreed to and are paying into escrow (see below) . . . which brings us to another recent victory for CIW.

Subway, the largest purchaser of tomatoes in the fast-food industry, agreed to a penny per pound pay raise for tomato workers. CIW had already struck similar deals with McDonald's, Taco Bell and Burger King after long, hard-fought campaigns. While a penny per pound doesn't sound like a helluva lot, it results in about a 75 percent wage increase for these workers— from $10,000 annually to $17,000—raising their living and working conditions and making them less vulnerable to those who would enslave them. Already, approximately $1 million is being held in escrow for the workers as they begin the second season with the deals in place.

As I have written previously, the only thing standing in the way of these workers and their million bucks-plus is the FTGE. The FTGE represents 90 percent of the state's growers and has threatened members who implement the penny per pound deals with fines of $100,000 for each worker benefiting from the pay raise. FTGE Executive Vice President Reggie Brown testified earlier this year at a Senate hearing chaired by Senator Bernie Sanders that these deals would result in buyers going to Mexico for their tomatoes. He's dropped that argument since it's the buyers themselves who are already agreeing to pay the workers the extra penny. But he continues to push a bogus legal argument—as the *Miami Herald* reported—that "they can't participate because of legal issues with a third party dictating the terms of its workers employment." (As Senator Sanders noted at the hearing on Capitol Hill, "I gather that McDonald's and [Taco Bell] have some money to hire some pretty good attorneys. You might want to reconsider the attorneys you are using and rethink this issue"; Sanders also presented Brown with a letter from twenty-six legal professors specializing in labor law, including anti-trust dimensions of labor standards, writing that "the ostensible legal concerns of the Growers Exchange are utterly without merit.") It's outrageous to now read Brown feigning sympathy for the workers as he did to the *Herald*: "I just wish someone would be a little creative and find a way to get the money to the workers. We would like to see the worker paid, but we can't do it," he said.

As long as the FTGE continues to be obstructive, you can bet Senator Sanders will be on their case. In addition to his own fact-finding mission in the fields of Immokalee, and the hearing on the Hill, Sanders recently single-handedly blocked tomato growers from getting $100 million or so that they wanted to tuck away into a continuing resolution before Congress recessed for the election.

"The Senator had a problem with a government bailout for folks who wink at slavery and can't figure out a way to let other people pay their pickers a penny a pound more for their back-breaking labor," Senator Sanders' press secretary, Michael Briggs, told me.

Sanders has spoken out not only on the pay issue, working, and living conditions, but also about closing a loophole which allows growers to use independent labor contractors and escape any liability for the enslavement of workers who work their fields. McElroy claimed that no "legitimate grower" is involved with slavery, but in fact the *Fort Myers News-Press* reported that the victims in the latest slavery case worked on "farms owned by some of the state's major tomato producers: Immokalee-based Six L's and Pacific Tomato Growers in Palmetto."

Senator Sanders indicated in an e-mail to me yesterday that he's determined to stay on top of these human rights issues: "It is beyond comprehension that in the year 2008 slavery still exists in America. I look forward to working with the new administration and Congress to finally end the scourge of modern slavery in the tomato fields of Florida. I will certainly advocate that every aspect of the businesses of those engaged in or indirectly benefiting from these scandalous activities be gone over with a fine-tooth comb by appropriate federal officials."

As for CIW, in addition to its continuing work to battle modern slavery, it's now turning its attention to signing penny-per-pound agreements with supermarket chains and food service companies. "With the agreement with Subway now done, the fast food industry in the main has now spoken, and they are clearly saying to the Florida tomato industry that it's time to turn the page. And so now we're turning to the supermarket and food service companies—like Kroger, Ahold, Safeway and Wal-Mart, and Sodexo and Aramark—and asking them, 'What are you waiting for? If you buy tomatoes and you're not looking to help improve conditions where they are picked, then you're part of the problem.'"

With a track record of successes, and Congressional allies like Senator Sanders fighting on tomato workers' behalf in Washington, CIW will continue to play an invaluable role in improving the deplorable working and living conditions that give rise to modern slavery.

# Van Jones and the Green Revolution
## *January 16, 2009*

Van Jones, president of Green for All and a *Nation* contributor, came to DC on Thursday to talk to the House Select Committee on Energy Independence and Global Warming about a Green (and fair) New Deal. Testifying along with Jones were Philadelphia Mayor Michael Nutter and Trenton Mayor Douglas Palmer.

Jones spoke of the "new tools . . . new training . . . and new technology" that would "begin to put some green rungs on America's ladder of opportunity." He took on the "falsehoods and confusion" spread by "vocal opponents and naysayers" who oppose investing in a new green economy and breaking our dependence on fossil fuels.

Jones set the record straight on the notion that green jobs are a fantasy—"Buck Rogers jobs, or science fiction jobs, or George Jetson jobs"—and pointed to the section of the Green Jobs Act (passed in 2007, but not funded—evidence he said of the need to "move aggressively from inspiration to implementation") that spells out the exact kinds of job-training programs and industries eligible for support, some of which are: energy efficient and retro-fitting construction jobs, renewable power industry, biofuels industry and manufacturing of sustainable products using environmentally sustainable materials. He addressed the myth that for every green job created a gray job will be lost—"the zero sum critique." He pointed to the report Green Recovery by the Center for American Progress and the Political Economy Research Institute (PERI), which suggests that investing in energy efficiency and renewable energy "creates four times as many jobs as the same money invested in the oil industry."

And then there is the myth that the green economy will hurt the poor by driving up energy prices. Jones spoke to the jobs created and costs saved through energy efficiency, and the economies of scale achieved through investment which will drive down the prices of technologies. "A well thought out shift to a clean energy economy offers more work, more wealth, and better health to disadvantaged communities than does any plausible business-as-usual scenario," he said.

In terms of making this shift to a new economy, both mayors talked about "ready-to-go projects," some of which—such as certain weatherization projects—would require as little as two weeks training. Mayor Nutter said Philadelphia hires high school graduates for its weatherization staff at a starting rate of $12 per hour plus benefits. The average salary of the staff is $35,000–$40,000 per year, with salaries and promotions tied to a standard industry certification process. Mayor Palmer spoke of 427 cities that have already identified 942 projects for potential Energy Efficiency and Conservation Block Grant funding, for an investment of $6.2 billion that would create 38,732 jobs. He said the US Conference of Mayors will be updating that survey this weekend based on responses from 779 cities. (It will be important to watch how recovery funds are allocated—through governors or mayors—and the tensions around that.)

After the hearing, Jones spoke to *The Nation* about this issue of who the green jobs will go to—if the market will ensure that lower-income communities get a stake in the new green economy as *New York Times* columnist Tom Friedman and others have suggested.

"Number one, there's nothing natural about a green economy, that will produce justice, equity, or opportunity. The gray economy didn't do it, and the green economy won't do it on its own," Jones said. "Solar panels do not have embedded within them equal opportunity. That's something that we have to as a community—working through government—insist upon. . . . If we fail to do that we have no excuse. Because this is not our great grandmother's economy, or our great grandfather's economy we're trying to fix and integrate. We're about to build an economy . . . and we need to do it in a way Dr. King would be proud of. If the market would take care of these things there would have been no civil rights movement. If the market would take care of these things we wouldn't have the suffragette movement. If the market would take care of these things we wouldn't have the labor movement. You need more than the market to have an inclusive, green economy. And, if it's not inclusive, it will not be sustainable politically or economically. . . . If you don't build in economic and political sustainability, i.e. spread the risk and the reward, share the burden and the benefits, then all you're doing is setting this up for a populist, anti-green backlash—an alliance between polluters and poor people. So when the poor say, 'You're just trying to impose green taxes on me,' the whole thing will become a house of cards. It's not just the moral thing to do—though that would be enough. It's also the only intelligent political and long-term sustainable economic thing to do.

So how are we doing in terms of the current recovery proposal?

"We have a way to go [for this]. . . . It's hard in the age of Obama when we're not supposed to talk about race anymore, to keep telling the truth," he said. "But here's the thing that I take my hope in: this is a new day. If you look at most of the people who are in the clean energy sector, politically they tend to lean more in a liberal direction. . . . There's an opening. This is not the kind of thing where in the past you had to just lay down in the streets, protest, picket, call folks racist and stuff like that. There is at least a hope and an opportunity that we can have a dialogue, and remind people that that Dr. King picture on their wall—should have something to do with who you're hiring."

There you have it—speaking truth to power about the green revolution.

With reporting from Capitol Hill by Greg Kaufmann, a freelance writer living in his disenfranchised hometown of Washington, DC.

# Senator Webb's Act of Strength
## February 12, 2009

Our criminal justice system is broken. The United States represents 5 percent of the world's population but accounts for nearly 25 percent of its prison population. We are incarcerating at a record rate, with one in 100 American adults now locked up—2.3 million people overall. As a *New York Times* editorial stated simply, "This country puts too many people behind bars for too long."

But people who have been fighting for reform for decades are seeing new openings for change. The fiscal crisis has state governors and legislators looking for more efficient and effective alternatives to spending $50 billion a year on incarceration. At the federal level, there is reason to believe that the Obama administration and our invigorated Department of Justice will take a hard look at the inequities of the criminal justice system and work for a smarter and more effective approach to public safety. Finally, there are Congressional leaders—none more prominent than Senator Jim Webb—who understand that the system isn't functioning as it should and there is an urgent need for reform.

Indeed, advocates for reform couldn't ask for a better standard-bearer than Senator Webb. As a decorated former Marine and Reagan administration official, no one is going to slap him with the politically dreaded "soft on crime" label that has stymied so many Democrats who have taken on this issue in the past. There is a "Nixon goes to China" quality to Webb's call for change—a law-and-order man who described his reform effort as "an act not of weakness but of strength."

As a journalist, Webb wrote on the need for reform after visiting Japanese prisons and seeing a fundamental fairness and effectiveness that he recognized as lacking in the US criminal justice system. As a Senator, he's held hearings which have highlighted racial disparities in sentencing, the staggering costs of incarceration and effective and cost-efficient alternatives, and a futile and racially biased drug policy.

Now Senator Webb has established a commission with a broad mandate to examine issues like drug treatment, effective parole policy, racial injustice, education for inmates, reentry programs— the myriad of issues intertwined in wasteful, ineffective criminal justice policies. Look for him to lay out that mandate with specificity in the coming weeks and make an aggressive push to bring this issue to the forefront in both Congress and the media, much as he was able to do with the GI Bill.

Webb sent me an e-mail saying, "I feel very strongly about the need to put the right people behind bars. But we're locking up the wrong people too often all across our country. Mental illness isn't a crime. Addiction isn't a crime. We need to make sharp distinctions between violent offenders and people who are incarcerated for nonviolent crimes, drug abuse and mental illness. We must raise public awareness about the need for criminal justice reform and find viable solutions. My staff and I are finalizing proposed legislation that could be introduced in the next two weeks to establish a national commission that will take a comprehensive look at where our criminal justice system is broken and how we can fix it."

While it's critical that Senator Webb is raising these issues at the national level where they have received so little attention, Marc Mauer, executive director of The Sentencing Project, points out that 90 percent of the US prison population is incarcerated in state prisons and only 10 percent in federal prisons. Mauer said there is a growing awareness at the state level that our drug and sentencing policies have "gotten out of hand" and that the fiscal crisis presents an opportunity to do something about it.

"The fiscal crisis gives governors and legislative leaders the opening to do what many of them have known should be done for some time, but [they] didn't have a political comfort level to do it," Mauer said. "Now they can talk about issues like excessive sentences for drug offenders, and too many people being sent back to prison for technical violations of parole."

One legislative reform effort is occurring in Senator Webb's own Virginia—a state that abolished parole in 1995 and is second only to Texas in number of executions. This session, a bill will be taken up that would allow prison officials to release nonviolent offenders ninety days before their sentences are up. This would primarily be achieved by offering drug treatment programs at the beginning of an individual's incarceration rather than only at the end. (Which begs the question—if we are truly serious about rehabilitation of inmates, why are we only offering addicts treatment for a disease at the end of a sentence?!) Upon successful completion of the treatment program, these individuals would be eligible for early release. The legislation also provides for more nonviolent offenders to be sent to community-based programs or be monitored electronically rather than incarcerated.

A similar program was undertaken in Washington State, and a four-year study of 2,600 inmates released early showed significant cost savings and no negative consequences in terms of recidivism. Mauer said the coalition rallying around the Virginia proposal is diverse and particularly encouraging in what has traditionally been a "tough on crime state."

Other states taking action on criminal justice reform include: Michigan is addressing re-entry issues and shifting resources to parole officers and community-based programs; Kansas cut parole revocations by 50 percent in a two-year period by increasing oversight of parole officers and using alternatives to incarceration such as increased drug testing and electronic monitoring; California issued a court ruling this week that the state must address its failure to provide adequate health and medical services in prisons by reducing the population by a third—nearly 55,000 persons—through "shortening sentences, diverting nonviolent felons to county programs, giving inmates good behavior credits toward early release, and reforming parole."

Now is also a hopeful, unique moment in New York State, where the top three political leaders all support real reform and there is a chance to repeal the wasteful, ineffective, and unjust Rockefeller-era drug laws—after thirty-five years! This week I moderated a panel—co-sponsored by *The Nation*, the Correctional Association of New York, and The New School's Center for New York City Public Affairs—of government officials and reform leaders working to downsize prisons, reform probation and parole, and provide effective community-based prisoner re-entry programs. The Correctional Association of New York is leading the "Drop the Rock" campaign that includes an Advocacy Day in Albany in March.

Greg Berman, director of the Center for Court Innovation—a non-profit think tank in New York—said, "The question is: can we come up with meaningful, cost-effective responses to nonviolent crime that do not rely on incarceration? Drug courts, mental health courts and community courts—the so-called 'problem-solving courts'—all show enormous potential. Most criminal cases are not complicated in a legal sense, but they are committed by people with complicated lives. Scratch the surface and you find addiction, mental illness, joblessness, etc. These problem-solving courts are linking offenders to drug treatment, counseling, job training in lieu of incarceration. But unlike some rehabilitation efforts in the past, they are requiring participants to return to court on a periodic basis to ensure accountability. There is a growing amount of evidence suggesting that this approach can change sentencing practice—dramatically reducing the use of jail, for example—while also reducing both substance abuse and recidivism."

Despite a fiscal crisis which has caused at least forty states to make or propose cuts in vital services like education and healthcare—and ample evidence of the effectiveness of alternatives to incarceration—the battle for reform on the state level is still a difficult one.

"It's far from a done deal that this will automatically lead to prison reductions," Mauer told me. "One option is to say let's reconsider sentencing policies, reduce the population, close prisons and save money. The other choice is to say let's cut out alternatives to incarceration, community-based drug treatment, and other programs, and you can see those cost savings very quickly. I think that would be a shortsighted way to go but it's going to be tempting for a lot of legislators to think about doing that. I think that's the battle that is going to be fought in different states."

That's why the effort of Senator Webb and his colleagues at the federal level is so critical. They can galvanize support for repealing unjust policies like those that treat a low-level user of crack the same as a major drug dealer, or five grams of crack the same as 500 grams of powder. They can ensure that we use needed federal dollars for public safety in smart and effective ways. For example, the Second Chance Act to provide job training, drug treatment, and other re-entry programs was passed with broad bipartisan support in 2008, but no funds have been appropriated. Finally, with Senator Webb's commission, we can begin the process of transforming our criminal justice system so that prisons are reserved for violent offenders and other vital resources are used to support alternatives like drug treatment, effective parole policies, education and re-entry programs.

# Gun (In)Sanity
*June 2, 2009*

Despite a Democratic Congress and president, it's been a bad time for common-sense measures to curb gun violence.

Earlier this year, a voting rights bill for the citizens of the District of Columbia was stalled by a Senate amendment that would strip the city of its right to regulate guns. And last month, the credit card reform bill was hijacked in the Senate and amended so that concealed guns are now permitted in our national parks.

Here's hoping the majority of Americans who support sane gun control begin to turn the tide.

Bills have now been introduced in both the House and Senate to at long last close the absurd and dangerous gun show loophole which permits the sale of guns without any criminal background check.

Background checks are required for any gun purchase at federally licensed dealers. The result? 1.6 million felons and other prohibited purchasers have been stopped from buying guns. But those same people can go to a gun show in more than thirty states and buy a weapon—no questions asked. It doesn't matter, for example, if Maryland requires a background check when the same individual can cross into Virginia and buy an assault weapon without a hitch. That's why four out of ten guns are sold by unlicensed sellers without background checks.

The Columbine killings were committed using two shotguns, an assault rifle, and a TEC-9 assault pistol—all four weapons were purchased from gun shows. The person who bought three of the weapons later said she wouldn't have done so if a background check had been required. Recently, the brother of a Virginia Tech victim was followed by ABC News into a gun show, where he was able to purchase ten guns in under an hour—again, no questions asked.

Senator Frank Lautenberg's Gun Show Background Check Act would require background checks at any event where fifty or more firearms are offered for sale. It wouldn't stop a grand-father from giving his prized handgun to his grandson, as the cynical NRA would have America believe. Nor does it take on the Second Amendment. Despite the NRA's whipping gun owners into a buying frenzy over the notion that President Obama and the Democrats are coming after their guns—a hysteria that has led to a surge of sales at gun shows nationwide—this legislation does no such thing.

It simply insists—in the interest of public safety—that you clear a criminal background check before buying a gun.

"There is no rational reason to oppose closing the loophole," Senator Lautenberg said when he introduced the bill with fourteen cosponsors last month just days after the tenth and second anniversaries of the shootings at Columbine and Virginia Tech, respectively. "The reason it's still not closed is simple: the continuing power of the special interest gun lobby in Washington." Which brings us to the politics.

The Senate bill is in the Judiciary Committee, chaired by Senator Patrick Leahy, who perhaps has made a decision in his career to never be outflanked by a pro-gun opponent—despite his generally progressive values. So, frankly, the prospect of the bill getting a hearing there is bleak. The House Judiciary Committee is chaired by Congressman John Conyers, so it might stand a better chance of consideration there. Conyers has supported similar legislation in the past and will in all likelihood support this bill too.

What seems more likely, however, is that the legislation might be offered as an amendment to a different bill—the same tactic the GOP has employed to try to get guns on Amtrak, in our national parks, and throughout our nation's capitol. In 1999, Senator Lautenberg successfully passed legislation identical to this bill as an amendment to a juvenile justice bill (it was later killed in a House-Senate conference).

The White House has clearly made a political decision at this time not to push for closing the gun show loophole or the assault weapons ban—both of which it clearly supports and would gladly sign into law.

So it's time for rational, concerned citizens to take matters into their own hands. Polls show over 85 percent of the public wants the gun show loophole closed now. That's a lot of voters. Speak out—let your senators and representatives know where you stand. Threaten to stop any contributions to representatives who won't listen. Hold house parties to get the word out. Ask MoveOn and bloggers to launch a day of blogging to ensure people know how wrongheaded this is.

Don't let the NRA's lies and fulmination hold sway over this life-saving measure.

# Rediscovering Secular America
## *July 3, 2009*

This Fourth of July, those who identify themselves as non-believers, or humanists, or atheists—or a whole host of other names which signify a nontheistic worldview—have much cause for celebration. After eight years in the Bush wilderness—and an even longer period of ostracism by the Washington political establishment—a rising demographic of like-minded Americans and a new president are guiding us back to our roots as a secular nation.

"We have generally been a pariah group in America," says Woody Kaplan, Advisory Board Chair of the Secular Coalition for America. "Pretty much unrecognized by the political establishment. Yet there's almost no religious group in America as large as us. . . . We were that third rail that politicians failed to touch."

Indeed, when the Obama administration invited the Coalition to the White House for a meeting in May, it marked a stark departure from recent history.

"Joe Lieberman famously talked about the constitution providing for freedom of religion but not freedom from religion—and questioned the possibility of non-believers to be ethical human beings," Kaplan says. "Suffice it to say we were never invited as an identity group into the Bush White House. But interestingly enough . . . we were only invited into the Clinton White House under the rubric of core civil rights or civil liberties interests, and not as an identity group of nontheists."

Things began to change shortly after then-Senator Obama announced his candidacy for president.

"He was on one of those talking head shows," Kaplan says. "And he was talking about Dr. King's arc of the moral universe bending toward justice. He followed that with 'no matter what your belief system'—and he made a list, a litany—'whether you're Christian or Jewish or Muslim or have no religion at all.'"

Within a week, the Coalition approached Obama. They let him know they had never been part of that "list" before—never had had a seat at the table—and they would appreciate it if he would continue to include them whenever appropriate.

As Herb Silverman, the Coalition's president says, "Lip service is better than no service at all."

"It's helpful in bringing us out of the closet," Kaplan says.

Obama agreed and remained true to his word. And then came the moment approximately 50 million Americans—who identify themselves with terms like agnostic, atheist, materialist, humanist, nontheist, skeptic, bright, freethinker, agnostic, naturalist, or non-believer—will never forget. In his inauguration speech, Obama said, "Our patchwork heritage is a strength, not a weakness. We are a nation of Christians and Muslims, Jews and Hindus, and non-believers." Two weeks later, he talked about "non-believers" and "humanists" at the National Prayer Breakfast.

Kaplan gives a sense of both the historical and personal significance of Obama's words.

"The shock came at the inaugural speech—arguably the biggest speech a President ever makes—and he listed us there" he says. "And he's continued to do that—he mentioned us twice at Notre Dame. And then he did it [this month] in Normandy.

I can't tell you what a pariah group feels about those statements. For the first time we have a seat at the table. We're not thought of, evidently, as automatically unethical."

After meetings with the Obama transition team in coalition with other groups interested in church-state issues, the Secular Coalition for America was invited to the White House for its own meeting with Associate Director of Public Engagement Paul Monteiro. Kaplan, Silverman, Legislative Director Sasha Bartolf and Associate Director Ron Millar all attended.

"It was the first time a nontheistic group met privately with the White House," Silverman says. "So in large part we just got to know each other . . . to have them learn more about our constituency, how many people we represent."

The Coalition described the "full spectrum of nontheists it represents" within its nine member organizations. (Now ten, with the recent addition of American Atheists.) Among those organizations are the Society for Humanistic Judaism, Military Association of Atheists and Freethinkers and the American Humanist Association. The Obama administration expressed particular interest in reaching out to the Secular Student Alliance. The Coalition also addressed some of the issues of greatest concern to nontheists, including coercive religious proselytizing in the military, faith-based initiatives and employment discrimination.

"We also pointed out that we are much more unified than we used to be, and so we hope our needs will be taken into account," Silverman says. "And that we watch legislation, we watch what politicians say. And we think that it could be beneficial to the Administration for them to take our point of view into account, just like they do for other interest groups. I think they did get the message in the White House. . . . We're hoping now to become players in all three branches of government."

As the Coalition continues to carry out its mission of increasing the visibility of—and respect for—nontheistic viewpoints, and protecting the secular character of our government, it seems to be moving forward with great confidence. This comes as no surprise, given the fact that there are now more nontheists in America than Methodists, Lutherans, Presbyterians, Episcopalians, Mormons and Jews combined, and the organization itself has made huge strides.

Kaplan describes the Coalition's transformation from its founding in 2002 with a sole employee and "half a year's money in the bank," to having a full-time lobby shop. That shop includes newly hired Executive Director Sean Faircloth.

Faircloth brings with him ten years of legislative service in Maine, including as the House Majority Whip. He also taught legal courses within the University of Maine system. In addition to advocating for the separation of church and state, he was active on children's issues and founded and managed the Maine Discovery Museum, the largest children's museum in New England outside of Boston.

Faircloth says that the Coalition is "very pleased" with the recognition it has received from President Obama. But he adds, "I think we still have some important issues to address."

Perhaps foremost among those issues is the Obama administration's continuation of President Bush's faith-based initiative. In a campaign speech in Zanesville, Ohio, then-candidate Obama declared, "First, if you get a federal grant, you can't use that grant money to proselytize to the people you help and you can't discriminate against them—or against the people you hire—on the basis of their religion."

But Bush's policy remains in place while the program is under review, so under current law, religious organizations can receive funding to provide social services, discriminate in hiring for those programs, and proselytize. The Coalition is advocating to end this clear violation of the separation of church and state.

"The President deserves great kudos for making his Zanesville statement. We would like him to [now] implement it," Faircloth says.

The Coalition is also pleased that the Obama administration has ended the global gag rule, allowed stem cell funding and largely ended funding for abstinence-only education programs. (There are some loopholes the Coalition is still working to address.) On the other hand, the nomination of Republican Congressman John McHugh as Secretary of the Army is a real concern. McHugh has one of the worst records of anyone in Congress on church-state issues. In fact, he voted against an amendment that would have required the Secretary of Defense to present Congress with a plan to prevent coercive and abusive proselytizing at the Air Force Academy.

Faircloth says the importance of the Coalition's advocacy extends beyond the specific issues themselves.

"I want to be involved in those lobbying issues," Faircloth says. "But also in terms of allowing people the comfort level and the opportunity to say, 'Yeah, that's what I happen to believe. I happen to agree with Mark Twain. I happen to agree with Clarence Darrow.' And allow those people to feel comfortable joining an organization, whether it's a humanistic association, chapter, whatever the case may be—saying, 'I care about these values because I view them as moral values, and they connect to these policies. . . .'"

Faircloth also sees the rise in the nontheistic demographic as an opportunity to reconnect with our nation's heritage.

"I see historical trends coming together that bring us back to our nation's heritage," he says. "Think if a presidential candidate were to say as Jefferson did, 'Religions are all alike, founded on fables and mythology.' . . . Abraham Lincoln said, 'The bible is not my book nor Christianity my profession.'" Faircloth adds, "these tremendously valuable leaders, I question whether were they to be a candidate for public office today . . . would they be [elected]? And that would be a great loss to the nation. . . . I think something has gone haywire when it seems that they were more free to speak their individual perspective—in some cases 200 years ago—than elected officials might feel today. We want to address that issue."

Indeed, when the Coalition ran a contest to find the highest ranking official who identifies as a nontheist (or one of the terms within the nontheist nomenclature), sixty members of the House and Senate were nominated. The Coalition spoke to each of them, and twenty-two admitted it but refused to go public. Only Congressman Pete Stark was willing to be identified.

Kaplan notes that the sample was skewed and that the number of nontheists in Congress is significantly larger. The legislators who were nominated were more likely to articulate their belief system than others, and some of the sixty nominees didn't admit to their belief system for fear it would be leaked.

"But we see at the very least there are 22 people who think that honestly admitting their worldview would cause them not to get reelected," Kaplan says. "That's an awful commentary on a pluralistic, liberal America."

Nevertheless, with its constituency growing—and growing more visible, assertive and respected—the Coalition is optimistic about the future.

"All that terminology has meaning, but to me what is of greater meaning is our shared set of values," Faircloth says. "We think that [our constituency] is a quiet, thoughtful, moral group that is significantly growing in our society and it's time to let that blossom. . . . The Founding Fathers specifically addressed the issues that the Secular Coalition for America raises, and they specifically took our side on these issues. So, we're very proud of the civil rights movement we're involved with and we feel its heritage goes back to the founding of this nation."

# Wealth for the Common Good
## April 6, 2010

The challenge for progressives and Democrats in these turbulent times is how to consistently and clearly explain the real causes of our current economic condition.

One problem is that we live in a center-left country with a center-right media that consistently misinforms people about the perils of debts, deficits and tax increases, and purveys misinformation about a good but modest health care bill that right-wing talk radio, tea partiers and GOPsters would have Americans believe is a "socialist" power grab.

It's against that political backdrop that a just-released report from Wealth for the Common Good—a network of business leaders, high-income households and partners working together to promote shared prosperity and fair taxation—is a welcome and common sense antidote. History is always important, especially in the "US of Amnesia"—as writer Gore Vidal once put it—and this tight, fact-filled report gives us the history we need to understand how enormous tax cuts over the last fifty years have favored the wealthiest Americans at the expense of a strong and secure middle class. Its must-read facts and common sense ideas deserve and demand as much media attention as the Tea Partiers' kvetching.

What's crystal clear in this well-documented report—whose title might have been "The Real Story Behind Today's Unfair Economy"—is that the middle class has largely been shafted by both Republicans and Democrats, whose campaign coffers are equally greased by wealthy donors. And the shift in the tax burden has fueled a rising inequality and concentration of wealth that weakens our democracy—as *The Nation* argued in its June 30, 2008, special issue, "The New Inequality."

That shift is clear just looking at the tax rates paid by the wealthiest Americans. From 1950 to 1963—even under that radical Republican President Dwight Eisenhower—the federal tax rate on personal income over $400,000 never dropped below 91 percent. Between 1936 and 1980, it never dropped below 70 percent. But today, the top personal income tax rate after the 2001 Bush tax cut is just 35 percent, and you can count on one hell of a fight with ConservaDems and the GOP just to let that expire at the end of this year so the rate will return to the modest 39.6 percent level of the Clinton years. The tax rate on capital gains—which most benefits those in the highest income brackets—dropped to 15 percent in 2003, down from as high as 39.9 percent in 1977.

With all the fury about the debt and deficits, it's worth reminding ourselves that if we close a few loopholes for the very rich, then presto, the current deficit would be significantly smaller. The Bush tax cuts for the wealthy between 2001 to 2008 cost the US Treasury $700 billion, with all of these billions added directly to the national debt. Retaining these tax cuts will cost $826 billion over the next decade. But while Bush exacerbated the tax shift, it was largely a done deal before he took office. Check out these stunning stats:

Between 1960 to 2004, the top 0.1 percent of US taxpayers have seen the share of their income paid in total federal taxes drop from 60 to 33.6 percent. The top 400 income-earners have seen the share of their income they pay in federal income tax alone plummet from 51.2 percent in 1955 to 16.6 percent in 2007.

In 2007, if the top 0.1 percent of taxpayers had paid total federal taxes at the same rate as they paid in 1960, the federal treasury would have collected an additional $281.2 billion. If the top 400 had paid the same rate as it did in 1955, it would have meant an additional $47.7 billion in revenue. (The incomes of the top 400 have multiplied by twenty-seven times—adjusted for inflation—since 1955, yet back then they paid over three times more of their incomes in federal income tax.)

Meanwhile, the middle class has seen their taxes increase. The report lays out that "Despite all the 'tax cut' political rhetoric and action of recent years, average Americans have seen no tax savings at the federal level."

Taxpayers in the middle—who made more than the bottom 40 percent but less than the top 40 percent—saw an increase in their taxes, paying 15.9 percent of their incomes in total federal taxes in 1960 and 16.1 percent in 2004. Adding insult to injury, "Our children and grandchildren . . . will be asked to pay back, with interest, the trillions our federal government has been borrowing to offset our loss of tax revenue from wealthy taxpayers."

The result of this imbalanced, unjust and out-of-whack tax shift?

A public investment deficit—seen in our crumbling infrastructure, lack of investment in a robust green economy and rising tuition costs at public universities, to name just a few areas—and a concentration of wealth and power that bought a deregulated casino economy and subsequent economic collapse that the rest of us are paying for.

Yet despite this historic shift in the tax burden, the debate we are having on tax reform is inadequate to say the least.

What's really shocking is we can't even manage Tax Reform 101—to tax the hedge fund managers like we do normal working people. They pay a stunning 15 percent on their billions— a lower rate than teachers, cops, even their own assistants! And a 2008 GAO report found that two-thirds of US corporations paid zero federal income taxes from 1998 to 2005. Twenty-five percent of the largest US corporations had $1.1 trillion in gross sales in 2005 but paid no federal income taxes. Where is the debate on corporate tax rates and loopholes? If corporations are now people, can't they start paying taxes like people too?

(Not if their new Supreme Court–sponsored campaign ads can help it.)

Here are some examples of what a smart tax reform program would look like as prescribed by the Wealth for the Common Good report: end the income tax cuts for households earning more than $250,000 and raise capital gains and dividend rate from 15 to 20 percent ($45 billion increase in revenues); a progressive estate tax on estates worth over $2 million or $4 million for a couple—taxing no more than one in every 200 estates—generating $40 billion immediately and over $100 billion a decade from now; end overseas tax havens used by the likes of Citigroup and Best Buy ($100 billion per year); a modest financial transaction tax ($100 billion per year); a new 50 percent tax bracket for income over $2 million ($60 billion per year).

This is the kind of common-sense, creative thinking that needs to be taken up by elected officials who understand that another generation of this tax madness will lead to ever higher concentrations of wealth, gut an already weakened middle class and unravel the American Dream.

# Healthcare, History and Kennedy
*August 26, 2009*

I was writing this column when I heard of Senator Kennedy's death.

I am heartbroken.

For more than five decades, my father, William vanden Heuvel, was a close friend and political ally of Kennedy's. When I called him this morning, he had been weeping. He'd just seen the footage on CNN of Kennedy's extraordinarily emotional visit to Ireland one year after his brother John's assassination. My father traveled with Kennedy on that trip, as he would on many others in the years to follow. He also shared memories of sailing trips on the coast of Maine, and the good times, and tough times, and the campaigns waged and won.

My father told me he was supposed to be on the small plane that crashed and nearly killed Kennedy in 1964, but what with Bobby running for the New York Senate that year, my father went to campaign for Teddy's older brother. He spent the next year shuttling to the Massachusetts hospital to visit Teddy, who was strapped down on a gurney to avoid paralysis.

My father wrote many speeches for Kennedy, and informed many others, including the eloquent and impassioned statements Kennedy made opposing the war in Iraq. Vietnam was never far from Kennedy's mind or the memories of those—like my father—who had served in President Kennedy's administration and watched Lyndon Johnson's Great Society destroyed.

When Kennedy was deciding whether to endorse Senator Barack Obama for president, he took counsel with friends and advisers, including my father.

Senator Kennedy was a fighting liberal, a passionate and exuberant lion to the very end—often among timid cubs. He will be remembered as the best and most effective Senator of the last century. Kennedy helped shape every major piece of legislation, with his powerful commitment to civil rights, labor rights, and women's rights—always fighting for equality, always standing with the underdog, the poor, the most vulnerable, who he believed deserved lives of dignity.

Kennedy's final fight was for quality, affordable healthcare for all. As recently as July, he called that fight "the cause of my life." In the coming months, President Obama and a Democratic Congress will determine whether that cause is realized.

Whatever one thinks of President Obama's presidency so far, he is one of the few reform presidents in modern history—a potential Senator Kennedy recognized when he endorsed his candidacy. A reform president takes on the status quo in order to improve the lives of the majority and ensure that America lives up to its potential and promise. Franklin Roosevelt was the very model of a reform president. Lyndon Johnson, in a sense, was pushed to become a reformer by the turbulence of the times.

When a reform president takes on the status quo, he confronts a ferocious, well-organized, reactionary opposition. What we're seeing today—with right-wing groups comparing Obama to Hitler and healthcare reform to socialism—Roosevelt faced with the American Liberty League calling him a socialist or a fascist (ironic, since it was Roosevelt who led the United States into war against fascism). Like Obama, Roosevelt also confronted well-funded business lobbies. And in the Catholic demagogue Father Coughlin, Roosevelt had his Rush Limbaugh or Glenn Beck in a Roman collar.

As Congressman Keith Ellison—vice chair of the Progressive Caucus—notes in a recent post, "The special interests and protectors of the status quo acted worse when America was on the brink of passing Civil Rights and Voting Rights legislation. They spread lies and fear when America was contemplating women's suffrage too."

The rabid protesters opposing Obama are representatives of a long national tradition: an irrational fear of a strong central government. Obama has found it more difficult to turn away from the contemporary edition of the fanatical right than his reform predecessors, partly because conservative ideology has been in the saddle for three decades and the recession began too late in the Bush administration to sufficiently discredit its free-market fundamentalism and those who still speak on its behalf.

Obama himself acknowledged parallels between now and previous battles for reform when speaking to a coalition of religious leaders on August 20. He said, "These struggles always boil down to a contest between hope and fear. That was true in the debate over Social Security, when FDR was accused of being a socialist. That was true when LBJ tried to pass Medicare. And it's true in this debate today."

Indeed, those words might be a valuable frame for a presidential speech after Labor Day, as Obama returns to presenting and—one hopes—truly fighting for his healthcare agenda. Obama would be wise to place his agenda in the tradition of reform in US history—especially the two most popular programs in modern history, Social Security and Medicare, which were staunchly opposed by the GOP.

The president, his Congressional allies and millions of Americans should also be inspired to honor and fight for the cause of Senator Kennedy's life. Surely the president recognizes that the Senate's fighting liberal would not place the fate of affordable health insurance back in the hands of the private sector without a viable public alternative that isn't driven by profit or greed.

This country now has the best opportunity since 1912—when Theodore Roosevelt included universal healthcare in his progressive party platform—to pass real healthcare reform and fulfill a moral imperative. A bill with a strong public option would be a victory not only for progressives but for all those who seek a healthier, more humane country where healthcare is a right, not a commodity.

One has to question the value of bipartisanship at this moment. This is not a Republican Party out to criticize or modify healthcare reform. This is a party out to cripple or kill reform, and with it the future of Obama's presidency. It's high time to part ways with the Party of No—which once opposed Medicare and Social Security and is now committed to fear-mongering about government takeovers and socialism coming to America.

Democrats must pass a strong reform bill by any means necessary (and Congressman Ellison makes a strong case here for using reconciliation to avoid a GOP filibuster). If the Republicans defeat it, let them explain themselves in the 2010 midterm elections to voters who remain at the mercy of insurance companies. If, on the other hand, Dems choose to enact a bipartisan sham reform bill instead of seizing this moment when they are in charge, they will shoulder the blame and see ugly results come 2010.

Every president, no matter how popular at the outset, has only so much political capital and must use it wisely and strategically. And if one looks at American political history—as Mike Lux explains in his valuable book *The Progressive Revolution: How the Best in America Came to Be*—every so often a window to change opens and the combination of crisis, leadership, and political movement makes big, positive reforms possible.

"That window is open right now," Lux writes, "and President Obama, to his credit, is trying to keep it open" to make changes that will make our nation immeasurably stronger. But if he gives up this fight and caves to lobbyists—or either the Congressional Democrats or the grassroots fails to deliver the support he needs—then that window will slam shut, and the next opportunity for reform might not come for another generation.

That would be a real tragedy—and also no way to honor the Lion of the Senate. Today, President Obama said, "The Kennedy name is synonymous with the Democratic Party." Now, for this fight, the Democratic Party must become synonymous with Kennedy.

# Metropolis Now
## *September 17, 2009*

America is a metro nation. About 80 percent of the US population now lives in metropolitan areas, which together cover about 20 percent of the country's land and create roughly 90 percent of GDP. The top 100 metros alone, on 12 percent of American land, account for 65 percent of the population, 75 percent of GDP, and comparable or greater shares of critical infrastructure, education and research institutions.

While cities have long been to a large extent invisible in American public life, the country now has a president who actually likes them and understands their centrality. He recognizes that almost all the big trends in US demographics (smaller households, aging), culture (more tolerant, less racist), economics (the need for innovation, less waste, greater self-sufficiency) and the environment (dying) either predict or recommend the growth of cities. And he thinks their present dysfunction—the source of most of the country's main domestic problems, such as inequality, unsustainability and declining competitiveness—can be cured.

During his campaign for president, Barack Obama promised to champion cities and, most urgently, to change the way that federal programs tackled their multiple but often interrelated problems. For years, initiatives touching many of the same people and places but originating from different departments—housing and urban development, energy, education, transport and environment—had too little shared purpose and coordination to get much done, and enough red tape to strangle innovation. They were victims of a bureaucracy driven by process rather than outcome.

Since taking office, Obama has made good on his pledge to address this. After a series of strong appointments, and with firm instruction, the various government agencies are collaborating as never before. Having formalized working agreements and joint staff teams, they are synchronizing complementary interventions (on matters of housing and transport, for example, or—to be more specific—regenerating homes and installing broadband access at the same time), and they are asking cities to match that coordination with their own.

This is still small-scale and, admittedly, good government on a pretty basic level—as is Obama's recent request that the Office of Management and Budget should carry out a formal review of the effectiveness of all urban programs (the first time this has happened in thirty years) and make recommendations on strategy. Yet in this particular area of US government, it is a spectacular breakthrough to common sense.

It has limits, however. One is that nobody in the administration has defined what success in a city means. Should it be measured by improvements in sustainability, such as reductions in carbon-dioxide emissions; or productivity, such as asset appreciation; or equity, such as the declining significance of family background, race or sex for educational attainment, income, wealth or health? Or some combination of all three?

The more glaring and urgent problem, however, is the stiff resistance that Obama has run into over his substantive domestic investment agenda. The original strategy was "do everything at once"—to spend his political capital while it was at its height in order to push through reforms in health, climate, transport and education, after which the direction on taxes would be clear. But this was immediately slowed down by two things.

The first was the continued mop-up of the financial disaster and Obama's deference to his Clinton redux treasury team in handling it. This led to a series of poorly defended and predictably unpopular decisions—to bail out favored banks and insurance companies but not others, to sell off good assets to hedge funds while keeping the worst for taxpayers, to approve colossal bonuses for those who nearly wrecked the economy, to decline providing direct relief to distressed homeowners—and has put unstated limits on the terms of future domestic spending.

The second spanner in the works was the Republican Party's decision to go into near-total opposition, attacking anything that Obama proposed. This was evident from his first piece of legislation, the American Recovery and Reinvestment Act. Widely proclaimed as gargantuan but in truth almost certainly too small, this was a straightforward effort to help an economy in freefall through tax cuts and public spending.

Virtually all economists (including former advisers to the Republican presidential candidate John McCain) agree that the act has done the trick, thus far saving several million jobs and about 2 percent of GDP growth in a huge contraction. When it came up for approval in February, however, it was denounced by Republicans as wildly irresponsible. Larded with tax cuts to lure their support, the act got only three votes from Republican senators.

Things have only gone downhill since. The Republican Party's opposition to Obama now amounts to an all-out war, in which it is prepared to enlist and support any willing lunatics and liars, such as a "birther" movement questioning Obama's citizenship, and others screaming about his plans for concentration camps and mass euthanasia of the elderly. These antics are aired 24/7 on Rupert Murdoch's Fox network, where right-wing populists such as Glenn Beck feed their audiences a steady diet of rage and character assassination. Fox/Beck's latest campaign, against the White House's "green jobs" adviser Van Jones, ended with Jones' resignation early this month.

So it is an uncertain time for cities. They won't go down if Obama goes down. The 2010 budget, all but approved, maintains support for the government agencies of greatest concern to them. But a defeat on healthcare and climate, and a failure to reform transport, will make things a good deal tougher for cities. And at the moment, nobody is certain that anything—not healthcare, not climate, not transport—is on track to success.

There is a deeper problem too. Despite the new president's concern for and engagement with America's cities, there is a stubborn legacy of hostility and indifference toward them. There is, for a start, racism. Postwar federal housing policy encouraged a distinctly white suburbanization. From the urban freeways of the 1950s, to Lyndon B. Johnson's Great Society reforms, to latter-day New Orleans or Oakland, urban renewal has meant black removal. Then there is the indifference of the mainstream left. Labor unions in effect dismantled their central labor councils and, outside the building trades, turned all their attention to industry or employer bargaining, without regard for spatial context. There is the immense power of the auto-industrial complex, the single biggest source of employment throughout the postwar period, and its unremitting hostility to any place or alternative in its way. There is political and cultural conservatism. The electorate in US cities, as in cities throughout the world, is more progressive than elsewhere. It believes in public goods, but it also admits vice, outlandish behavior and other interruptions to middle-class order. As Jane Jacobs observed, cities create the middle class; they don't attract it.

A further obstacle is the fierce competition fostered among local governments, which severely hinders them from working together constructively on metropolitan or regional schemes. Public spending in the United States, as a percentage of GDP, is about ten points lower than the OECD average, and about fifteen points below the EU one—that's roughly $2 trillion not spent in the United States on the social wage and public goods. As a result, a citizen in need of assistance in the United States is not first and foremost a concern for local government, but a cost. The federal government compounds this public poverty by encouraging states and local governments to compete for business capital through tax, regulation and subsidies. Last year alone, states and local governments handed out more than $70 billion in relocation subsidies to lure firms (or keep them from moving) across jurisdictions, often only a few miles apart. Only in a handful of cases—San Francisco, Portland, the Port Authority of New York and New Jersey—has regional government emerged from and survived the stranglehold of such divisively competitive local politics.

Despite all these difficulties, however, there is hope for US urban policy, and for the president most likely to reform it. First, there is widespread recognition among the elite that the irrationality of the current system is creating costs that will eventually be unbearable to social peace, competitiveness or the environment. Second, the demographic and cultural trends are on the side of cities, and the property market tells us that ordinary people—not just Generation Y computer graphic artists and designers—prefer to live in them. At some point, it just gets hard to move the mountain of consumers who would like something other than empty suburbs and rural McMansions.

But the greatest cause for hope is the development of far more positive and successful metro politics. This can be seen in the huge success of referendums on funding more city transport; the speed at which organized labor and communities of color (for so long divided in US cities) are joining together in vast regeneration projects; the emergence of pro-planning/pro-tax business groups; and the astonishing range of innovation and experiment by communities and local political leaders on issues encompassing schools, public safety, healthcare delivery, new property forms and types of financing.

This new politics breaks with many of the divisions that largely defined city politics and urban decline during the second half of the 20th century: the endless wars between business, labor, environmentalists and communities of color. Now, by virtue of learning and necessity, these groups recognize that they cannot succeed with their old strategies. At least some parts of business recognize they cannot forever divest from a society on which they depend; labor knows that it must be productive as well as redistributive; environmentalists understand that they need economic power and an economic argument for saving the planet, not just a moral one; communities of color know that protest has diminishing returns when the society in which they've only sought respect might finally be prepared to give it. And although these four groups are by no means at complete peace with one another, they do have a shared political project, centered in the economy.

That project is to develop cities as "high road" places. That means valuing economic self-sufficiency; competing on distinctiveness and performance, not commodity price; recognizing the productive use of democracy and the value of place; and developing by using democracy to organize places to better add value, reduce waste and capture and share the benefit of doing both. This project is Obama's own (if not that of all of his advisers)—to develop our metro nation in ways that make it more self-sufficient, productive, sustainable and inclusive—and those now pursuing it across the country provide his real base. If they get a bit more mobilized, we think we're going to be all right.

Written by Joel Rogers and Katrina vanden Heuvel. Joel Rogers, a *Nation* contributing editor, teaches at the University of Wisconsin, where he directs the Center on Wisconsin Strategy.

# Modern Slavery
## March 28, 2010

Updated April 1, 2010.

CIW today announced another major victory—its eighth fair food agreement, this one with food-service giant Aramark. Like previous agreements struck by CIW, this one establishes a supplier code of conduct developed by the farmworkers themselves. Aramark also agrees to pay an extra 1.5-cent premium for every pound of tomatoes picked, with the premium distributed directly to the harvesters. That doesn't sound like much, but it makes a huge difference in the workers' wages.

Equally important, this agreement helps build momentum in the fight to ensure that buyers (and consumers) hold their food suppliers accountable for their labor practices.

On its website, the CIW wrote:

> This newest agreement is significant on several levels. It consolidates the historic advances established in the Compass agreement. It lays the groundwork for the further expansion of those advances in the foodservice industry. And it sends a powerful message to the supermarket industry—and to Publix in particular—on the eve of the Campaign for Fair Food's biggest action of the year. With this agreement, the four largest companies in fast-food, and now the two largest companies in foodservice, are standing with the CIW. It is time, finally, for the supermarket industry to do its part to clean up the farm labor poverty and human rights abuses from which it has profited so handsomely for so many years.

»»»

In textbooks across the country, students are still taught that slavery in the United States ended with the adoption of the Thirteenth Amendment in 1865.

But the Coalition of Immokalee Workers (CIW) knows better, and its Modern-Day Slavery Museum is traveling throughout Florida to drive that point home—that slavery persists in the agriculture fields of the state right up through this very day.

The *Village Voice* recently described the significance of the museum this way: "Though it's unlikely to compete for crowds with Disneyworld, the Modern-Day Slavery Museum may be Florida's most important new attraction."

The bulk of the museum is housed inside of a twenty-four-foot box truck—a replica of the one used by the Navarrete family in Immokalee to hold twelve farmworkers captive from 2005 to 2007. The workers were beaten, chained and imprisoned inside of the truck, and forced to urinate and defecate in the corners. US Attorney Doug Molloy called the operation "slavery, plain and simple."

Inside of the truck, visitors learn about seven cases of farm labor servitude in Florida successfully prosecuted by the US Department of Justice over the past fifteen years. Workers were held against their will through threats, drugs, beatings, shootings and pistol-whippings. These cases meet the high standard of proof and definition of slavery under federal laws and resulted in the liberation of over 1,000 farmworkers—CIW worked with federal and local authorities during the investigation and prosecution of six of the seven cases.

Barry Eastabrook described his experience in the truck for *The Atlantic*: "Inside, the vehicle was stacked high with cardboard tomato cartons. The floor was chipped and scuffed. There was a plywood sorting table—which doubled as a 'bed' for the workers. But what stays with me was the heat. Outside, the day was chilly and overcast, but inside the truck, even with the cargo door all the way open, the temperature became borderline unbearable. The stale air was uncomfortable to breathe. Sweat soaked the back of my shirt. And I was in there for less than five minutes, not two and a half years."

But it's not just the contemporary slavery examples one finds inside the box truck that educates the visitors. The museum is designed to look at the history of slavery and forced labor—the evolution of it—and the fact that there has never been a period in Florida agriculture when there wasn't some form of forced labor. The exhibit was vetted by historians, slavery experts, economists and other academics, including *Nation* editorial board member Eric Foner, who said, "A century and a half after the Civil War, forms of slavery continue to exist in the world, including in the United States. This Mobile Museum brings to light this modern tragedy and should inspire us to take action against it."

Before entering the truck, the museum-goer is given a booklet and sees two large exhibits which provide historical context—examining slavery from Spanish settlement through Edward R. Murrow's acclaimed CBS documentary *Harvest of Shame* in 1960. Forms of slavery include chattel slavery, the convict-lease system through 1923 and debt peonage.

Another display plays a 1993 *60 Minutes* piece on Wardell Williams, a former crew leader in Florida who kept workers in debt while also supplying some with drugs and alcohol.

Inside of the truck, the seven cases are described powerfully through the use of primary sources—court documents, indictments, criminal complaints, testimony. Miguel Flores and Sebastian Gomez held 400 workers under the watch of armed guards and assaulted—even shot—those who tried to escape. Abel Cuello held more than thirty tomato workers in two trailers in the isolated swampland west of Immokalee. Once out of prison, Cuello was able to resume supplying labor to Ag-Mart Farms in Florida and North Carolina. Michael Lee recruited homeless US citizens to harvest oranges, creating debt through loans for rent, food, cigarettes and cocaine. Ramiro and Juan Ramos had a workforce of over 700 farmworkers and threatened with death those who tried to leave. They also pistol-whipped and assaulted at gunpoint van service drivers who gave rides to farmworkers leaving the area. Ronald Evans also recruited homeless citizens throughout the southeast with promises of good jobs and housing, then kept them in a labor camp surrounded by a chain-link fence topped with barbed wire. He also made sure they were perpetually indebted to him, deducting money from their pay for food, rent, crack cocaine and alcohol.

When the visitor steps out of the truck, he sees a panel which gets to the heart of CIW's analysis around modern slavery—that it's not something that takes place in a vacuum, but it's tied to the broader conditions in the agriculture industry—sub-poverty wages and substandard working conditions; from the earliest days of slavery through today, farmworkers in Florida are among the least paid and least protected workers in the nation.

On the panel are two artifacts to drive home that message: the bloody shirt of a 17-year-old boy who was beaten in 1996 for stopping to take a drink of water while working in Immokalee. In response, there was a nighttime march by 400 workers to the crew leader's house. This was a significant moment in CIW's history because that kind of violence was routine and never received a widespread organized response.

There is also testimony blown up from a 1970 Senate hearing convened by Minnesota Senator Walter Mondale illustrating that these same issues were being discussed forty years ago. Next to it is a video by Iowa public TV of a similar hearing held just two years ago by Senators Bernie Sanders, Edward Kennedy and Richard Durbin.

At the foot of the panel is a thirty-two-pound bucket of tomatoes. Harvesters fill it up 100 to 150 times per day, on average. For that bucket, the worker receives forty-five cents—a nickel more than the wage earned in 1980 (and that nickel is the result of general strikes organized by CIW in the mid-and late '90s). The museum-goer can pick it up, getting a sense of how hard the work is for stagnant wages.

All of these exhibits allow CIW to make the arguments that they have been pushing for over fifteen years very tangible. It's one thing to tell people about the conditions that persist in the fields. It's an entirely different thing to show it inside of a rolling replica of the most recently discovered slavery truck where people were held captive.

"The museum has made it possible to lay out our argument about slavery from A to Z, in a sort of irrefutable package of completely documented and totally unimpeachable facts," says CIW staff member Greg Asbed. "And when you can see the whole history and evolution of 400 years of forced labor in Florida's fields assembled in one place, then all the false assumptions about what drives modern-day slavery just fall away. It's not workers' immigration status today, or a few rogue bosses, but the fact that farmworkers have always been Florida's poorest, most powerless workers. Poverty and powerlessness is the one constant that runs like a thread through all the history. In short, you see, it's not about who's on the job today. It's about the job itself."

But the last thing CIW wants is for people to simply leave, shaking their heads, saying, "Isn't that terrible. I can't believe slavery exists." The goal isn't just to educate people about what's going on, but also to show them what they can do about it.

The final panel outside of the truck lets people know there is a solution underway with the Campaign for Fair Food. Since 2001, farmworkers have been focusing on the retail level of the food industry—forcing companies to take responsibility for the conditions of their supply chain in order to alleviate the poverty and powerlessness at the root of the industry.

"The key to making change happen—the absolute fundamental key to making change happen—is for the major buyers to move their purchases from the farms where bad stuff is happening, to the farms where good stuff is happening," says Asbed. "Of course, there are no farms that you can say are good across the board yet, that could be certified as 'fair food.' The industry has a ways to go before it gets there. But you can encourage better behavior by moving your purchases to follow the best behavior, and you can eliminate the worst abuses by making sure growers will lose business, and maybe even lose the ability to do business, if abuses like slavery happen in their fields."

CIW has signed code of conduct agreements and penny-per-pound pay raises with the four largest fast food companies in the world; the largest food service company in the world, Compass Group; and the largest organic grocer, Whole Foods. In fact, the latest slavery case—in which the farms that used slave labor were identified—led to growers losing business for the first time thanks to the code of conduct agreements.

CIW has now turned its attention to supermarkets, asking them to end their tradition of buying tomatoes with no questions asked.

In the southeast, that means Publix. When asked whether the supermarket continues to purchase from farms that were recently found to use slave labor, a Publix spokesperson "said the chain does purchase tomatoes from the two farms but pays a fair market price." That's the kind of mentality CIW is up against in trying to get them to change their ways and pay attention to working conditions and wages. In the northeast, the focus is on Ahold, a Dutch company which owns Giant Food and Stop and Shop. Ahold continues to purchase tomatoes from

Six L's, one of the growers that used enslaved workers to pick tomatoes in the Navarrete case. Ahold will take up this issue on April 13 at its shareholder meeting.

The final panel of the museum allows people opportunities for action. They can get on the CIW e-mail list, take a postcard to send to Publix or get information on the upcoming farm-worker Freedom March on April 16–18—twenty-five miles from Tampa to Publix Corporate Headquarters in Lakeland. Visitors can also sign a guest book to share some reflections. Some of those comments over the last three weeks of exhibits include: "Such a national shame—it must stay on the front burner until it is no longer." "I will be making choices that will help stop this horrible situation." "Seeing injustice should move us to action!"

Indeed, people across the state have been moved to action. At churches, universities, high schools and other venues, the responses from what one CIW member described as "scores and scores of focus groups" have been amazing.

"They range from I had no idea this is going on, to what can I do to help, to wanting to get involved," said CIW staff member Leonel Perez. "And part of it's the presentation—once you're inside the truck, and the use of primary sources—I think there's a very visceral component. It really has been a pretty easy pivot to 'and here's what you can do about it'."

This week in St. Augustine, two older African American workers who used to work for Ron Evans (US v. Evans, 2007) visited the museum. They described their experience in servitude and vouched for the museum's accuracy in portraying the Evans' operations. One of the men had escaped by slipping away in the middle of the night after working for Evans for eleven years. They talked about the beatings they received if they tried to leave the labor camp and how Evans used to gather up the workers' shoes at the end of each workday so that even if they escaped, they wouldn't be able to get far running barefoot through the fields and forest.

The Modern-Day Slavery Museum stops us from running in a very different way. It forces us to confront the horrible truth that slavery still exists in America, and that too many consumers and leaders in the food industry simply turn a blind eye.

When the museum has finished traveling Florida, I hope legislators will take an interest in bringing it to the National Mall. It's time to make the fight against modern slavery part of our national consciousness.

---

# Michelle Obama's Food Fight Revisited
## *April 6, 2010*

Michelle Obama is not at war with Twinkies. But she does want food manufacturers to "rethink the products that you're offering, the information that you provide about these products and how you market those products to our children." For this, she has been accused of "federalizing fat" and labeled "the first nanny." But it's not the federal government that's playing the role of nanny here.

After all, food and beverage marketers spend about $2 billion a year to reach children, and most of those ads hawk the least healthy foods. So when a child begs for fruit-free Froot Loops, he's simply doing what he's been commanded to do, clean-your-room style, by the marketing nanny.

This advertising juggernaut is proving to be a governess with influence not seen since Maria convinced the Von Trapp kids that Anschluss was no fun. A recent study published in the *American Journal of Public Health* demonstrates that as a sedentary activity, television-watching alone doesn't contribute to childhood obesity; rather, it's the incessant bombardment of ads associated with television-watching that "robustly" correlates with obesity. In other words, a PBS-watching couch potato is less likely to become obese than his commercial TV–watching counterpart.

The federal government has tried before to eliminate this well-funded voice inside the machine—a move that would strengthen parents' roles, not interfere with them. Three decades ago, the Federal Trade Commission proposed restrictions on television ads that marketed sugary foods to America's youth. The FTC, of course, has the power to put the kibosh on predatory marketing tactics. And the Supreme Court's 1934 decision in FTC v. Keppel was commonly interpreted to mean that promotion aimed at audiences incapable of protecting themselves—such as young children—necessarily qualified as predation.

But the *Washington Post* published a derisive editorial attacking the FTC proposal, declaring, "It is a preposterous intervention that would turn the agency into a great national nanny." Ratcheting up the sarcasm, the *Post* continued, "But what are the children to be protected from? The candy and sugar-coated cereals that lead to tooth decay? Or the inability or refusal of their parents to say no? The food products will still be there, sitting on the shelves of the local supermarkets after all, no matter what happens to the commercials. So the proposal, in reality, is designed to protect children from the weakness of their parents—and the parents from the wailing insistence of their children. That, traditionally, is one of the roles of a governess—if you can afford one. It is not a proper role of government. The government has enough problems with television's emphasis on violence and sex and its shortages of local programming, without getting into this business, too."

With the government-as-governess idea gift-wrapped by the national nanny neologism, the advertising lobby detected an opening and pressed Congress to rein in the FTC. In 1979, Congress temporarily cut off FTC appropriations, and in 1980, it passed the FTC Improvements Act, which barred the agency from devising industry-wide rules governing promotion and marketing. President Reagan further neutered the agency by appointing James Miller, a free-market fundamentalist out of American Enterprise Institute central casting, as chairman.

And so we've had thirty years of expanding waistlines, decaying teeth and skyrocketing rates of diabetes.

Only today is the federal government demonstrating a willingness to risk the nanny-state accusations. In addition to Michelle Obama's obesity initiative, Congress has charged an interagency task force, encompassing the FDA, FTC, USDA and CDC, with the task of developing industry-wide guidelines on child marketing. "The guidelines won't have the force of law, but should have a lot of moral force," says Michael Jacobson of the Center for Science in the Public Interest. "And noncompliance would give the FTC or Congress the foundation for doing something stronger, from publicly shaming noncompliers to legislation." (Proposals for these guidelines were due in final format the end of 2011.)

Still, as long as these industry standards are voluntary, they may well prove illusory; there are simply too many consumers—and too much money—involved. One solution, then, is for the FTC to educate, not regulate. "No one is suggesting that we engage in regulation," says David Vladeck, head of the FTC's Bureau of Consumer Protection, about his agency's educational efforts. "Industry may be unhappy with some of what we're doing, but they have steered clear of the nanny rhetoric because they know that if the hammer comes down, Congress, not the FTC, will be holding it."

On this point, it could also help to have a new *Post* editorial, this time redirecting the outrage once reserved for the FTC onto the fundamental problem of deliberately targeting children with advertising.

We could do without manipulative, profit-driven nannies. But we do need the FTC as a cop on the beat of wayward marketers.

# Happy 75th Birthday, Social Security
## *August 13, 2010*

On its 75th anniversary, Social Security is once again under attack and so are its defenders.

Those who would axe benefits are spreading myths designed to make you think there's a looming crisis. Well, it's just not true.

The stark reality is that it will be several decades before the program encounters any financial problems. The program's trust fund will have a $4.3 trillion surplus by 2023 and can pay all its obligations for decades to come. And strengthening Social Security is easy—making the very rich pay their fair share by lifting the cap on contributions by the wealthy would allow the program to pay all its obligations indefinitely.

So on this 75th anniversary, rather than fighting these Social Security–busters, we should celebrate what has been one of the nation's best anti-poverty programs—a lifeline for millions of Americans—and a reminder of what effective government can do. Indeed, the Center on Budget and Policy Priorities reports that without Social Security benefits, over 45 percent of elderly Americans would have incomes below the poverty line. In contrast, with Social Security, only 9.7 percent are poor. (Still too many.)

Social Security was a centerpiece of FDR's New Deal reforms that helped this country recover from the Great Depression. These programs provided Americans a measure of dignity and hope and lasting security against the vicissitudes of the market and life. FDR therefore accomplished what the venerable New Deal historian David Kennedy says is the challenge now facing President Obama—a rescue from the current economic crisis which will also make us "more resilient to face those future crises that inevitably await us."

This anniversary is also a reminder of how major social reforms in this country have come about—in fits and starts. As former Clinton adviser Paul Begala observed in a *Washington Post* op-ed, "No self-respecting liberal today would support Franklin Roosevelt's original Social Security Act. . . . If that version of Social Security were introduced today, progressives like me would call it cramped, parsimonious, mean-spirited and even racist. Perhaps it was all those things. But it was also a start. And for 74 years we have built on that start."

Indeed, when Social Security was first passed, it left out African Americans and migrant workers. It was an imperfect piece of legislation but one that progressives built on to create the program we know today—a program like Medicare (which just marked its 45th anniversary last month)—that people feel an emotional connection to and will fight to protect. A new campaign from MoveOn and Campaign for America's Future will tap into that energy, enlisting candidates to pledge their support to Social Security this election season—opposing any cuts in benefits, including raising the retirement age. And these candidates would be wise to pay attention: A just-released poll shows that 65 percent of voters reject raising the retirement age to 70. And a separate AARP poll shows the vast majority oppose cutting Social Security to reduce the deficit, and 50 percent of non-retired adults are willing to pay more now in payroll taxes to ensure Social Security will be there when they retire.

Progressives can also mark this anniversary by not only rededicating themselves to defending Social Security, but also going on the offensive to expand and improve our Social Security system to provide economic security for everyone.

# No Holiday for Labor Unions
## *August 31, 2010*

Labor Day this year comes draped in mourning. More than half of all workers have experienced a spell of unemployment, taken a cut in pay or hours, been forced to go part time or seen other such problems during and after the Great Recession. Collapsing stock and house prices have destroyed a fifth of the wealth of the average household. Nearly six in ten Americans have canceled or cut back on holidays. Amidst all this, workers increasingly don't even have labor unions as a potential answer to their insecurities—despite the fact that, of all the institutions in America, they more often than not got it right on the big issues facing the country, generally in the face of a bipartisan political and elite consensus.

Unions are in trouble. They represent less than 13 percent of the workforce and less than 8 percent of private workers. Union workers still receive higher wages and are more likely to have employer-provided health insurance, pensions and paid sick leave than non-union workers. But when unions represented over 33 percent of all private workers in the 1940s, they drove wage increases for everyone—non-union firms had to compete for good workers. Now, unions struggle just to defend their members' wages and benefits. Over the past decade before the Great Recession, productivity soared, profits rose and CEO pay skyrocketed, but most workers lost ground.

Unions face constant attacks from corporations and conservatives. The most recent campaign—designed as always to divide workers from one another—assails the pay and particularly the pensions of public employees. Why should they have pensions, when many workers have lost theirs and get, at best, a retirement savings plan at work? In fact, in a civilized society, we would ask the reverse question. How do we create pensions—beyond Social Security—for workers across the economy, leveling up rather than down?

Indeed, if we had listened to unions more often in the past, America wouldn't be in the predicament it's in now. For years, labor warned about the dangers of growing trade deficits, the folly of letting Japan and China and others play by a different set of rules. But a bipartisan consensus forged by Wall Street and embraced by both Presidents Bush and President Clinton championed corporate-defined free-trade accords.

The results are calamitous. US trade losses totaled $5.8 trillion over the past decade alone. The US manufacturing sector lost nearly one in three jobs. Federal Reserve Chairman Ben Bernanke notes that the global trade imbalances helped create the bubble and bust that drove the global economy off the cliff. Now, growing imbalances impede recovery from the Great Recession. Last quarter's disappointing 1.6 percent growth would have been a robust 5 percent except for the increase in the trade deficit. Now even Intel's Andy Grove and GE's Jeff Immelt agree that we've been feckless in shipping manufacturing jobs and production capacities abroad.

On corporate governance, a bipartisan consensus preached the cult of the CEO, championing "linking pay to performance" with stock options. Labor unions were scorned as impediments to "flexible labor markets." Union leaders argued strongly that corporations should be responsible to more than the next quarter's financial statement. They pushed unsuccessfully for stakeholders, including labor and the community, to have a greater say on corporate practices. The result: CEOs launched a crime wave. Enron, WorldCom, Global Crossing, Adelphi. Hundreds of corporations "restated" earnings reports once the CEOs were made personally responsible. Dozens of executives were caught backdating stock options. Big banks made bigger and bigger bets, with taxpayers covering the losses. Executives were given multimillion-dollar personal incentives to cook the books; it isn't surprising so many found creative ways to do so.

On government regulation, labor fought a pitched battle against privatization and deregulation that Reagan conservatives and New Democrats made fashionable. Now in one area after another, privatization has been revealed as a source of waste, fraud and abuse—from Halliburton to Blackwater. Deregulation contributed directly to the corporate and financial debauch that brought the economy down, with the human costs apparent from the Gulf of Mexico to Appalachia to the eggs we eat.

Last Saturday in Washington, Glenn Beck tried to lay claim to the civil rights movement. That same day in Detroit, we saw the real thing: The UAW, SEIU and AFSCME joining with the Rainbow PUSH Coalition, the NAACP, the Urban League, ministers and civil rights activists to march for jobs and justice. Union support was vital to the Rev. Martin Luther King's march on Washington forty-seven years ago. And union support is vital to civil rights movements—from immigration reform to equal pay for women to the fight for jobs—today.

For all of their flaws, unions give voice to workers, and not just their members. Their small-"d" democratic strength is a vital counter to the special-interest big money that has so distorted our politics. And their revival is central to building a new foundation for this economy, one that will ensure that it works once more for working people.

# As 44 Million Americans Live in Poverty, a Crisis Grows

*September 28, 2010*

When the government released new US Census data on poverty last week, our warp-speed news cycle paid too little attention to what these numbers tell us—and what the government could do to tackle this moral, economic and political crisis.

It's clear that the Great Recession battered those on the bottom most heavily, adding 6 million people to the ranks of the officially poor, defined as just $22,000 in annual income for a family of four. Forty-four million Americans—one in seven citizens—are now living below the poverty line, more than at any time since the Census Bureau began tracking poverty fifty-one years ago. Shamefully, that figure includes one in five children, more than one in four African Americans or Latinos, and over 51 percent of female-headed families with children under 6.

These numbers are bad enough. But dig deeper—as Georgetown University law professor Peter Edelman has been doing for nearly fifty years in his battle against poverty—and the story told by these figures is even more staggering.

Edelman points out that 19 million people are now living in "extreme poverty," which is under 50 percent of the poverty line, or $11,000 for a family of four. "That means over 43 percent of the poor are extremely poor," said Edelman, who served as an aide to Sen. Robert Kennedy and in the Clinton administration before resigning in protest over welfare reform that shredded the safety net. "That's over 6 percent of the population, and that figure has just been climbing up and up."

Edelman says that the number of people living at less than two times the poverty line ($44,000 for a family of four) is equally significant.

"Data shows that's really the line between whether or not you can pay your bills," said Edelman. "That has reached 100,411,000 people. That's 33 percent of the country. That's the totality of the problem—whether you call it poverty or not."

For too long we have accepted the narrative—promoted by well-funded conservative think tanks—that claims people who are struggling are to blame for their troubles, and at the same time we don't have effective anti-poverty policies. So tackling the problem is seen as wasteful.

"So many people think it's their own fault," said Edelman. "They don't see the structural problem in our economy."

But with so many in poverty, that narrative has become harder to sustain during the Great Recession, and so renewed work is being done to take on poverty and its structural underpinnings.

Half in Ten, a coalition working to cut poverty by half in ten years, is pushing Congress to renew the TANF Emergency Fund, which is set to expire on Thursday. Thirty-six states and the District of Columbia have used the program to provide 250,000 low-income and long-term unemployed workers with subsidized jobs. The coalition is also pushing to make the Obama administration's Recovery Act reforms to the child tax credit and the earned-income tax credit permanent. These progressive policies keep families from falling into poverty and reduce long-term costs such as crime, public benefits and lost consumption. Estimates of costs associated with childhood poverty run at $500 billion annually, or 4 percent of gross domestic product.

And then there are the Bush tax cuts for those making over $250,000 a year, a centerpiece of the GOP's just-released "Pledge to America." Edelman says that it's difficult to see how we can help the 44 million Americans living in poverty today without that revenue.

Beyond what Congress can do immediately, it's clear that America needs a broader movement to create a more just and higher-wage economy. Edelman and other advocates say that we will need to push to make it easier for people to join labor unions through the Employee Free Choice Act or at least reduce legal barriers to organizing. The minimum wage should also be indexed to half the average wage.

"But you're still going to have a gap," said Edelman. "And you essentially have to invent some new idea of a wage supplement that starts from the premise that the so-called good jobs went away a long time ago and we've become a nation of low-wage work."

That's why 100 million people are struggling to make ends meet on less than $44,000 per year.

This devastating economic reality has the potential to create new political alliances—and shape a 21st-century anti-poverty movement. Such a movement is urgently needed because the voices of the poor, of workers and of those struggling to get by are barely heard in the halls of power these days. Anti-poverty groups and advocates with ideas for a more equitable economy are often marginalized within even Democratic Party policy circles that seem hardwired to reject them.

We know what needs to be done to reduce poverty. The question is who will fight that fight? And who will listen?

## Just Say Yes to Common Sense on Pot Policy
*October 26, 2010*

With all the hand-wringing over a Democratic "enthusiasm gap," one effort to turn out young people at the polls this November is showing real energy and promise. What's the secret? In a word, as 78-year-old John Burton, chairman of the California Democratic Party, put it, "Pot."

Proposition 19 would make it legal for Californians over 21 to possess and cultivate marijuana for personal use, and it would authorize city governments to regulate and tax commercial production and sales. Its passage would signal a major victory for common sense over a war on drugs that has been an abysmal failure in the Golden State and throughout the country. As states devastated by the fiscal crisis look for more efficient and effective alternatives to spending $50 billion a year on incarceration, a shift in California might presage changes across the nation.

It would be great if young people would take to the streets and the voting booths on issues like Afghanistan, historical levels of inequality and poverty, or to protect Social Security from a Republican takeover. But they're not. And if it's reforming an ineffective, wasteful and racially unjust drug policy that mobilizes young people—who are at the core of the rising American electorate along with African Americans, Hispanics and unmarried women—so be it. According to Public Policy Polling, for those who cite Prop 19 as their top reason for voting, 34 percent are under age 30.

"There's nothing that motivates young people more than this issue," Aaron Houston, executive director of Students for a Sensible Drug Policy, told me. "So much of this comes down to young people saying they don't want this war on drugs to be waged in their name anymore."

The case for Prop 19 is clear and strong. Between 1999 and 2009, nearly 570,000 residents were arrested for misdemeanor pot possession. Harvard economist Jeffrey Miron, a prominent libertarian, estimates the annual cost of enforcing prohibition in California at $1.8 billion. The new statute would save as much as $200 million per year on enforcement, prosecution and incarceration. But for all the time and resources the state has pumped into targeting these nonviolent, low-level offenders, there has been no corresponding drop in reported use. (In fact, according to surveys by the US and Dutch governments, 41 percent of Americans have used marijuana, compared to 22.6 percent of residents of the Netherlands, where it is legal.) There has, though, been a spike in racial disparities. Black adults across California are arrested for pot possession at higher rates than whites—sometimes by a factor of twelve. The same ugly imbalances apply to black youth, even though government surveys consistently show that their white peers are more likely to use pot.

Legalization would also help balance the budget. California is facing a $19 billion shortfall and can ill afford to waste so much money on a failed war on drugs. But it can surely benefit from a regulated cannabis market; advocates estimate that the state could capture $1.4 billion a year in taxes and fees.

Unions, progressives and community activists see Prop 19 as a jobs engine and revenue generator—especially for economically depressed communities—which would increase resources available for healthcare, public safety, parks, roads, transportation and more. But it's critical to not only fight for approval of the ballot initiative but also for the infrastructure for production and distribution. Oakland's city council, for example, has already approved permits for four indoor marijuana plantations.

Because the reasons to support Prop 19 are so diverse, promising alliances are being formed that might be sustained beyond this election. Libertarians and progressives, civil rights advocates, law enforcement groups, unions and young activists all see the value of ending prohibition. (As editor of *The Nation*, it's not often that I find the magazine in a bipartisan alliance with *Reason* magazine. And the *National Review* was on board for legalization when William F. Buckley Jr. served as editor a decade ago.)

So Prop 19 is good policy and good politics. States across the country struggling with these same issues are watching with interest, as are Democratic strategists who see the potential for similar ballot initiatives to drive people to the polls in 2012.

On November 2, 201, California voters rejected Proposition 19 by a 54–46 percent margin. Following this defeat, the state's legalization movement immediately turned its attention to 2012—in March, the Coalition for Cannabis Policy Reform (CCPR) officially announced they would file another Prop 19–style initiative for the 2012 ballot.

# The Horror in Arizona
## *January 11, 2011*

A colleague invoked Robert Frost: "Poetry is about the grief. Politics is about the grievance." This is a time of grief, not grievance. The crazed act of a clearly unstable man in Arizona has taken six lives and wounded fourteen people, with Rep. Gabrielle Giffords still fighting for survival.

This was an assassination of democracy, an armed assault on citizens gathered to exercise the most precious of American rights—the right to free speech and assembly. Rep. Giffords was doing the essential work of politics, meeting with her neighbors and constituents outside of a grocery store in a "Congress on Your Corner" gathering. This small "d" democratic act is so central to our Constitution and our republic that its protection is enshrined in the First Amendment, the same amendment that Giffords read aloud on the opening day of Congress.

Nothing is more corrosive to democracy than the use of violence to terrorize the public square, to shut down speech, to slay those seeking its exercise. Among the lives so wantonly taken was that of Christina-Taylor Green, a third-grader who had just been elected to her school's student council. She died because of her love for political engagement. Her loss diminishes us all.

The rampage has led, as it should, to a broad indictment of the vitriol and venom on the right that has come to characterize too much of our political dialogue—particularly, since the election of Barack Obama. Arizona has been, as Pima County Sheriff Clarence W. Dupnik stated, "a mecca for prejudice and bigotry" and a hotbed of Tea Party anger and hatred toward immigrants.

John M. Roll, the chief federal judge of Arizona, killed in the rampage, lived with hundreds of death threats. Talk radio hosts fomented rage over his decision to allow to go forward a lawsuit filed by undocumented immigrants against a rancher. Giffords, a moderate Blue Dog Democrat, was demonized in her reelection campaign as a socialist, a communist, a fascist, a job-killer, a traitor and much more. Her office was vandalized after she voted in favor of Obama's healthcare plan. On her webpage, Sarah Palin put Giffords' district in the cross-hairs of a gunsight, while Giffords' Republican opponent invited supporters to "shoot a fully automatic M16" with him.

Mendacious and vicious rhetoric is destructive. Honesty, more tolerance and the jettisoning of violent imagery in our politics would be a good thing. Yet it's worth reminding ourselves that passion and vitriol in political disputes are as American as apple pie—with a lineage tracing back to Tom Paine and Thomas Jefferson. Violent rhetoric is deplorable, but we still don't know whether it was responsible for last weekend's horror.

Acts of violence by unstable people happen in all societies. Yet they are more than random acts. The unstable are inflamed—sometimes more than others—by the conditions around them, including a climate of hate and fear and overt (or even implied) appeals to violence.

And we live in a flammable atmosphere. For young people like accused gunman Jared Lee Loughner, a community-college dropout apparently rejected by the military, these are brutal times. In an economy where many Americans are struggling simply to keep their heads above water, where poverty is spreading and young people without college educations face bleak futures, fury and depression are certain to spread.

Combine that with a culture awash in violence—from Afghanistan to video games—and then throw in our ridiculous gun laws, which make it easy to purchase rapid-fire weapons and, in too many states, make legal the carrying of concealed guns. The 22-year-old Loughner didn't need a gun to commit an act of violence, but surely easy access to a Glock-19 semi-automatic with an extended clip of thirty bullets exponentially increased the danger he posed to society. Loughner was able to buy the gun legally because the federal ban on assault weapons expired in 2004. It's time to reinstate it.

Then add the reality that mental illness gets too little treatment in America. Counseling is expensive and often not readily available. Loughner, existing on the margin, was not likely to get treatment for his instability. But consider the veterans of our wars, those scarred by the horrors of conflict who return home to face bleak job prospects. Even they get far too little help for their mental health needs. (It's worth noting that Rep. Giffords fought for expanded mental health benefits for veterans.)

Violence or incitement to violence (see Sharron Angle's talk of using "Second Amendment remedies") has no place in a democracy that needs a robust exchange of ideas. But even while we condemn it, the violent imagery at Palin's website should be of less concern than the real cross-hairs of guns readily available across the land; the vitriol of politics of less concern than the shrinking opportunities in our economy; the passions of partisans less dangerous than the absence of help for the mentally unstable among us.

# Wisconsin—It's About Democracy
## *February 22, 2011*

As demonstrators in the tens of thousands flooded the Capitol in Madison, Wisconsin, a sign captured the spirit: "I didn't think Cairo would be this cold." Even conservative Republican Rep. Paul Ryan saw the parallel: "It's like Cairo moved to Madison."

Got that right. As the demonstrations for workers' rights head into their second week, Madison has become ground zero in the battle for democracy in this country.

Don't fall for the dodge that this is about money, the pay and perks of public employees. This is about basic democratic rights, and the balance of power in America. This is a fight in which every US worker has a direct stake.

Wisconsin faces budget deficits in the wake of the Great Recession, although not nearly as severe as in many states. In the 2010 election, Republicans captured control of the statehouse and both houses of the legislature. Scott Walker, the newly elected, self-declared "Tea Party" governor, signed off on tax cuts for businesses and then demanded harsh concessions from public employees, forcing them to pay more for pensions and healthcare. He coupled this with a direct attack on teacher and public employee unions, seeking to ram through legislation curtailing their right to bargain collectively, limiting any pay raise to the increase in the cost of living, and requiring an annual vote of members to continue the union. These measures aren't about the budget crisis; they are about eliminating the unions. And to make the power grab blatant, Walker exempted those unions—police and firefighters—that supported him in the last election. This is straight ugly, folks.

And it isn't limited to Wisconsin. Corporations and their right-wing allies have launched a final offensive against America's unions. With unions representing less than 7 percent of the private workforce, the target is public employee unions. With Republicans now in control of twenty-one states, hundreds of bills have been introduced seeking to cripple unions, if not ban them completely. States that are considering either weakening or removing entirely the ability of public-sector workers to bargain collectively include not only Wisconsin but also Ohio, South Dakota, Colorado, Michigan, Nebraska, New Hampshire and Oklahoma.

Unions, described by right-wing gadfly Grover Norquist as one of the "five pillars" of Democratic strength, have been central to the rise and fall of the American middle class. There is a strong correlation between states with right-to-work laws that outlaw majority rule on unionization, a worse quality of life for workers and a more hostile climate to any progressive cause. The average worker in a right-to-work state earns $5,333 less than his or her counterpart in a pro-worker state. Twenty-one percent more people lack health insurance in right-to-work states. In a country which, by some measures, suffers greater inequality than Egypt or Tunisia, the stakes in Wisconsin are high.

But they are more than economic. At stake is the strength of our democracy itself. The Supreme Court decision in *Citizens United* opened the floodgates for the money of corporations and billionaires to corrupt our elections. The unions provide virtually the only counterbalance for working Americans. It is no coincidence that America has grown more unequal and the middle class has declined as union representation has been weakened.

In Wisconsin, stunningly, workers drew the line. The public employee unions agreed to accept Walker's economic demands, but rallied against the union-busting provisions. State Democrats joined, leaving the state to block the vote on Walker's legislation and allowing the demonstrations to gain traction. Students and activists rallied to the workers' side. The demonstrations swelled to levels not seen since the Vietnam War protests. Yet other than former House Speaker Nancy Pelosi and Sen. Dick Durbin (Ill.), joined by President Obama, national Democrats have been virtually invisible. More Green Bay Packers have spoken in support of the demonstrators than national Democrats.

The teachers, nurses, police officers and public workers in Wisconsin, in the spirit of their progressive and populist forebears, have stood up against the assault on basic rights. Their fight poses a classic question: Whose side are you on? With basic rights at stake, it is time for outrage.

# Real Political Courage
## *May 31, 2011*

In August 1964, President Johnson went to Congress to ask for far-reaching authority to conduct military action in Vietnam. The "Gulf of Tonkin Resolution," as this authority was called, would give the president broad power to engage in a war of any size, for any length of time, without the need for a formal declaration of war from Congress. It was popular within Congress and throughout the country, and Johnson rightly expected it to pass without much opposition.

Out of that uncritical unity, Sens. Wayne Morse (D-Ore.) and Ernest Gruening (D-Alaska) rose to give a scathing and extraordinarily prescient critique of the resolution and of our involvement in Vietnam. "Mr. President," said Morse, on the Senate floor, "criticism has not prevented, and will not prevent, me from saying that, in my judgment, we cannot justify the shedding of American blood in that kind of war in Southeast Asia. I do not believe that any number of American conventional forces in South Vietnam . . . can win a war, if the test of winning a war is establishing peace." He called the Gulf of Tonkin Resolution "an undated declaration of war" and urged his colleagues to join him in opposing it.

They did not. Ninety-eight senators voted in support of the resolution. Only Morse and Gruening (who had been a longtime editor at *The Nation*) opposed it. Four years later, Morse's opposition to the war would become the central issue in his reelection campaign, a campaign he would lose by just half a percentage point of the vote. Gruening was defeated that same year in a Democratic primary.

There was a time when this is how we defined political courage in America: a politician standing up for deeply held principles, in opposition to his party and a popular president, regardless of consequence. But today, we have adopted a new and distorted definition of political courage, one that rewards those who claim to be making hard choices, when in truth there is nothing hard about what they've chosen.

Case in point: Rep. Paul Ryan (R-Wis.). Ryan has been called courageous, a hero of sorts, by members of his party, by members of the media and even by some Democrats. And what is it that Ryan so bravely did in order to receive the outsized praise heaped upon him these past two months?

He proposed a federal budget that, in every respect, articulated extremist Republican ideology. He balanced the budget using faulty assumptions that no respected economist outside the Heritage Foundation has called reasonable. And he did it by slashing healthcare benefits for the elderly and the poor, for children and the disabled, all while giving $4 trillion in tax cuts to the wealthiest Americans. For this, he has become a hero within his own party (someone Dick Cheney claims to "worship"), even though he made his proposal from a perfectly safe

Congressional district, where he has no reason to expect political consequences at the ballot box. While his proposal may cost his party control of Congress, it will cost him nothing.

Despite the pomp and circumstance, despite the laudatory columns and glowing testimony from DC elites, what Ryan did is not, nor will it ever be, a true measure of political courage. Real political courage means bucking party orthodoxy when the leadership has strayed. It could be seen in Russ Feingold's vocal opposition to the Patriot Act and the bank bailouts, or in John McCain's scathing critique of those in his party who advocate torture. It could be seen in Gary Johnson's impassioned plea to end the war on drugs or in his support for gay marriage, which he calls a "civil rights issue." It can be seen in Dennis Kucinich's demands that President Obama seek authorization for military efforts in Libya. And it could be seen in Rep. Barbara Lee's brave decision to stand alone, among both parties and both houses of Congress, as the sole vote against the far-reaching Authorization for Use of Military Force in the aftermath of Sept. 11.

Real political courage also means standing up for those whose voices carry least in Washington, not for those who least need a voice. Such courage can be seen today in the House Progressive Caucus's attempt to pass "The People's Budget," a budget that will create jobs and economic growth and will bring down deficits, not by stripping benefits from the poor and middle class, but by making the wealthiest Americans pay their fair share of taxes.

And political courage means a willingness to sacrifice for the sake of principle, to put the obligations of office ahead of re-election to office. That could be seen on full display last March, when members of Congress such as Betsy Markey (D-Colo.), and Tom Perriello (D-Va.) voted to extend healthcare access to 30 million people, knowing that it would almost certainly lead to their defeat (as it did) in the fall.

That is what true political courage looks like. But too often, too much of the media fails to portray it that way. John McCain is more likely to be called courageous for his vote for the Ryan budget than for his stance against torture. He's more likely to be called courageous for standing with his party than for breaking with it. The Progressive Caucus was not called brave for defending the poorest among us; it was virtually ignored. Russ Feingold was not called brave for being one of the few Democrats to stand up to a popular president in opposition to the Patriot Act; he was called brazen.

If we applaud false courage, we'll only get more of it, and less of the real thing, at a time when we need real courage more than ever. Solving this problem, then, must be a shared responsibility. It is the media's obligation, as much as it is our own as citizens, to highlight genuine political courage for what it is and to reject Ryan-style courage for what it isn't.

*Part VI*

## PERFECTING OUR DEMOCRACY

# Ways to Perfect Our Democracy
*May 4, 2009*

The first 100 days of the Obama presidency have come and gone in a state of crisis. For supporters of democracy reform, however, that could describe the last eight years since *Bush v. Gore*. If the 2008 election vindicated their work, it was only a first step toward redressing the fundamental flaws of our democracy.

In the words of Miles Rapoport, democracy reform advocate and president of the think tank Demos, "A lot of the focus for Demos and for other organizations over the last ten years has been work on the state level. That was a result of the fact that Washington was so hopelessly gridlocked on these issues, it was almost better not to have Washington take them up. The situation is different now. The possibilities for federal reform are better now than they've ever been before."

As the data-crunchers digest the numbers, it's clear that 2008 had the highest turnout of any presidential election since the voting age was lowered to 18 in 1972: 62 percent of eligible voters. More African Americans, Latinos and young voters made it to the polls than ever before, and the electorate on Nov. 4 looked more like America than it ever has in the past (proportionally speaking). However remarkable, this milestone was partly the result of a slightly lower turnout (in relative terms) by white and elderly voters, and it was far short of the record-setting spectacle many had hoped for. Voting rates in the United States continue to lag far behind many of the world's other oldest democracies. There's still much to do to make it possible for all Americans to make their voices heard, from enacting election-day registration and early voting to making election day a holiday.

As advocates for election reform are quick to observe, the fact that the turnout didn't shatter records may have been a blessing in disguise. The seven-year-old, nonpartisan Election Protection coalition declared in its report: "Election officials nationwide were grossly under-resourced." Election Protection's hotline took nearly 100,000 calls on election day alone. As Common Cause's Tova Wang put it shortly after the election: "We must . . . wonder what kind of system breakdown would ensue should we ever achieve the turnout levels that are routine in most countries around the world, where participation rates are in the 75–94% range."

At 62 percent, Election Protection reported that "hundreds of thousands" of voters still had to wait for hours to cast their ballots. In Detroit, some waited for five hours; in St. Louis, six; in the battleground of Chesapeake, VA, seven.

Just over a third of the problems reported to Election Protection's hotline involved registration. Seemingly unrelated problems—with absentee ballots or polling places, for example—were often really issues with registration as well. As Election Protection director Jonah Goldman observes, "Registration was really the big cancer in the whole voting process." An MIT study estimates that 2.2 million voters were turned away from the polls due to problems with their registration, and another 2.2 million due to problems with their identification.

The voter suppression tactics the 2004 election made disconcertingly familiar resurfaced as well. In the weeks running up to the election, the Election Protection hotline received nearly daily calls about deceptive practices. "Traditionally it's been targeting minority communities," Goldman says. "This year we saw a couple of really unfortunate developments. One: the tactics have been updated for the 21st century. We saw them on Facebook, we saw them on MySpace. There are text messages and e-mails going out. Now they're often targeting first-time voters and young voters." The threat of voter caging and challenges was also brandished yet again; if these practices were held in check, it was thanks to the rapid legal response by national democracy reform groups in Ohio, Montana and elsewhere.

It's long past time to declare voter suppression a crime and focus on encouraging voters, not discouraging them. On Nov. 10, 2008, Tova Wang could still write, in reference to deceptive practices, "Currently, the Department of Justice does not believe there is a federal statute that explicitly criminalizes this activity."

Rep. John Conyers is one of several elected officials working to change this. He has resurrected Obama's Deceptive Practices and Voter Intimidation Act in the House (it awaits an answer in the Senate), and advocates think the bill would be an important step. Rep. Conyers has also introduced the Caging Prohibition Act—Sen. Sheldon Whitehouse (D-RI) has advanced a companion bill in the Senate—which would ban the practice of using undeliverable mail to challenge a voter's registration. Along with these measures, a law restricting the power to challenge a voter's registration to election officials would check the most egregious ways of keeping voters from voting.

Challenges and caging were pioneered by the defenders of Jim Crow and segregation; deceptive practices and registration problems disproportionately impact African American and Latino voters. Even as these practices persist, both sides in an upcoming Supreme Court case are drawing on Barack Obama's election to argue over the continuing relevance of a major provision of the Voting Rights Act.

Last week, the Supreme Court heard oral arguments in the innocuously named Northwest Austin Municipal Utility District Number One v. Gonzales. The VRA requires jurisdictions with a history of discrimination—eight states including Texas, and any number of municipalities and counties—to clear any changes to their electoral procedures with the Justice Department or a federal court. Attorneys for the Texas district are arguing that Obama's election demonstrates the VRA's safeguards are no longer necessary. And the Roberts' court seems to be receptive to the argument, with the Chief Justice declaring rhetorically: "You know I have this whistle to keep away elephants. Well, there are no elephants, so it must work." With Justice Kennedy reportedly leaning in Roberts' direction, there's some chance the Court will decide against pre-clearance. If the Court essentially overturns a major provision by which the VRA is enforced, democracy reform advocates and Congress will have to act quickly to ensure the gains of the civil rights movement.

While a conservative Court considers whether the VRA is still relevant, the 18th-century compromise that is the electoral college remains in place, even after effectively overturning the will of the people in 2000. The electoral college succeeded in infiltrating the three-fifths compromise into the election of the president, and long after that shameful deal was overturned, the college has persisted. Slowly, the push for a national popular vote for president is gaining ground across the country. One state legislature after another is passing bills that declare that once states representing a majority of electoral college votes sign on, they will award their electoral votes to the winner of the popular vote. The principle of "One person, one vote" will finally be represented at all levels of government.

"These are a series of issues all related by the empowerment of ordinary voters in a democracy," says Nick Nyhart, dedicated campaign finance reformer, Public Campaign CEO and occasional *Nation* contributor. With Obama in office and a Democratic Congress, "a number of these issues go from existing on the drawing boards to actually existing in practice," Nyhart says. "They go from hopes to actual possibilities."

Campaign finance reform is one of those possibilities. If the Supreme Court's decision in Buckley v. Valeo essentially rules out public financing of campaigns, the Fair Elections Now Act sponsored by Dick Durbin (D-Ill.) may be the next best thing. The act uses public funds to give leverage to small donors, matching contributions of $100 or less at a 4:1 rate. "We want a public financing system strong enough that Barack Obama would not have opted out," Nyhart says.

In the 2008 election cycle alone, the Center for Responsive Politics reports that the finance, insurance, and real estate industries gave more than $463 million to the duopoly, splitting it almost equally between Democrats (51 percent) and Republicans (49 percent). As backroom bailout deals and black-site torture tactics slowly continue to come to light, calls for transparency provide another possible rallying point for a democracy reform movement.

The Sunlight Foundation is a two-year-old organization dedicated to "changing the focus in terms of who's a gatekeeper for this information," says Gabriela Schneider, a spokesperson for the non-profit. The Foundation works to achieve this goal both by supporting the work of other organizations, like the Center for Responsive Politics (a recent grant for more than $1 million required the Center make its data available under a Creative Commons license) and through the work of Sunlight Labs, their open source development team. Their first annual "open source application" contest generated dozens of new tools for keeping track of the sort of things elected officials would often rather no one kept track of, like Filibusted, which lets anyone keep track of just which Senators are refusing to vote for cloture.

"This is the next generation of civic engagement," Schneider says. "There's increased apathy and mistrust of government. We think that the solution to that is greater transparency. It's a way to empower people—the more they know, the more they feel part of the process. We see it as a way to revitalize democracy. The transparency work is a catalyst for the greater democracy reform movement."

Another potential catalyst is the creation of an Office of Civic Engagement within the executive branch. "There needs to be a place in the White House whose job it is day in and day out, to figure out how, in all the welter of issues, what role citizens have in this," says Miles Rapoport. "How can we do this in a way that encourages people to think of government not as this kind of other, but that gives people a larger stake in the decisions that are made. And we'll get better decisions that way. It's easy in the crisis mentality that can often pervade for civic engagement to be lost. So having someone or some group in the White House that's really thinking about this is a good thing." On the second day of his administration, President Obama issued an executive order calling for "a system of transparency, public participation, and collaboration." The Obama administration has since opened an Office of Social Innovation within the White House, placing the emphasis on new forms of technological innovation. An Office of Civic Engagement would still be invaluable for achieving those goals.

Our democracy still needs defending. But the best defense is a good offense.

# Let's Make Every Vote Count
## May 14, 2009

Quick: When did we elect the president last year? If you said November 4, you're more than a month off. Try December 15. That's when the electoral college convened in each state to formally "elect" Barack Obama president. Despite overturning the popular vote in 2000, efforts to establish direct election of the president—which would require amending the Constitution—have been unable to gain traction in Congress. Now two election reform organizations, relative newcomer National Popular Vote and the more established FairVote, have a promising proposal to use the electoral college for the very end it was intended to circumvent.

On April 28, Washington became the fifth state in the nation to enact legislation in favor of a national popular vote for president. "Being a blue state since '88, in the primary cycle we draw some attention, but in the general election we draw very little attention from the national campaigns," says State Sen. Joe McDermott, the prime sponsor of the bill in the Washington State Senate and a former elector himself. "National Popular Vote would blow that open. Whether the Democrat won by 52 or 57 percent would make a difference nationally. Assuming Washington was still a blue state, what the margin was suddenly becomes important."

When it comes to how electors are awarded, all the Constitution has to say on the matter is that "Each state shall appoint, in such a manner as the legislature thereof may direct, a number of electors, equal to the whole number of Senators and Representatives to which the state may be entitled in Congress."

The plan for direct election of the president first advanced by National Popular Vote (NPV) is nothing short of ingenious: instead of awarding electors by Congressional district (as both Maine and Nebraska do) or by state, states would award their electors to the winner of the popular vote in the country as a whole. This would only go into effect once states representing a majority of electoral votes had passed similar legislation. With Washington joining Maryland, New Jersey, Illinois and Hawaii, we're about a quarter of the way to transforming the way we elect a president.

"We seem to have a national election for president, but when you look under the hood you realize it's really just an election by a handful of states," says NPV Chairman John Koza. "Every vote is not equal. We have a system where votes in certain states and certain years are very important, and two-thirds of the voters every year are basically ignored." A report by FairVote bears this out: even in an election in which the political map seemed to be transformed, just ten—or a fifth—of the states enjoyed almost 90 percent of campaign events. Almost half those events took place in a mere three states: Florida, Ohio, and Pennsylvania. Rob Richie, FairVote's executive director, is succinct on this disparity: "Big state, small state—it's all swing state versus spectator state."

A report from the Nonprofit Voter Engagement Network describes in stark detail how lopsided this contest is: 95 percent of the $495 million the candidates, parties, and interest groups spent on TV advertising in the final six weeks of the campaign went to fifteen battleground states. More than half that prodigious sum was shoveled into Ohio, Florida, Pennsylvania, and Virginia alone. And voters respond: voter turnout in those same fifteen swing states averaged seven points higher than voter turnout in the spectator states. Whether that's driven merely by their swing-state status or the increased attention it brings from the campaigns, the states that the electoral college favors are those most closely divided along partisan lines.

"The Electoral College system fails to realize some fundamental principles of what representative democracy should be about," says FairVote's Richie. "One is that every voter's participation should be equal and that the candidate with the most votes wins. That I'm of equal weight with someone who lives in Florida. And right now I'm not." In 2008, Florida was second only to Ohio, with 15 percent of campaign events being held in the state. "Equality needs to be at the core of democracy, but the current system just throws it out the window."

The last time there was a serious effort to dissolve the electoral college was in the late '60s, when a proposed constitutional amendment made it through the House but not the Senate. The elections of 1960 and 1968 both saw a fair amount of chicanery in the electoral college; during the former, electors in Alabama, Oklahoma and Louisiana all attempted to deny John F. Kennedy (the "labor Socialist nominee" in the words of one Republican elector) the presidency. In 1968, one "faithless" Republican elector went so far as to cast his vote for unrepentant segregationist George Wallace instead of Richard Nixon (a move that remains legal).

The history of the electoral college is intertwined with that of slavery and segregation. While the college itself was adopted as much if not more out of political compromise than anti-democratic principle, it effectively imported the three-fifths compromise (under which slaves were counted as three-fifths of a person for the purposes of distributing seats in the House) into the selection of the president. "That was intended. That certainly was something of which the Southerners were very much aware," says George C. Edwards III, a scholar of the presidency and author of *Why the Electoral College Is Bad for America*.

As Alexander Keyssar noted in a keen analysis published in the *New York Review of Books*, with the Fifteenth Amendment and the subsequent collapse of Reconstruction (the result of a deal bartered through the electoral college), the South effectively came to enjoy a five-fifths advantage, as African American men were counted as citizens but effectively denied the right to vote. And the electoral college continues to frustrate attempts to exercise voting power today; Rob Richie observes that in 1976, three out of four African Americans lived in states where they made up 5 percent of the electorate and therefore constituted a swing vote. Today, as Edwards observes, "There's a lot of blacks concentrated in the deep south. Their votes are basically irrelevant, because they can't be aggregated across the country."

NPV's Koza reports that national popular vote legislation already has sponsors in all fifty states; over the last four years, bills have passed twenty-seven separate legislative chambers in seventeen states. Some of this support has even come from battleground states, with chambers in Michigan, Nevada, New Mexico and Colorado all passing a version of the bill. National polls have consistently shown support in the 60–70 percent range for direct election of the president.

Even with this broad support, governors in Vermont, Rhode Island and California have vetoed the legislation, suggesting those states are out of reach for the moment (Schwarzenegger killed the bill not once but twice). Nor is it certain that the legislation will retain the ground it has gained: in Washington, the opposition is attempting to gather the roughly 120,000 signatures necessary to force a public referendum in November. At the same time, New Mexico, Colorado and Massachusetts have all come close to joining the states which have rallied behind a national popular vote.

In New Mexico, a lesser swing state in 2008 (at #12 on FV's list of battlegrounds), State Rep. Mimi Stewart sponsored national popular vote legislation that passed the House but not the Senate during this year's session. "I think it'll be fairly easy to pass the national popular vote out of the House again," Rep. Stewart says. "Our work really is in the Senate." She's hopeful that Governor Bill Richardson will make the bill a priority for the legislature's 2010 session.

In Colorado, the State Senate passed a bill twice in previous sessions only to see it die in the House; this year State Rep. Andy Kerr sponsored a version of the bill that finally passed the House only to see it die in the Senate. "I've carried bills dealing with renewable energy, education, all sorts of things," says Rep. Kerr. "When I go to my town hall meetings and make appearances around the state—this is the bill people talk about. Ten years ago, most people couldn't tell you what the electoral college was, let alone how it worked. Since the election of 2000 especially, but 2004 as well, people are starting to understand better that in the 21st century, the winner-take-all system that forty-eight of the states have really isn't in the best interests of the country." Although the Colorado state legislature has ended its 2009 session, Rep. Kerr plans to reintroduce the bill, perhaps as early as 2010.

With twelve electoral votes, Massachusetts would be a significant victory for a national popular vote. In the 2007–2008 session, the bill nearly made it to the governor's desk. "Massachusetts has changed the way it apportions its electors eleven times in its history," says State Rep. Garrett Bradley, who sponsored the legislation in the House. "I never understood the electoral college, even in school. When I try to explain it to my 9-year-old, I can't do it. If I can't explain it to my kids, then something's wrong. I can't explain how the person with the most votes doesn't win." He continues: "Nobody ever campaigns in Massachusetts. They only come here for money; they know we're going to vote Democratic. Let's get it back in play."

FairVote's Rob Richie believes a national popular vote is "very much in play for 2012," and John Koza agrees with him. Richie argues it would remake the political map: "There's value in a long-term investment in the infrastructure of participation. Parties will have greater incentive to build themselves and make their case over time, and in all parts of the country."

It's a vision of a country in which there are no spectator states or swing states, in which volunteering is just as relevant in New York, California, Texas or Alabama as in Ohio, Pennsylvania, Florida or Virginia, and in which every vote is finally equal.

# A Call For Universal Voter Registration
## May 22, 2009

Between 2 and 4 million Americans were unable to vote in the last election because of problems with their registration. And that's just people who tried to vote; in 2006, there were more than 65 million who were eligible to vote, but weren't even registered. That's a third of potential voters.

It doesn't have to be this way. Registration rates in other countries frequently run upwards of 90 percent (both Canada and France hit that mark, for example. Now reformers are seizing the moment to use existing law to expand registration, as well as considering new laws that could finally put the United States on an equal footing with many of the world's other democracies.

"That's a pretty staggering number," says Project Vote's executive director Michael Slater of the millions unable to cast a ballot in 2008. "We don't have the egregious problems with voter registration that we had in the past, but it's still a system that's far from perfect and it's still a system that's preventing people from voting in America."

As with too much else in America, the divide between the registered and the unregistered isn't neutral. The think tank Demos estimates that while 80 percent of citizens in households making $100,000 or more a year are registered to vote, only 60 percent of those making less than $25,000 a year can say the same.

The National Voter Registration Act, passed in 1993 and often known as the "Motor-Voter" Law because it made it possible to register to vote at your local DMV, was intended not only to make registration easier, but to begin closing the chasm between rich and poor voters. Section 7 of the act instructed public assistance agencies to offer everyone who walked through their doors an opportunity to register to vote. At first states complied and registrations jumped, but as of 2006 voter registration applications from public assistance agencies had plummeted from over 2.5 million to below 500,000.

Along with Project Vote and the Lawyers' Committee for Civil Rights Under Law, Demos has set about challenging states to comply with the NVRA. In Missouri, the state's public assistance agencies had collected a measly 15,500 registrations in 2005 and 2006. In the six months after the coalition won a court ruling against the state in July 2008, those same agencies saw 90,000 new registrations. North Carolina saw a similar six-fold increase in registrations, while Virginia saw monthly registration applications leap eight-fold.

Iowa offers an even more compelling demonstration of the benefits of enforcing the NVRA. Even though Iowa had one of the highest voter registration rates in the country, after the Governor lit a fire under its public assistance agencies (or ordered its public assistance agencies to comply with law), the state still saw a stampede of new voters through those agencies' doors: a mind-boggling 3000 percent increase over 2003. As a report issued by Project Vote and Demos concludes, if this is what happens in a state with a strong registration rate, states with low registration rates can expect even more dramatic results.

On the other side of the scale, there's the state of Maryland. In the two years after the NVRA was passed, Maryland registered a mere 982 voters via its public assistance agencies. After a private party filed suit, the state got its act together. In 1999 and 2000, those same agencies registered 32,250 people. Then the agreement by which the suit had been settled came to an end in 2001, and public assistance registrations tumbled back down to around 1,000. "Most states which are covered by the NVRA are not in compliance," says Project Vote's executive director, Michael Slater.

"The lesson that we draw from this is the old line that vigilance is the cost of liberty. Performance needs to be monitored and states that are failing need to be taken to task." Project Vote and Demos have already issued "notice letters" to six of the forty-four states covered by the act that they're failing to comply, the first step toward taking legal action against them.

"The good news is the Justice Department is actually interested in enforcing this again," says Regina Eaton, the Deputy Director of the Democracy Program at Demos. "We've already seen a marked change in attitude." 13 million people who make less than $25,000 a year aren't registered to vote. Their chances of voting just got a whole lot better.

Placing the burden on voters to register before they can participate in elections was first done in Massachusetts in 1801, but it was only after the 15th Amendment granted African-American men the right to vote and waves of immigrants began arriving on the country's shores that such laws gained traction. Under the original Massachusetts law, town assessors drew up lists of voters, which were then publicly posted. If come election day your name wasn't on the list, you could simply present the necessary documents and register to vote. Since then, many states have shifted the burden onto the voter and closed the window in which it's possible to register. "Voter registration deadlines vary widely across the nation," says Demos' Eaton, observing that "these cut-off dates bear little relevance to a state's ability to run smooth elections."

As evidence, Eaton cites the experience of the nine states which now allow voters to register and cast their ballot on the same day. Usually referred to as election day registration (EDR)—except in those states like North Carolina where election day is off limits, but voters can still register and cast their ballot early, where it's therefore known as same day registration—this simple reform holds the potential to dramatically increase participation in our democracy. Every one of the five states with the highest percent turnout in 2008 used EDR, and on average, states with EDR saw turnout rates 7 percent higher than those without. Historically, states with EDR have enjoyed an even greater advantage, usually leading the rest of the country by between 10 and 12 percent.

In the wake of the 2004 election, the AGs of New Hampshire and Wisconsin both launched investigations of EDR voters for fraud. In both states, the practice was vindicated. Demos' early estimates suggest that in the last election over 1.1 million Americans used EDR and SDR to vote. Iowa, which enacted EDR in 2007, saw the highest turnout in state history in 2008, even as the number of provisional ballots cast (between 20 and 33 percent of which often go uncounted) plunged by almost 70 percent between 2004 and 2008. Young voters in particular benefit from EDR. As young Americans, especially college students, are highly mobile, EDR ensures that they can show up at the polls and vote on Election Day. Research suggests that EDR could raise turnout of young voters in presidential elections by 14 percent.

Yet these reforms still leave the burden of registration on the voter. The holy grail of registration reform remains universal registration. As the Election Protection coalition states in its report on the 2008 election, this would mean a registration system that was automatic, permanent (providing voters an opportunity to update their registration when they changed their name or address, for example), and allows for voters to correct any mistakes on election day. "A system where everybody's registered in some fashion automatically is much better than the patchwork system we have now," says Regina Eaton of Demos. "But that doesn't mean we don't need a way to make corrections. And there will be errors." In her analysis, EDR is part of the foundation of universal registration.

Michael Waldman, executive director of the Brennan Center for Justice at NYU, calls universal registration "potentially the most significant improvement since the Voting Rights Act of

1965." He sees it as the surest path toward giving those 65 million more potential voters a voice in our democracy. "Roughly a third of eligible Americans still are not registered," Waldman says. "They tend to be less educated. They tend to be people who are locked out of the system. We don't expect people who are going to court to rustle up their own juries. Making sure that every citizen is registered should be a core responsibility of government."

Project Vote's Michael Slater is quick to sound a note of caution. He points to the troubled implementation of the Help America Vote Act's requirement that states implement statewide voter registration databases. "Creating a brand new untested system has a real risk of making the system worse rather than better," he says. While he agrees with "the central tenet," that the state and not the individual should be responsible for registration, "we need to roll it out over a period of time so we know what we're getting. In the meantime we need to enforce what we have already, which would get us a long way toward universal registration."

As of this writing, Senator Chuck Schumer is reportedly considering introducing legislation to this effect in Congress soon. We may not have such a long way to go.

# True Populism
*January 29, 2010*

A very sweet victory in Oregon this week, where voters passed two ballot initiatives to raise taxes on the wealthiest 3 percent of its residents—individuals earning over $125,000 and couples exceeding $250,000 annually—and also on businesses which have until now enjoyed "one of the lowest corporate tax rates in the nation."

The $1 billion in increased revenues will go toward public education and social services, averting significant cuts which would have been made worse by the loss of approximately $250 million in matching funds from the federal government.

Charles Sheketoff, executive director of the Oregon Center for Public Policy (OCPP), told the *New York Times* this was a victory for "true populism" and that conservatives and Tea Partiers had "tried to hijack the term."

Indeed, this victory was won through the hard organizing work of teachers and public employees unions, and the crafting of a smart tax proposal. The campaign wasn't about class warfare or taking on the banks as evil beasts (though there's nothing wrong with that!); it was about progressive taxation, an art form in economic policy that has somehow been lost over these many decades. It's worth remembering that under President Eisenhower, the top marginal tax rate was over 90 percent.

The Oregon campaign was based on the notion of shared prosperity and common sense—that people who are more affluent can pay a little more for services that they too benefit from—especially in these tough times. To take a line from President Obama's State of the Union address, "Let's try common sense. A novel concept."

Steve Robinson, senior policy analyst at OCPP, honed in on the broad appeal of the campaign.

"The lesson here is if you want funding to keep schools open, care for seniors, and other vital services, ask who is in the best position to help with that project?" Robinson told me. "People who are doing just fine, making over a quarter-million dollars a year even in the recession. The state is just taxing 1.8 percent of whatever is earned over that threshold. Oregonians also said that isn't appropriate for corporations to pay just $10 a year in income taxes. We need to look at who can afford to help in difficult times."

Doug Hall, director of the Economic Analysis and Research Network at EPI, spoke of another key reason to celebrate this victory. "This was achieved through ballot measures," he said. "The people had an opportunity to weigh the relative merits of draconian budget cuts versus strategic revenue increases, and they have decided to support the revenue increases. I think that sends a powerful message to the rest of the country and it's a message that we hope other states hear as well. Pretty much all states are struggling with significant revenue shortfalls. And enacting high-end income tax increases is actually the least harmful way to close those revenue gaps."

Hall said budget cuts "not only hurt vulnerable populations" but it's like "slitting their own throat in terms of the state economy's ability to recover," since states aren't permitted to run deficits in order to grow the economy.

Oregon got it right with its appeal to common sense and fairness, and crafting a progressive tax policy. Twenty-nine states have now passed tax and fee increases totaling $24 billion this fiscal year, up from $1.5 billion a year earlier. Here's hoping this latest victory is a sign of more budget sanity to come.

---

# Supreme Power
## *March 12, 2010*

The *Citizens United* campaign finance decision by the Court's conservative judicial activists is a dramatic assault on American

democracy and a real threat to the prospects of an Obama reform presidency.

Tensions between the Court and the administration rose
even higher last week, when Chief Justice John Roberts criticized
President Obama for expressing his disagreement with the *Citizens United* decision during the State of the Union address.
Roberts called Obama's comments "very troubling."

"What is troubling is that this decision opened the floodgates
for corporations and special interests to pour money into elections—drowning out the voices of average Americans," White
House Press Secretary Robert Gibbs shot back.

And when those voices are drowned out, the ability to move
economic, political and social reform legislation becomes even
more difficult, especially in the face of already too powerful
corporate lobbies that keep campaign coffers flush with cash.

The Court and the administration's fundamentally different
visions for the country are reminiscent—though far less dramatic at this stage—of the conflict between FDR and the
Supreme Court as he worked to save the nation from its last
great economic crisis. So much of the commentary pro- and
con-Roberts' challenge to Obama is on whether he's a "crybaby,"
or whether Supreme Court justices should attend the State of
the Union. These arguments ignore the deeper, historic conflicts
between the two branches of government, especially with reform
presidencies.

That makes a new book by author Jeff Shesol all the more
important and timely. *Supreme Power* describes the conservative
assault on FDR and the New Deal, and how right-wing hopes
came to rest on an activist obstructionist Supreme Court—a
narrow but determined majority that struck down the central
pillars of Roosevelt's reform agenda.

In an April 2002 speech to the Century Association, my father, William vanden Heuvel, founder and Chair Emeritus of

the Franklin and Eleanor Roosevelt Institute, described just how far the Supreme Court reached in its effort to thwart Roosevelt.

"The anti–New Deal forces literally started thousands of legal actions to stop the fulfillment of programs which the president had initiated, that Congress had legislated, and the people in landslide elections had approved," he said.

The Supreme Court invalidated the Railroad Retirement Act, the National Recovery Act, and Mortgage Moratorium legislation. In 1936, it ruled the Agricultural Adjustment Act unconstitutional. It overturned legislation designed to bring order and safety to the desperate coal mining industry, the Municipal Bankruptcy Act created to save local governments across the country and the New York State law establishing minimum wages, outlawing child labor and regulating the hours and labor conditions affecting women.

The Court was about to rule on the constitutionality of the Social Security Act and the Wagner Act establishing collective bargaining and protecting the right of labor to organize, and the minimum age and employment laws.

In February 1937, FDR struck back.

He proposed that when a federal judge, including those on the Supreme Court, reached the age of 70 and chose not to retire, the president could add a new Justice to the Bench. The legislation would have expanded the Court to fifteen justices, allowing FDR to appoint New Deal–friendly judges.

*The Nation* is something of a minor (and feisty) character in the book. Shesol describes how "the editors of *The Nation* refused to rule out packing the Court, 'though this strikes us as a repugnant idea.'" But what *The Nation* really wanted was a constitutional amendment to strip away the Court's power to nullify legislation.

"We must repeat with wearisome iteration, a constitutional amendment is necessary," the editors wrote.

The magazine ended up supporting Roosevelt's plan because "it will clear the blockage of New Deal legislation." Otherwise, as Thurman Arnold wrote, "the menace of the Supreme Court will continue to hang like an ominous cloud over all legal attempts to solve the social problems that are crowding upon us."

(The magazine's support for FDR's plan caused then-owner Maurice Wertheim to blow his stack and sell it off to the next editor, Freda Kirchwey, in an unusual arrangement. He demanded $30,000 or else he'd sell to the highest bidder. When Kirchwey could only come up with $15,000, he loaned her the rest. So even in his anger, Wertheim managed to uphold and support *The Nation*'s tradition of editorial freedom.)

Of course, neither of those things—FDR's Court proposal or amending the Constitution—happened.

The Court abruptly changed course in the middle of the fight—upholding the Wagner Act, Social Security legislation, and even the state minimum wage laws it had previously ruled unconstitutional—with the "switch in time that saved nine."

As *Supreme Power* describes, the switch was most likely the result of sustained political pressure from FDR and progressives. But as Shesol hastens to add, this conversation became a transformation—"the Constitutional revolution of 1937," as it is known—primarily because of the appointments Roosevelt made to the Court. By the time of his death, FDR had appointed all the justices of the Supreme Court but one.

Which brings us back to our time, and another 5–4 conservative majority that threatens to cut off avenues to economic, political and social reform.

We occasionally hear interesting ideas about Court reform, but realistically, change will come to this Court—or the federal courts generally—only through new appointments. So far, the prospects are not encouraging. During Obama's first year in office, progressives rightly lamented not only the slow pace of nominations—Obama has been far slower to fill judicial openings and reshape the federal courts than was President Bush. The opportunity to gain ground on nominations while the Democrats enjoyed a sixty-vote margin has been lost. The midterm elections may erode that margin further.

In August 1937, as Shesol recounts, FDR finally got to appoint his first Supreme Court justice: Hugo Black. *The Nation* called the choice "courageous."

What is needed today—in the face of a sustained conservative assault on the courts—is a series of appointments to the Supreme Court and the federal bench that could truly be described as "courageous." Not as "clever," in a political sense, not as "expedient," but as bold. John Paul Stevens has been such a justice— his retirement will reportedly come at the end of this term—and we will need more like him if reform is not to hit an insurmountable obstacle at the courthouse door.

George Bush pushed the courts sharply to the right, and we've seen the consequences. At the end of his first year in office, Obama has made just half of the appointments of his predecessor to the federal appeals and district courts, despite a similar number of vacancies.

It's impossible to overstate the challenges currently on the president's plate. But the *Citizens United* decision serves as a reminder of the fact that he can't lose sight of judicial appointments. President Obama must use this moment to move aggressively and boldly to restore balance and sanity to our courts.

# How to Turn Congress, Inc.
# Back to Just Congress
## *May 12, 2010*

What is the biggest scandal of 2010 so far?

Allegations of fraudulent misrepresentation from Goldman Sachs? An oil spill that poses a threat to our environment and economy for generations? Mining operators freely ignoring safety violations and treating workers as disposable?

Each of these is bad. But perhaps the biggest political scandal is the one that aids and abets these others—the pay-to-play system that buys up Congress, pollutes our political system with special-interest cash and deep-sixes the kind of bold reform agenda that we voted for and need.

The healthcare industry has contributed more than $200 million to Congressional candidates in the 2008 and 2010 election cycles, according to the Center for Responsive Politics. Is it any wonder that there was no public option in the final bill or that Medicare isn't able to negotiate lower drug prices for seniors the same way the Veterans Administration does for veterans?

Big banks and Wall Street financial firms spent more than $500 million since the beginning of 2009 on lobbying and campaign contributions, the Center reports. In just the first quarter of 2010, the finance, insurance and real estate sectors spent more than $123 million on 2,057 lobbyists. Any bets on whether the final financial reform bill will create the kind of robust, independent Consumer Financial Protection Agency that would serve as a watchdog with teeth?

Big oil and gas spent nearly $170 million lobbying in 2009—nearly $1 billion in the past twelve years—and has given more than $140 million to members of Congress in the past twenty years. Is it any surprise that we've seen so many exemptions from environmental studies for oil-exploration plans? Or that the climate bill is stalled and insufficient to confront the global warming crisis?

It is clear that the kind of strong reforms we urgently need won't be achieved simply by electing a new president or new members of Congress. Despite the voters' mandate for change, the underlying problem of Washington—what author and *Washington Post* reporter Robert Kaiser calls "so damn much money"—remains unaltered and is in many ways more powerful than ever before. In the wake of the Supreme Court's recent *Citizens United* decision—which awarded corporations the rights of citizens when it comes to electioneering, allowing them to use their coffers to manipulate political discourse—the prospect of a Congress "brought to you by (insert corporate sponsor here)" has only grown.

Americans must fight back with legislation that will help organized people defeat organized money. I'm not speaking of the Disclose Act—a good response to *Citizens United* that would make corporate campaign funding more transparent. Democratic leaders must recognize that such efforts are mere triage and fail to get to the heart of the money problem in Washington. Congress should also pass the Fair Elections Now Act.

This legislation would sever ties between big-money campaign contributors and members of Congress, who, in the Senate, must raise an average of $27,000 every week they are in office in order to run competitive races. The bill would bar participating Congressional candidates from accepting contributions larger than $100 and allow them to run honest campaigns with a blend of small donations and public matching funds.

Sponsored by Senate Majority Whip Richard Durbin and Rep. John Larson (D-Conn.), the bill has eighteen Senate co-sponsors (twelve of whom signed on since the *Citizens United* decision) and 149 bipartisan cosponsors in the House. Activists are hopeful there will be a House vote as soon as this summer, and Durbin reportedly will push for the Senate to take it up after the House does.

Fighting for this bill is good policy and good politics. A recent Greenberg/Mark McKinnon poll found that voters support the Fair Elections Now Act by a two-to-one margin, 62 percent to 31 percent. Independents support it 67 percent to 30 percent. Is there a candidate in the country who wouldn't gain votes by saying, "I want a political system in which someone who doesn't take more than $100 from anybody can run a competitive race for Congress. I want a political process that makes Congress listen to their constituents and allows them to ignore the lobbyists with fat checks in hand"?

It was a Republican president, Teddy Roosevelt, who had it right when he told Congress, "All contributions by corporations to any political committee or for any political purpose should be forbidden by law." He was so worried about the power of the trusts that he called for public financing of elections. More than 100 years later, we can take a desperately needed step to protect the public interest and clean up our politics by passing this legislation.

## A Coalition Builder's Lesson for Progressives
*July 6, 2010*

Some 500 days into the Obama administration, the White House touts passage of its economic recovery program and healthcare reform legislation and the expected approval of the financial reform bill. They are impressive accomplishments. Yet corporate lobbies and their minions in Congress significantly weakened each. Sure, we can't expect the president to fix everything in a year. But, as I've argued before, if progressives are to alter the hostile political environment that arms the lobbies and forces President Obama—and, even more, fearful centrist Democrats in Congress—to shrink from bolder reforms, they must build and mobilize a broad reform movement that transcends left-right divisions.

Now, we have a compelling blueprint of just how to do that. A new book—*The DeMarco Factor: Transforming Public Will into Political Power*—shows that that kind of organizing is no pipe dream. Written by Michael Pertschuk, former chairman of the Federal Trade Commission and co-founder of the Advocacy Institute, the book focuses on the strategies and leadership of organizer Vincent DeMarco, who has waged successful advocacy campaigns in Maryland and Congress for twenty years.

DeMarco and his allies mobilized nonpartisan advocacy coalitions outside of the usual progressive groups and scored legislative victories over such potent corporate and ideological adversaries as the National Rifle Association, the tobacco lobby and conservative opponents (including Wal-Mart) of healthcare expansion. Electing even the best-intentioned president and legislators will never be enough to achieve major policy change. DeMarco's approach demands a parallel, long-term effort to elect people based on their commitment to vote for proposed legislation. That means waging campaigns that force candidates to sign concrete pledges of support for particular bills.

This approach often requires more than one election cycle, and it means waiting to lobby legislators until after broad coalitions have been formed and all members have helped shape the legislative objective, so that their commitment is strong, deep and lasting.

DeMarco's campaigns begin with aggressive public education to raise awareness and build intense public support. "When you fight for a bill that Vinny has organized on," said Maryland Democratic Rep. Chris Van Hollen, who worked closely with DeMarco as a state senator, "you know that there is an army of voters behind you."

Consider DeMarco's successful fight against the tobacco industry. After building strong health and faith coalitions in many states for the national Campaign for Tobacco-Free Kids, he and his colleagues mobilized the national Faith United Against Tobacco coalition to press for federal legislation to give the FDA expansive powers to regulate tobacco products and their marketing—legislation that had languished for more than a decade.

The coalition spanned the religious and political spectrum, from the liberal United Methodists to the conservative Southern Baptists. And despite heavy opposition from all but one tobacco company (New York's Altria, formerly Philip Morris), it is the only major legislation on Obama's agenda that garnered close to a majority of Republican votes, even from conservative tobacco states. According to DeMarco, the critical time for achieving success is not when the legislature convenes, but when its members are most vulnerable—during the primary and general elections. For candidates, the allure of campaign money is that it funds successful elections. The only thing legislators fear more than alienating big donors is losing. Citizens maximize their electoral power by making a candidate's refusal to support proposed legislation a real threat to his or her election.

Pertschuk describes the thinking behind this tactic: "Get concrete, redeemable pledges from candidates before they are elected, and defeat even a handful of candidates who refuse to pledge, and you have erected a bulwark against the otherwise seductive pleading, lubricated by campaign contributions, of insider lobbyists."

There is no shortage of veteran community organizers who can apply their skills and strategies to DeMarco's successful template. Twenty thousand of them engaged in the Obama presidential campaign, and many are waiting for such an opportunity now. One proposal is for philanthropists interested in building a progressive infrastructure to find and fund a De-Marco-like organizer in every state. *The DeMarco Factor* is a must-read for these challenging times. It shows us how to bring people into the fold, rather than just folding.

## Chamber of Commerce Backlash
### *November 2, 2010*

Decades ago, the Chamber of Commerce enjoyed a Norman Rockwell–like image in the minds of many Americans: working in the interest of mom-and-pop stores everywhere and sponsoring community events such as Little League baseball and holiday parades.

And while there may still be some local chambers that fit that bill, this election cycle has given a much clearer picture of what the US Chamber of Commerce is all about—except when it comes to lobbying to make their healthcare more expensive, privatize their Social Security and outsource their jobs.

The US Chamber stated that its goal has been to spend $75 million on a midterm election that will break fundraising records. Its war chest is devoted almost entirely to defeating Democrats who take on big corporate interests. While Chamber President and Chief Executive Tom Donohue would have Americans believe that his organization is still working in the interest of small and mid-sized businesses, that's simply not true. In 2008, a third of its income came from just nineteen members—big companies to whom the Chamber is beholden. That probably explains why only 249 of 7,000 local chambers are now members, and why more and more are dropping out.

Just days after the Supreme Court's *Citizens United* decision opened the floodgates for corporations to spend on electioneering, Donohue announced a budget of $40 million for "the most aggressive voter-education and issue-advocacy effort in our nearly hundred-year history." That budget quickly ballooned to $75 million as the money rolled in from undisclosed foreign and national corporate interests. It's the perfect stealth arrangement for members—they remain anonymous while the chamber does the dirty work to take down the candidates and policies they oppose.

In what historian Tony Judt described as "the age of forgetting," it's important to track the historical evolution of the US Chamber's power and politics. In 1971, corporate lawyer and future Supreme Court Justice Lewis Powell—a board member of Philip Morris and its defender against health charges—wrote to the chamber board what is now known as "the Powell Memo." Serving as a corporate Paul Revere, Powell sounded the alarm on the threat posed to capitalism and corporate power by consumer rights crusader Ralph Nader, an emerging Beltway public interest community and its Democratic Party allies.

Powell—who would be appointed to the Court just two months after the memo—urged the Chamber to rally against these new corporate watchdogs. "Political power is necessary," he wrote, and "when necessary, it must be used aggressively and with determination. . . . The Chamber [should] consider assuming a broader and more vigorous role in the political arena."

In the decades since, and most brazenly in this election, the Chamber has emerged as a 1,000-pound gorilla of corporate political revanchism, fighting for Big Tobacco, Energy and Finance.

Now, with a new deluge of well-organized corporate money polluting our campaign finance system, perhaps the best antidote to the chamber's reactionary agenda is organized people—including organized business people.

Take, for example, the American Sustainable Business Council (ASBC), a recently formed group that has received far too little mainstream media attention. The ASBC already has a network of twenty-four business organizations representing 60,000 businesses and more than 150,000 entrepreneurs, owners, executive, investors, business professionals and individuals from diverse regions and sectors. Its member organizations include the South Carolina Small Business Chamber of Commerce, the National Latino Farmers & Ranchers Trade Association, the Manhattan Chamber of Commerce and the Association for Enterprise Opportunity.

Executive Director David Levine said that the ASBC was founded because of the tremendous growth in the number of businesses that believe in pursuing "the triple bottom line"—practicing social and environmental responsibility, as well as creating profitable businesses.

"The piece that was missing is that they weren't necessarily engaged in policy," says Levine.

Too often, the US Chamber position is accepted as the single business voice. "So," as Levine argues, "sound policies—especially those bringing financial, social, or environmental benefits—haven't been implemented because the policy dialogue in this country gets cut short because at the end of the sentence is 'it's bad for business.' Bad for whose business? Bad for business in which greed becomes the overarching goal at the expense of everything else. We're really offering the media and legislators an opportunity to engage in dialogue with forward-thinking business leaders."

Recently, the ASBC partnered with the Investor Environmental Health Network to send a letter to Congress urging support for reform of the Toxic Substance Control Act. It was signed by investors with $35 billion—not chump change—in assets under management. ASBC has also taken progressive positions on public financing of elections, the Bush tax cuts, offshore tax havens, and climate and energy policies.

In the wake of the *Citizens United* decision, polls showed majorities—across our fractured political spectrum—anxious about overweening corporate power. Given the US Chamber's recent spending spree and the regressive policies it has sought to advance, those fears seem more than justified.

If we're to successfully challenge unbridled corporate power, new and unlikely coalitions will be needed—including partnering with an enlightened business community.

---

## Filibuster Reform at Last?

*December 28, 2010*

As the lame-duck session drew to a close, progressives were reminded of the capacity of Congress to accomplish important things but also of what we are giving up as a new session begins. In the House, Democrats have lost their majority and will be dealing with the possibility of John Boehner and Eric Cantor wielding their new power to do real harm and undo real progress. In the Senate, Democrats will maintain their majority, though that may be little consolation. With a loss of five Democratic Senate seats, the caucus finds itself seven votes—and many miles—away from the ability to stop the filibuster.

Considering the damage the filibuster has done over the past two years, our new circumstances are, indeed, distressing. Back when Lyndon Johnson was majority leader in the Senate, he needed to file for cloture to end a filibuster only once. During President Obama's first two years, Harry Reid filed for cloture eighty-four times. To put that in perspective, the filibuster was used more in 2009 than in the 1950s and 1960s combined.

Even as we acknowledge the progress we've made these past two years, we must never forget the policies that lie dead on the Senate floor at the hands of the filibuster. We got a Recovery Act, but a filibuster prevented it from being sufficiently large. We got healthcare reform, but a filibuster killed the public option. We got Wall Street reform, but a filibuster killed provisions to break up the big banks. We got an extension of unemployment benefits, a payroll tax cut and more, but the threat of the filibuster killed our chances to do that without giving handouts to the wealthy.

That is an impressive, albeit decidedly mixed, record of two years when Democrats held fifty-eight to sixty Senate seats. Undoubtedly, in the years when they have only fifty-three seats, the record will be bleak.

That is, unless we reform this outdated and anachronistic tool. The filibuster was never intended to be wielded as a weapon of obstruction. Its current abuse was not contemplated by those who created it. Used this way, the filibuster does not just check the power of the majority; it cripples it. It is the very definition of minority tyranny, a concept as antithetical to democratic principles as any in the republic.

There is only one day in the year when the Senate can make changes to its rules without the fear of that process itself being filibustered—and that day is fast approaching. Jan. 5, 2011, will be the first day of the 112th Congress and, as such, the only day where a simple majority can vote to change the Senate rules (on all other days, sixty-seven votes would be required).

Some of the most junior members of the US Senate have expressed frustration and, at times, outrage (rightly so) over the use of the filibuster and the rigging of the rules. Democratic Sens. Jeff Merkley (Ore.), Tom Udall (N.M.), Claire McCaskill (Mo.) and Michael Bennet (Colo.) have spent much of their time drumming up support for reform, not just of the filibuster itself but of the procedures that allow it to eat up valuable floor time. They have faced pushback from more veteran senators, such as Chris Dodd (D-Conn.), who, having become accustomed to the Senate rules, are averse to change. Other veterans, however, including Sen. Tom Harkin (D-Iowa), joined forces with the freshmen.

The options they offer are simple and unquestionably reasonable. Sens. Udall and Merkley have put forward what has become known as the "constitutional option," a basic two-step process in which fifty-one senators first agree to adopt new rules, and then fifty-one senators agree on a reform package. Their package probably would not end the filibuster altogether. But it wouldn't need to. Procedural changes—such as preventing a filibuster on the motion to proceed, shortening the amount of debate allowed between cloture motions and ending the unconscionable practice of anonymous holds—have the potential to remake the Senate.

These reforms would prevent a single senator from wielding the filibuster against the entire body and would allow the majority to challenge the minority without wasting precious floor time. Perhaps most important, the act of revising the rules in response to abuse may in itself serve as a check on the minority, a warning that the overreach of the type the GOP perfected during the 111th Congress will not be tolerated in the future.

Until recently, the biggest challenge to reform appeared to be getting a majority to agree to take action on Jan. 5. But now, thanks in large part to a grassroots movement, the chances for reforming the filibuster may be the best in a generation. For the past several months, a coalition of labor unions and progressive organizations have pressured Congress to take action, launching a website called Fix the Senate Now and drumming up support among progressives. Those efforts helped reformers in the Senate gain momentum, culminating in a letter to Harry

Reid that called for reform and that was signed—amazingly—
by every returning Democratic senator.

We may be about to witness history as a result of the efforts
of this dedicated coalition and a group of freshman senators
who refused to accept the outdated rules of the establishment.
Democracy may be restored to a long-broken institution, with
the paralysis of obstruction becoming a thing of the past.

# Reversing *Citizens United*
## *January 18, 2011*

It will be a year this week since Chief Justice John Roberts and
his conservative activist colleagues on the Supreme Court joined
together in a dramatic assault on American democracy. Their
decision in the *Citizens United* case overturned more than a century's worth of precedent by awarding corporations the rights
of citizens with regard to electioneering. The Court did away
with limits on when corporations can spend on elections, how
much they can spend and how they can spend their money, allowing unlimited contributions from corporate treasuries to
flood the electoral landscape.

As *The Nation* noted in the days after the case was decided,
"This decision tips the balance against active citizenship and
the rule of law by making it possible for the nation's most powerful economic interests to manipulate not just individual politicians and electoral contests but political discourse itself."

According to Bill de Blasio, New York City's public advocate,
*Citizens United* spending—that is, spending that was only made
possible by the Court's ruling—accounted for 15 percent of the
roughly $4 billion spent on the 2010 midterm elections. Eighty-

five million dollars of *Citizens United* money was spent on US Senate races alone. Worse, 30 percent of all spending by outside groups was funded by anonymous donations, an illegal action prior to the ruling. Forty million of the dollars spent on Senate races came from sources that might never be revealed.

But as striking as these consequences might be, the 2010 election was just an experiment, the first opportunity to test the new law. In future elections, corporations and shadowy organizations will have a clearer understanding of the boundaries they are operating within, a reality that is sure to translate into more undisclosed cash. And the savvier corporate players know that the mere threat of a corporate onslaught of funding for or against a candidate is enough to win legislative favor, in effect blunting prospects for sound regulation, consumer protection and fair tax policies. As former Senator Russ Feingold (D-Wis.), himself a victim of *Citizens United* spending, said, "It is going to be worse in 2012 unless we do something much worse."

Yet even as we lament this decision, we should recognize the opportunity it presents. Justice Roberts and his allies overreached so brazenly that they have created an opening for genuine reform.

There are multiple steps that can be taken, both short term and long term, to roll back the corrosive impact not just of *Citizens United* but of preceding campaign finance cases and statutes that already had flooded the electoral landscape with special-interest spending. At the more modest end of the spectrum is the option of reviving the Disclose Act or introducing similar legislation that would require corporations to show how they spend money on elections and provide disincentives to spending it. This would be a good step, but it is mere triage; if not accompanied by a broader push for a bolder set of reforms, its success would do little to curb the corporate takeover of American elections.

One potential policy change that could accompany greater disclosure would be the introduction of a public financing system, which would empower small donors. Legislation has already been introduced in Congress—the Fair Elections Now Act, which has more than 160 supporters in the House. A similar system has been adopted in Arizona, and in 2007, New York City adopted an intriguing mechanism of public finance in which the city matches small donations at a six-to-one ratio, boosting grassroots fundraising.

The result? According to the *New York Times*, the changes "drastically curtailed the role of businesses, political committees and lobbyists in campaigns" and, importantly, "caused a major drop in donations from those doing business with the city." Such a system, implemented on the national level, could greatly increase the influence of average citizens. In the post–*Citizens United* era, there are already efforts afoot to weaken such systems. In Arizona, for example, the Chamber of Commerce is working aggressively to overturn the state's clean-money legislation. A push for national public financing, then, must be accompanied by a strong defense of those systems already in place.

The clearest and boldest counter to the court's ruling would be a constitutional amendment stating unequivocally that corporations are not people and do not have the right to buy elections. Rep. Donna Edwards (D-Md.) introduced such an amendment to counter *Citizens United* during the last session of Congress and views it as the only sure way to beat back the Court. "Justice Brandeis got it right," she noted last February. "'We can have democracy in this country, or we can have great wealth concentrated in the hands of a few, but we can't have both.'"

Campaigns for constitutional amendments demand a great deal of patience and tenacity. But as Jamie Raskin, a Democratic Maryland state senator and professor of constitutional law at American University, notes, "American citizens have repeatedly amended the Constitution to defend democracy when the Supreme Court acts in collusion with democracy's enemies."

Not only is a push for an amendment a worthy act, it also provides a unique opportunity to educate the broader public, raise the profile of this important issue and force elected officials to go on record as to where they stand. The campaign could create enormous pressure on state legislatures and Congress, prompting changes to campaign finance even before an amendment is ratified.

Success will require a coalition that transcends party. In this case, there is promising news. An August 2010 Survey USA poll found that 77 percent of all voters—including 70 percent of Republicans and 73 percent of independents—view corporate spending in elections as akin to bribery. Broad majorities favor limiting corporate control over our political lives. A coordinated effort, executed right, could unite progressives, good-government reformers and conservative libertarians in a fight to restore democracy.

The multitude of reform groups working to build a more just and democratic political system understand that if this issue is to grip people's imaginations, it must be about more than process. In a nation where recovery still feels like recession, the suffocating grip of corporate money is anything but abstract. Mobilizing the American people to make reform a priority will demand making the clearest possible link between the rise of corporate power and the challenges of everyday lives.

That's not a tough pitch.

In just the past two years, corporate money can be blamed for watering down consumer protections and diluting healthcare and financial reform. In truth, there is almost no conversation we have in American politics in which corporations don't occupy all the seats at the table. As Sen. Dick Durbin (D-Ill.) acknowledged while talking about big banks during last year's financial reform debate: "They frankly own the place."

Changing that dynamic might well be the central challenge of this generation. Reversing *Citizens United* is about more than any one issue or court case—it is, at its base, a question of whether American democracy itself can beat back a corporate takeover, whether our most cherished principles of self-government can ultimately prevail.

# A Time for Resistance
## *February 17, 2011*

A friend e-mailed me this morning, "Do you think events taking place in Wisconsin might be as important as what's happening in Cairo, if the media really got the word out? Might it be the spark to halt the Tea Party Express?" Another friend e-mailed, "It's possible that this labor strike in Wisconsin could become our Uncut." (In response to Britain's draconian public spending cuts, citizens there formed UK Uncut, a Twitter-organized movement, to protest wealthy tax evaders. If the rich paid for their fair share of taxes, the movement argues, the pressure on the state budget would diminish or disappear.)

Wisconsin's Republican governor and Republican-dominated legislature are moving to destroy organized labor, moving to abolish democratic rights that were the essence of the New Deal, and treating working-class Americans as though they were meaningless in our country's mosaic. Meanwhile, those who are responsible for the catastrophic financial crisis are riding high—and in the name of deficits they largely caused, they insist that those who worked a lifetime to build and own their homes, to send their children to public schools, to have security in their retirement years, to have decent medical care—that those citizens should pay the price for budgetary crises in honor, dignity and decency.

There are some who still respect the contributions of working people: Contrast what Governor Walker is doing in Wisconsin with the constructive steps the new Democratic governor of Connecticut, Dannel Malloy, is taking to address the same problems. But there are too many cheerleaders for fiscal austerity roaming our political landscape, abetted by a mindless mainstream media's suffocating consensus.

However, as the events in Cairo, and now Wisconsin, show us, this is a moment of extraordinary possibility. It is a time for global, nonviolent challenge to anti-democratic forces, wherever they may be—forces that have enriched themselves while promising stability based on coercion, suppression of rights and profound corruption.

This remarkable moment is captured in a small book by Stéphane Hessel, a 93-year-old distinguished French diplomat, leader of the Resistance, survivor of Nazi concentration camps and drafter of the UN's Universal Declaration of Human Rights.

Published last October in France, Hessel's *Indignez-Vous!* (which could be translated as *Get Angry!* or—my preference—*Time for Outrage!*) and its message of resistance and nonviolence became a publishing phenomenon—unexpectedly reaching the top of France's bestseller list and selling close to 2 million copies.

We are proudly publishing Hessel's 4,000-word manifesto in the next issue of *The Nation.*

*Time for Outrage!* forces us to ask how we can look at today's trends and not be angry. Hessel calls on the young, in France and around the world, to engage actively in defense of human and economic rights. His fervent advocacy of nonviolent activism captures the spirit of the revolutions in Tunisia and Cairo. It has also moved women marching in Italy to protest Silvio Berlusconi's barbarism to display the book's title on placards. It is a spirit that now animates brave and defiant workers, students and their allies all over the world.

In rousing language, Hessel reminds us:

The motivation that underlay the Resistance was outrage. We, the veterans of the Resistance movements and the fighting forces of Free France, call on the younger generations to revive and carry forward the tradition of the Resistance and its ideas. We say to you: take over, keep going, get angry! Those in positions of political responsibility, economic power and intellectual authority, in fact our whole society, must not give up or let ourselves be overwhelmed by the current international dictatorship of the financial markets, which is such a threat to peace and democracy.

There is a new spark in the world and in our country—lit by citizens of conscience resisting forces that would trample economic justice, decency and dignity.

"To you who will create the twenty-first century, we say, from the bottom of our hearts,
TO CREATE IS TO RESIST.
TO RESIST IS TO CREATE."
—*Stéphane Hessel, October 2010*

# Let's End the Secret Money Arms Race
## *May 15, 2011*

The post–*Citizens United* drive for secret money is now a veritable arms race.

As a *New York Times* editorial recently noted, Bill Burton, former White House deputy press secretary, is leading a group called Priorities USA to "raise unlimited money from undisclosed sources to aid in the president's re-election campaign."

While I'm sympathetic to the notion that Democrats cannot afford to cede ground in these exorbitant, no-holds-barred campaigns—as one colleague put it, "You don't fight with one hand tied behind your back"—this isn't news to be welcomed by pro-democracy reformers. By accepting the same opaque money they are arguing against, the Democrats' case for campaign finance reform becomes morally ambiguous at best.

Instead, Democrats could use this moment to seize the overwhelming bipartisan sentiment across this country that we need to curb the influence of money in our elections—even 62 percent of Republican voters and 60 percent of Tea Partiers agree!

Democrats are already on record—unlike nearly every Republican—to make campaigns cleaner and more democratic. Whether supporting the DISCLOSE Act, Fair Elections Now Act or state clean election laws, Democrats have demonstrated their commitment in rhetoric and votes. Some are even speaking out for a constitutional amendment to overturn the *Citizens United* decision granting corporations the "right" to spend unlimited money influencing elections.

Yet leadership on public financing and clean elections needs to begin at the top. President Obama's rhetoric has been tremendous on occasion—his campaign language, response to the *Citizens United* decision, statements on the DISCLOSE Act—but he could also do more to forcibly push for the Fair Elections Now Act, a presidential public financing fix and passing the DISCLOSE Act, which was defeated by a Republican filibuster.

He could immediately draw a stark contrast between the parties by signing his draft executive order requiring any company vying for a government contract to disclose details of its political giving. Not surprisingly, the GOP and its gravy train (aka Chamber of Commerce) have already gone bonkers over this little bit of sunlight, calling it "pay-to-play" politics, according to the *Baltimore Sun*. Seriously, let's keep those political gifts in the dark, that way everyone will know that corporations aren't receiving any favors in return. Say what?

This represents a canyon-wide opening for President Obama to drive home his original campaign message—remember that one—about changing the culture of Washington. Indeed, the need and political opportunity for all Democrats to step up couldn't be clearer.

Across the nation, conservative courts, Republican legislatures, and corporate front groups are attempting to reverse hard-fought pro-democracy gains. In Arizona, GOP legislative leaders and the Chamber of Commerce are pressing for a repeal of that state's effective clean elections law, despite the fact that 79 percent of Arizonans support it. In Maine, Republican Governor Paul LePage has gone after his state's clean election law—attempting to defund it, repeal its use in gubernatorial races and more than tripling the private contribution limit for gubernatorial candidates. (Here's hoping the 80 percent of Mainers who support the law have the last word.)

"The bottom line is that people want a political system that is responsive to their needs," says Nick Nyhart, president and CEO of Public Campaign. "Elected officials who stand in the way of that could pay a price down the line."

The fight for campaign finance reform can't be separated from the fight to preserve collective bargaining rights, prevent restrictive voter ID laws and protect an already tattered safety net from an onslaught of pro-rich/anti-everyone else budgets. These fights are all about power and voice in our democracy.

"Our country's biggest problems won't be solved for the many if the process is fixed by the money," says Nyhart.

Instead of traveling down the worn path of pay-to-play politics with Republicans, Democrats—led by President Obama—should double-down on the high road. Most Americans are already there waiting for them.

*Part VII*

REFLECTIONS

# Address to the Return to Chicago Rally
## Chicago, July 1996

Good afternoon. It's nice to see you all here today. I think one of the most valuable legacies of the 1960s was the idea of combining politics with celebration. And at the opening of a week of nothing but politics, it's nice to have this celebration.

We're also here to commemorate 1968. Unfortunately, I was not in Chicago then. I would have liked to have been there, but at the time I was 9 years old. And, like so many 9-year-olds of my generation, I was still living at home.

But *The Nation*, which is the magazine that I have had the privilege of editing for the past two years, was the ripe old age of 103 in 1968. And in that year's upheavals, it was decidedly on the front lines. During the 1960s, *The Nation* strove—as it has throughout history—to be an independent voice of conscience, an energetic and unflinching challenger of the status quo.

On what was then the paramount issue of the day, the Vietnam War, *The Nation* and its contributors spoke out early and often. Senator Ernest Gruening, a longtime *Nation* editor and associate, was one of only two senators to vote against the fateful Gulf of Tonkin resolution. And Dr. Martin Luther King Jr., who was a regular contributor to *The Nation*, made his first public speech opposing the war at a *Nation* conference in Los Angeles in January 1967. I'd like to quote a few lines from that speech, not only because Dr. King's words are so eloquent, but because they have a particular resonance even today:

> We cannot remain silent as our nation engages in one of history's most cruel and senseless wars. America must continue to have, during these days of human travail, a company of

creative dissenters. We need them because the thunder of their fearless voices will be the only sound stronger than the blasts of bombs and the clamor of war hysteria.

Today, thirty years later, the bombs in Vietnam have been silent for quite some time. Yet, unfortunately, it seems, so have we. The Vietnam War, in all its brutal horror, was a galvanizing force for the left. Since then, the strength that we achieved in our unity has largely dissipated. Yet we need that strength now more than ever, because while the challenges we face today are very different from those of 1968, they are no less grave.

As we gather here today in the shadow of another Democratic convention, it's worth remembering our collective duty to replenish the ranks of that company of creative dissenters that Dr. King summoned to action three decades ago.

Because in 1996, young Americans are not dying by the thousands in a war fought in the jungles of Southeast Asia. They are dying right here at home, in the streets of South Central Los Angeles, on the South Side of Chicago, and in the South Bronx. It is a war that rages every day in neighborhoods all over America, but because our freeways do not pass through and our television crews refuse to enter these war-ravaged neighborhoods, we are free to ignore the crisis even as it simmers to a boil.

The casualties in this war are even more numerous than those in Vietnam. And most of them, tragically, are children. Yet at a time when these children cry out for our help as never before, our government has elected to turn its back. It seems that moral imperatives and plain common sense have run headlong into craven political expediency.

The welfare reform bill recently passed by Congress and signed by President Clinton is not merely a step in the wrong direction—it is a moral and political failure.

Yet the conventional wisdom applauds it. And why? Because for too long, we on the left were too quiet in the face of relentless propagandizing by the Social Darwinists of the right. We allowed them to define the terms of the debate, and after sixteen years of scapegoating and demagoguery that began with Ronald Reagan's cruel and utterly false caricature of the welfare queen who drives a Cadillac, we have reached a point where a member of Congress can stand on the floor of the House of Representatives and, in urging the repeal of welfare, hold up a sign that says, "Don't feed the alligators."

The dehumanization of the poorest and most disadvantaged members of society would have been unthinkable twenty years ago. Yet the unthinkable has now become the status quo. And it is time once again to challenge the status quo.

This is not an easy task because American politics—more so now than at any point in our recent history—is driven not by conviction but by cash. Can anyone deny that the influence of money in the political process is worse than ever? In an age of widespread disgust with politics as usual, how do we explain the fact that men like Ross Perot and Steve Forbes can make themselves heard, while the Ralph Naders of the world toil in obscurity—how do we explain this, except through a direct comparison of their bank accounts?

I don't mean to stand here and tell you that the sky is falling. In many ways, let's face it, it's already lying around our ankles. But the job of putting it up again is not an impossible one.

There are those on the left who would seek to blame our current predicament on the combined efforts of big business and a zealous right-wing minority which appropriates the name of Christ in the service of political ends that bear little resemblance to Christianity as we know it.

But our problem is not so much a zealous minority as it is a quiescent majority, put off by what it sees as the futility of conventional politics and so weary from the ever more difficult effort to put food on the table that it has given up on politics as a means of solving its problems.

One of our greatest concerns at *The Nation* is how to revitalize this majority, to win it over to the cause of a spirited and energetic progressivism. And we believe that the majority of Americans are our natural allies, for what we seek is an America in which the rising tide of economic progress lifts all of our boats, not just those of the 20 percent in the top income bracket.

We have an opportunity here today to provide a spirited, impassioned alternative to the lifeless and pre-scripted proceedings that will take place this week inside the Convention Hall. But to truly succeed—to once again change the political direction of the country—we must be willing to fight long and hard, to have the courage of our convictions in confronting our party's and our nation's shameful accommodation to the agenda of a well-endowed corporate minority.

My colleagues and I at *The Nation* will continue to fight the good fight. For 121 years, our magazine has been known for two things. The first is its steadfast willingness to speak truth to power. The second is its inability to turn a profit. We are convinced the two are related. And while we have high hopes of reversing the latter, we will never do so at the expense of the former.

We will attempt, to the best of our ability, to remain faithful to Dr. King's call for a company of creative dissenters. And we hope that you will join us in that task, because unless we rediscover our common voice in numbers sufficient to make a difference, the America we leave our children will be a far less hospitable place than the America we inherited. Thank you.

# On Political Alternatives
## *November 19, 2002*

When people receive an award, they always begin by saying it is a special honor. In my case, tonight, it truly is a special honor to receive an award from President Mikhail Gorbachev. I've known President Gorbachev for many years (as he has said). What he didn't say is that I have long had a deep admiration for him both as an individual and as a political leader who used his great power so courageously to change his country and the world. And now he has set a precedent for future Russian leaders by using his post-presidency to continue to work for a safer and more just world.

This award is a special honor for me also because my life has been so closely connected to Russia for nearly twenty-five years. In particular, with my husband, Stephen Cohen, I had the extraordinary opportunity to be present in Moscow for many months during the six and a half years of Perestroika, as President Gorbachev called his reforms. And I should say, because she is here tonight, our 11-year-old daughter, Nika, is a Perestroika baby. She was conceived in Russia during the Gorbachev years, made her first visit to Moscow in 1991 at the age of two months, and since then has been back to Russia some thirty more times.

Thinking about the Gorbachev years and about *The Nation* magazine, which I have edited since 1995, I certainly see parallels between the magazine's political philosophy and the ideas and policies advocated by President Gorbachev—what he often called "new thinking."

Historians will debate the significance of President Gorbachev's role in history for many decades to come.

But certain things about his leadership are beyond dispute. Over the years, President Gorbachev has often said, usually referring to himself, that all great reform ideas and movements begin as heresy and as a minority. Much as Gorbachev was seen as a heretical leader in his own country, *The Nation* magazine is often accused of heresy for its espousal of unconventional, unorthodox ideas and policies, and much as President Gorbachev took pride in being called heretical, we at *The Nation* also consider charges of heresy to be confirmation of (what we see as) the magazine's essential role in American political life. From the time *The Nation* was founded by abolitionists in 1865, to our current editorial opposition to a reckless and unnecessary war against Iraq, the magazine has tried, week in and week out, to challenge the prevailing orthodoxy and narrow consensus of our public debate by bringing minority ideas into the mainstream of American political life.

I see another parallel between President Gorbachev's "new thinking" and *The Nation* magazine. From the moment he came to power, he insisted that there are always alternatives in history and politics . . . alternatives that are better than the status quo. It was this conviction, I think, that moved President Gorbachev to fight for fundamental changes at home and in the world. As you in the room know, his leadership and the changes they produced transformed the idea of alternatives into real opportunities for all of us to escape the Cold War and its arms race. (Whether those opportunities have been used wisely or not is another matter.)

We at *The Nation* and I as the editor also believe that there are alternative ideas and policies that would make our country and the world more humane, just and secure.

*The Nation* magazine is being honored here tonight for its coverage of the nuclear danger. And this too is a very special honor. Because President Gorbachev was the most radical and committed arms reductionist ever to lead a nuclear country. As a visionary leader, he was willing to move in the direction of an actual abolition of nuclear weapons.

Here I must pay special tribute to *The Nation's*—and the nation's—leading writer and thinker about nuclear issues, Jonathan Schell. Jonathan has commanded an even wider audience since September 11—but long before that, he was America's most eloquent and forceful voice both on the nuclear dangers we face and the necessity of nuclear abolition. His influence is felt across the country, even in certain offices of those few bold members of Congress, as Congressman Kucinich, who is here with us tonight, can testify to.

I want to end by saying that while most people still insist that the abolition of nuclear weapons is an unachievable and therefore utopian goal, I would echo a principle stated many times by President Gorbachev over the years: if we don't attempt what seems impossible, we will risk facing the unthinkable.

In short, this honor encourages *The Nation*, and me personally, to do what we have always done: to struggle to transform the political heresies of a minority into the movement of a majority and to transform the political alternatives we propose into the new American realities at home and abroad.

Once again, on behalf of *The Nation* and myself, I thank President Gorbachev and Global Green USA for this special honor.

# Remembering Studs Terkel
## *December 7, 2008*

"You're Peachy," Studs would bellow through the phone. I loved it when Studs called me that, who else would have? He'd also tell me, "You're swell and nifty" and he'd ask, "Whatever happened

to those incomparable adjectives?" I never had a good answer . . .
they sure seemed alive to me if Studs used them. He'd always
tell me to "pass those feelings on to your mother—who's probably too young to remember the adjectives, though she deserves
them too."

My mother, by the way, considers herself a minor disciple of
Studs. She's tried her hand at oral history. *Edie* was one of her
books. I think there was one day when she and Studs met up—
she wanted to interview him—but the grandmaster of oral historians had come equipped and he pulled out his taping
equipment. After all, as he liked to say, "I tape, therefore I am,"
and he'd add, "only one other man has used the tape recorder
with as much fervor as I—Richard Nixon!" Well, in my mother
he met someone with about as much fervor for taping as Richard
Nixon. So they sat for a while—like friendly cowboys in a high-
noon standoff, two people so used to listening, getting stories
out of people who didn't even know they had stories to tell.
And I think, after a bit, Studs decided the hell with this, I'll just
start talking. And a great interview he was.

One of my proudest and happiest moments as editor was
when, with a measure of trepidation and some chutzpahmoxie,
I called Studs to ask if he—at age 92—would write a tribute to
his friend Pete Seeger, who was about to turn 85. And he happily
agreed.

I had seen Pete and Studs together just a couple years earlier . . . at FDR's stomping grounds, Hyde Park. That November,
Studs was getting the Four Freedoms Award. Studs loved FDR
and the New Deal way before it got fashionable like it is today—
after all, Studs worked for the WPA's federal writers' project,
and when FDR died, Studs remembered "leaning on a lamppost
and weeping." So, Studs was at Hyde Park to get a Four Freedoms Award . . . and while his award was for freedom of speech,
he could have qualified for any one those four freedoms.

Studs regaled people that afternoon—Senator Robert Byrd, Dolores Huerta, Senator George Mitchell, Anne Roosevelt—with tales of how he had imagined arriving at Hyde Park and asking FDR, "Mr. President, could you fix me one of your superb martinis?" And Studs and Pete took special delight in being there that November day because it just happened to coincide with the dedication of the Henry Wallace Visitors Center spitting distance from the FDR library. Studs had worked for and voted for Wallace in '48.

So, fast forward, happily. Two years later, Studs agreed to write a tribute to his friend Pete Seeger, and I quote from his wonderful piece because it's as much about Studs as it is about Pete:

> It is hard to think of Pete Seeger as an elderly gaffer, because the boy in him, the light, remains undimmed . . . the night when I first encountered the four wandering minstrels of the almanac singers was a cold Chicago beauty. At 2 in the morning, my wife heard the doorbell ring. I was away rehearsing the first play in which I had ever appeared. It was waiting for lefty, of course. There, at the door, were the four of them. The first was a bantam—freckled, red-haired and elfin. He handed my wife a note saying: "these are good fellas. Put them up for the night." Putting them up was a rough assignment, even for a depression-era social worker, what with the only spare bunk being a murphy bed that sprang from the walls. Freckles announced himself as Woody Guthrie. The second was an Ozark mountain man named Lee Hayes. The third was a writer, Millard Lampell. The fourth, somewhat diffident, more in the background, was a slim-jaw of 20 or so, fretting around with his banjo. He was Pete Seeger.

And Studs closed, "Hail Pete, at 86, still the boy with that touch of hope in the midst of bleakness."

That was Studs. A touch of hope amidst bleakness . . .

A hopemonger, and for someone who lived through so many -isms, if he had an -ism, his was underdogism or joyism or to be grand-leftie humanism.

And all the while, with tape recorder in one hand, martini in another, Studs stood for the radical idea of the long memory. How could he not—vigilant optimist that he was—for a man who was born the year Jack Johnson was denied passage on the Titanic and who lived to see an African American from his beloved Chicago on the verge of the presidency?

Last time I spoke to Studs it was in July and it was to ask if he'd sign our open letter to Obama—holding the candidate to his promises and possibilities. "Sure," Studs said, "sign me up . . . but he needs to counterpunch," Studs bellowed through the phone. Remember his roots as a community organizer. Studs especially wanted to make sure that Obama was moved to launch a new New Deal.

As Studs said of Pete Seeger, I say of Studs.

"There ain't no one like him." Loved the man. He was peachy.

# Remarks to the 28th Annual Bill of Rights Dinner
### ACLU Foundation of Massachusetts
### Boston, May 28, 2009

In 1918, two years before he founded the ACLU, my godfather, Roger Baldwin, went to prison. As a leader of the American Union Against Militarism, he refused to sign up for the World War I draft. A judge sent him to jail for a year.

At the time, most people assumed Baldwin wouldn't actually have to serve his sentence. After all, he had friends in high places, and some of them offered to write to President Wilson personally and have him pardoned. Baldwin turned them down. Later that year, a clerical error took two months off his sentence, and Baldwin was the only one who noticed. So what did he do? He wrote the judge in his case to say, "Listen, there's been a mistake," and he served those two months.

Why did he refuse to leave prison early? Was it simply that he was contrary? Well, maybe a little. But at the heart of Roger Baldwin's philosophy, at the heart of the ACLU, at the heart of America, is an absolute faith in the Rule of Law. In a democracy, nobody has a get-out-of-jail-free card.

Over the past eighty years, there is no single organization that has done more to protect the rule of law for more people in more places in more ways than the ACLU. As my friend Molly Ivins once wrote, "The ACLU exists to protect every citizens' rights as defined in the Bill of Rights in the Constitution of the United States."

I imagine some of you even received the letter she wrote shortly before she died, in which she announced that she was remembering the ACLU in her will and hoped others would do the same. "Just think," she wrote, "about all the hell the ACLU can raise with your money. I can't think of anything I'd rather do with my worldly goods than fund folks who will be a pain in the ass to whatever power come to be."

I am pretty sure that somewhere, Molly and Roger Baldwin are probably driving somebody crazy right now. But if they could be here, I know how proud they would be to see James Yee receive the 2009 Baldwin Award for his strength and courage in standing up to the entire chain of command at Guantánamo in defense of Muslim prisoners' basic human rights. I know how delighted they would be to see Kerry Kennedy carry on the work of her uncle Senator Edward Kennedy and her father,

Senator Robert Kennedy. And I know they'd both find a kindred soul in Baratunde Thurston and his work—as his book says—to keep Jerry Falwell away from his Oreo cookies.

At *The Nation*, of course, we are proud of the many, many battles we have fought together over the years. I like to think we help keep each other strong. And we have been honored to join the ACLU in recent years in trying to bring a little more sunlight into the black hole of the Bush administration and its policy on torture. A year ago, we were especially proud to join with the ACLU in a lawsuit filed in the US District Court of New York challenging the constitutionality of the FISA Amendments Act, also known as the Warrantless Wiretapping Act, which simply argued that it is possible to defend this country from terrorists while also protecting the rights and freedoms that define our nation.

My godfather always believed that no matter how dark things get, America will always find a way back into the light. From his prison cell, he wrote a friend: "Time will justify the strength of those of us who do not yield to blind authority and mob opinion."

The past eight years have taken this country to some dark places: to Guantánamo Bay, to secret CIA jails, to the "Salt Pit," where an Afghani prisoner died of hypothermia, chained naked to a wall outdoors.

But when President Bush told us that only illegal prisons could keep us safe, you, the members of the ACLU, did not yield. When too many in Congress were too scared to stand up to the Patriot Act or to warrantless wiretapping, you did not yield. When too many in the media turned a blind eye to abuses of power around the world, you did not yield.

And then, after eight long years, we elected a president whose first act was to re-criminalize torture; who declared in his Inaugural Address that "we reject as false the choice between our safety and our ideals;" who said at the National Archives just last week that "those who argued for these [torture] tactics were on the wrong side of the debate, and the wrong side of history. We must leave these methods where they belong—in the past."

This was a conviction reflected in his first 100 days, in which he announced plans to shutter Guantánamo . . . in which he ordered the release of the infamous torture memos of the Bush Administration, and said as plainly as he could: "I know some have argued that brutal methods like water-boarding were necessary to keep us safe. I could not disagree more."

Of course, the president said those words on May 21, an hour before the dark lord of water-boarding himself, Dick Cheney, embarked on what has rightly been called his "tortured logic tour." In a speech at the American Enterprise Institute, he said that water-boarding—which was torture when Americans did it to Filipino prisoners in 1898, and was torture when Japanese soldiers did it to Americans in 1945—suddenly was a legal part of what he called "asking questions."

We now know that "enhanced interrogation techniques" produced false confessions: confessions which were used to justify the war in Iraq. Just last week, Colonel Lawrence Wilkerson, the former chief of staff to Secretary of State Colin Powell, went on the *Rachel Maddow Show* and said that one of the main uses of the Bush-Cheney era torture was to persuade detainees to "confess" to ties between Saddam Hussein, Al Qaeda, and 9/11.

I know how happy it makes Democrats to see Dick Cheney and Rush Limbaugh compete to be the face of the Republican Party. Somehow, I think Cheney believes that speaking out now in defiance will somehow make us forget that the attacks on 9/11 happened on his watch, or that he ignored every piece of credible evidence about bin Laden beforehand.

And yet, here he is, lecturing us, as he did last week, that "when just a single clue that goes unlearned or one lead that goes un-pursued can bring on catastrophe, it's no time for splitting differences. There is never a good time to compromise when the lives and safety of the American people hang in the balance."

To Dick Cheney, I say: there is never a good time to compromise America's highest ideals. As the ACLU has believed for its entire history—and I quote—"Time and again, our values have been our best national security asset."

Nobody envies President Obama as he tries to undo the illegal and shameful Bush-Cheney detainee policy. At *The Nation*, we believe that America will never truly find its balance again until we get off the permanent war footing we are on today. Another thing Cheney did last week was mock the Obama administration for not using the phrase, "War on Terror." Let's not forget that Donald Rumsfeld and the rest of the neocons didn't call it the War on Terror either. They called it "the long war." Because that's what Bible-quoting Christian soldiers like Rumsfeld want more than anything: a war without end; a permanent vacation from the Constitution.

It's this fear of never-ending war that led Roger Baldwin to form the American Union Against Militarism, and then the ACLU. And he was right: this century's greatest abuses of civil liberties, from Japanese internment to My Lai to Abu Ghraib, have occurred while our nation was at war.

The collateral damage to our liberties has never been more evident than it's been the past eight years. This permanent military paradigm has been used as justification for almost anything, from unlawful spying on Americans, to illegal detention policies, to hyper-secrecy, to equating dissent with disloyalty.

Dick Cheney can complain as he did last week that his illegal surveillance campaign was secret until it ended up on the front page of the *New York Times*, but they never seemed to understand that how we defend America is just as important as what we defend. If permanent war footing allows us to permanently suspend our constitutional rights, America will have lost a lot more on 9/11 than even the terrorists could have imagined.

Terrorism is a brutal tactic which must be condemned. But fighting terror requires genuine cooperation with other nations in policing; in lawful, targeted intelligence work; and in smart diplomacy. We need to confront the danger of inflating a very real—but limited—threat of terrorism into an open-ended global war. We need a blueprint for how to exit this "long war." Because until we break with this paradigm, we will confront plans for what President Obama called in his National Archives speech "prolonged detention."

This idea, as Senator Russ Feingold wrote the president, "is a hallmark of abusive systems that we have historically criticized around the world."

In 1987, Justice William Brennan gave a remarkable speech in Jerusalem to the Hebrew University Law School. Listen to what he argued. And I quote: "Our history has taught us how difficult it is to establish civil liberties against the backdrop of security threats. But while difficult, it is our work to build bulwarks of liberty that can endure the fears and frenzy of sudden danger—bulwarks to help guarantee that a nation fighting for its survival does not sacrifice those national values that make the fight worthwhile."

This is the never-ending task of the ACLU. With each passing week, we see that our work to reclaim our moral compass—not just for the sake of our position in the world, but for the sake of our own national conscience—is not over. When President Obama strives to keep us true to our values, we are right to support him. And when he is tempted to compromise those values, it is still our responsibility to hold his feet to the fire.

I spend a lot of time in Washington, doing battle on those Sunday talk shows. One thing I am sick of hearing from all the Beltway pundits is that somehow, it's only the ACLU or the press's left-wing base that is demanding accountability. Really? When did supporting and defending the Constitution become the concern of the limited few? As Molly Ivins wrote, "The

ACLU works solely through the legal system: without advocating violence, terrorism, or any other damn thing except the Bill of Rights. Since when did that become extremism?"

One place we need to continue to raise our voices, I believe, is the need for a commission to find the truth about the abuses and the crimes of the past eight years. If we are indeed in the early stages of a long war, we cannot go forward with a foundation built on lies. We cannot look forward with integrity if we are unwilling to look back responsibly.

We must demand a nonpartisan, independent commission to find out who did what, when they did it, and why. President Obama wishes to "move on"—perhaps out of a belief that investigating the abuses of the past eight years will be an obstacle to dealing with the crises of today. But as Paul Krugman pointed out, "would investigating the crimes of the Bush era really divert time and energy needed elsewhere?"

I believe America is capable of uncovering the truth and enforcing the law even while it goes about its other business. And as to the danger of undermining the political consensus, the president needs to pursue his agenda: What political consensus? Cheney's "Tortured Logic Tour"—replete with his family on the talk show circuit—suggests there is little political consensus to be achieved from failing to establish a commission, which is about justice, not vindictiveness.

This commission—let's call it the 9/12 commission—needs to be nonpartisan and independent—and it needs to have subpoena power. It should be led by people who have national respect and experience—perhaps even military experience. I think of Major General Antonio Taguba, who was pressured to resign by the Bush administration in 2007 following the 2004 leak of his report detailing abuses by the US Armed Forces in Abu Ghraib prison. To build credibility with the rest of the world, maybe James Yee should be included on the commission too.

As General Taguba declared in the preface of the 2008 Physicians for Human Rights publication, "Broken Laws, Broken Lives": "There is no longer any doubt as to whether the Bush administration has committed war crimes. The only question that remains to be answered is whether those who ordered the use of torture will be held to account." Taguba is also a man who understands that the real so-called "bad apples" were at the top of the civilian chain of command in Washington.

Such a commission should investigate torture memos written by John Yoo, Jay Bybee and Steven Bradbury—and if the legal reasoning behind those memos is as pathetic as it seems, those lawyers should be disbarred and, possibly, impeached.

The commission must investigate reports that, even by their own outrageous standards, Bush administration officials broke the law. Call Colonel Wilkerson and ask him to restate under oath that the Bush administration first authorized "harsh interrogation" during the spring of 2002—when its principal priority for intelligence was not aimed at preempting another terrorist attack, but rather discovering a smoking gun linking Iraq and Al Qaeda.

Now, some people, including some people in the Obama administration, are worried that we could be setting a bad precedent by trying these officials. But if we don't try them, we set a precedent that is far worse: if a lawyer says it's legal, it's legal. We can't allow the administration to write the law. If we do, the rule of law is meaningless.

And we need to remind President Obama of his obligation on another issue as well: ending the military commissions. Today, President Obama justifies military commissions by telling us that they'll only be used in a few cases.

But military commissions present a larger problem: open-ended detention without trial. This has been discussed by the administration only in the context of the current detainees at Guantánamo Bay. But as Russ Feingold wrote last week, "From a legal as well as human rights perspective, these are unlikely to be the last suspected terrorists captured by the United States. Once a system of indefinite detention without trial is established, the temptation to use it in the future will be powerful."

I think President Obama knows that just because you only violate a few peoples' rights, that doesn't make it okay. But he is under tremendous pressure, assault even, from the Cheney Corps and Abu Ghraib apologists. He will need us—ACLU members, citizens who support and defend our Constitution, people who understand torture is not only illegal, but immoral and provides unreliable evidence and information and opens our troops to retaliation. We must push the president in the right direction and support him when he does the right thing—the same role this organization has played for decades.

In 1981, sixty-three years after this nation first locked Roger Baldwin up, it granted him the highest honor a civilian can receive, the Presidential Medal of Freedom. He was 98 and he couldn't make the trip to Washington. So my father, William vanden Heuvel, had the honor of presenting him with the medal at the New Jersey nursing home where Roger spent his last weeks. Watching this weathered man—a man who had spent a lifetime taking two steps forward and one step back—my father later said, "It could have been Jefferson or Thomas Paine or Samuel Adams speaking to their countrymen."

At that speech—one of his last—Roger Baldwin said something which perfectly summed up the faith, at once conditional and absolute, that he had in this country: "If America has a claim to glory among the nations, it is her service to human liberty."

This service to liberty is our nation's soul. It is what makes us great. The battle to reclaim our soul is just beginning. We are still finding our way out of dark places. Think about how hard it will be to just close Guantánamo. This fight is far from over.

But if Roger Baldwin could see us today, could see us standing strong for our values no matter who the president is, no matter how powerful the opposition is, no matter how tired or frustrated we feel, I think I know what he would say: time will justify our strength. Thank you.

## Intellectuals and Pop Culture
### *Winter 2010*

Some questions are really not worth asking, even as they nag. What relationship should American intellectuals have toward mass culture: television, films, mass-market books, popular music, and the Internet may be one of them. Before answering it, let me first attack any effort to do so.

I don't think we have a recognizable group of American intellectuals of real political weight, at least not intellectuals of the sort celebrated by and occasionally inhabiting the old *Partisan Review*. That is, we don't have an identified bunch of very smart and socially interconnected people—of course, often neurotic, passionate, and sometimes delusional—who judge their life by its contribution to human science or art and who see themselves as the guardians of its standards before a debasing and resolutely meretricious mass culture. One reason we don't is that, whatever the searing inequalities of the American economy, talented Americans of almost every conceivable background have access to higher education. Another is that technology has erased virtually all barriers of entry to broadcasting individual opinion. A third is that America now lacks anything like a responsible business elite or a working class that might provide a natural audience. The well heeled abandoned this country some time ago.

The democratic public, without much organization or political leadership, is still not fully formed. We don't have standards of public discussion in this country. We don't even have political debate requiring rhetorical regard for the public interest. I also don't consider myself such an intellectual. I consider myself a reasonably intelligent editor and publisher, running an independent magazine of opinion, whose chief social interests are political. I'd like to make a contribution to achieving this country and making peace in the world. The most immediate way I know to do that is by getting the next issue out, making it as interesting as possible, and by disseminating its values and opinions on radio and television.

Perhaps I mistake myself. The word "intellectual" traces to the Dreyfus affair. It was the new collective name taken by those diverse writers and artists who, in sudden and articulate concert, condemned the injustice of his treatment. I'm sure I would have joined them. A generation ago, Noam Chomsky said the responsibility of intellectuals was to tell the truth and expose lies. I try to do that every day. However, I think of intellectuals as not only fearless truth-tellers but as people materially contributing to that truth by advancing science or art. I don't do that.

I also don't think "mass" means much these days. Most of the commercial boundaries between high-brow and low-brow culture have long since dissolved. Certainly that distinction isn't policed by the technologies themselves. It's not as if book readers are high brow and blog readers are low—after all, Stephenie Meyer's *Twilight* novels and Glenn Beck's screeds dominate book sales while scholars like Juan Cole and Michael Bérubé reach their largest audiences via blogs. Cornel West has over 12,000 Twitter followers. And how would one describe the phenomenon of Oprah's Book Club, which can instantly put works by William Faulkner and Leo Tolstoy on the middle-brow *New York Times* bestseller list through the magic of TV talk and paperback mass marketing? Did "high-brow" opera (Puccini's *Nessun Dorma* from Turandot) become "low-brow" trash when cell phone salesman Paul Putts turned it into a global hit on the reality TV show *Britain's Got Talent?* Or was it when Luciano Pavarotti popularized it during the 1990 soccer World Cup games? These distinctions have long since stopped making sense—if they ever did.

These caveats entered, I guess my answer to the question would be "critical embrace." And in giving it, I'll use "intellectual" in the broad sense of "a thinking American with interests in public affairs" to include myself.

I take it to be manifestly crazy, even were it possible, for such intellectuals to ignore or shun mass culture. It's too important. That's where most Americans, especially but surely not only the young, get most of their information, opinions and general take on politics. Their other source is their friends, who are generally watching and reading the same things. So of course we should engage. Frank Rich must have written a dozen columns using AMC's *Mad Men* to frame these times. And *24* may have influenced how a generation thinks about torture. As Judge Sonia Sotomayor admitted of herself, *Perry Mason* and *Law & Order* shape popular thinking about law. Before Twyla Tharp choreographed to Billy Joel, the Joffrey Ballet danced to music from the Purple Paisley god himself—Prince. The cheapest forms of popular culture (comic books, TV, pop music and so on) have forever shaped the imagination of current and future artists and presidents and offered the consolations of escape and control and pleasure.

It's also true that the profit imperative and relentless consolidation of corporate media, and more than a little of human nature, means that much of mass culture is utter junk or worse—indeed degraded, inhumane, politically backward (sexist, racist, materialistic and so on) or just stupid. But nothing's new here except its totalizing reach—total because of the continued decline of alternative sources of authority. That's the way of a depoliticized capitalism: no real secular community, politics and society as largely spectacle, mass privatization of civic culture. It may be that changes of degree have produced a change in kind, that people have actually become lobotomized, not just idiotically entertained. But I doubt it.

For one thing, the notion of "mass" in our culture is transforming before our eyes. At the ground level, the fact that the costs of broadcasting and information retrieval have dropped to near zero, and the limitless possibilities of peer-production and self-organizing made available by the Internet is the greatest social technology fact of our time. The Internet has already changed political campaigning and social movement organization and advocacy. It is well on its way to transforming government and almost all critical economic relations: the structure of the firm, the divisibility of property rights, national and local strategies of economic development. I think this opens enormous possibilities for progressives. They should stop congratulating themselves for cottoning to the Internet just a tiny bit faster than the right and devote themselves to collectively mastering and diffusing liberation technologies.

»»»

A little higher up, the expansion of the number of commercial broadcast channels and segmentation of audiences has of course increased the dangers of only listening to oneself. But it has also manifestly opened up a host of mid-sized audiences for good content. I can get as much opera and political satire as I want, along with home-shopping networks and reality TV. What I miss from television is my own Fox, a source of intelligent analysis and widely resourced coverage that I can rely on in the same way its current audience relies on its lethal distortions. But even here, I think we're a bit better off than a while ago. Would Rachel Maddow, a decidedly intellectual, openly gay, and progressive commentator, have commanded an audience of any size ten or twenty years ago? Would an academic like Charles Ferguson have gone into business and then decided to make an Oscar-winning political documentary? I doubt it. We're also seeing the rise of a new generation of intellectuals who freely combine high and low culture, demanding and easy analysis in ways that find a decent-sized audience. Whatever else one thinks of him, Michael Moore exemplifies this, as does Spike Lee, whose mostly rigorous documentary *When the Levees Broke* was broadcast on HBO the same year his crime drama *Inside Man* hit theaters.

This is all to the good. They and others are producing smart, nuanced, thoughtful mass-culture products that also find an audience, even if that audience isn't the same size as, say, the one for *The DaVinci Code* or *Dancing with the Stars*.

So I don't worry about intellectuals being able to penetrate mass culture. I assume the next generation of them will assume, with everyone else in our Internet-united humanity, that there are a variety of technologies available to make their arguments and art and a variety of genres and styles that can be mixed in making it. What I am worried about is that their contribution will become merely another form of niche entertainment with no real bite. I want the public itself to have the information and capacity to act on arguments, and I worry that that is diminishing. This is almost entirely a political matter, and this is where the critical part of the embrace comes in. We need to declare, to one and all, that in the mass of commercial speech, we also need easily accessed, publicly driven or public-minded sources of news and information. In news, it's past time that the United States join the rest of the world in having some public-minded alternative to the major commercial networks. And in the United States and the rest of the world, I think it essential that we stop the commercial erosion of the democratic global space opened up by the Internet. Here I think intellectuals have some intellectual work to do—to design a more public-minded communications system than the one we have, while keeping the barriers of entry to its use low, and to design an intellectual property rights regime, globally, that will not choke off humanity's current capacity for improvement. In truth, I think most of the work is political—to make the case for why that's important at all. As with other public goods, a democratic media and communications system will be hard to achieve without a public.

## Rising to the Task of Slowing Down
### August 10, 2010

The pace of life feels morally dangerous to me.
—Richard Ford, novelist

"Slow" is not a quality I'm used to embracing, nor is it often a realistic option. As a person who runs a round-the-clock website and a weekly magazine, I race through each day—assigning stories, writing stories, editing stories and then assigning more, writing more, editing more. I rush from editorial meetings to business meetings and back again. And though I sometimes manage to disconnect briefly—to have dinner with my husband or friends—I'm reliably online late at night and early in the morning.

I realize I have good company in living life at this frenetic pace. In fact, this sort of life is increasingly the rule rather than the exception. Juliet Schor notes that the average US worker in 2006 worked nearly a month more than he or she did in 1969. Of course, the distinction between working and not working has diminished too. We're expected to be on call at all times—and we feel guilty about taking a break from our smart phone-driven, perpetual overtime. *Salon's* Rebecca Traister puts it well:

"Now, it often seems, there is no 'gone for the weekend.' There is certainly no 'gone for the night.' Sometimes there's not even a gone on vacation. . . . I don't think the notion that we have to be constantly plugged in is just in our heads: I think it's also in the heads of our superiors, our colleagues, our future employers and our prospective employees." Forget smelling the proverbial roses; we're so busy sprinting from point A to point B—with our cell phones and Kindles and iPads, e-mailing and texting and Tweeting—we don't even spot the roses in the first place.

This August, I'm trying to do things differently. I've been inspired in part by Carl Honoré's wonderful book *In Praise of Slowness*. "The problem is that our love of speed, our obsession with doing more and more in less and less time, has gone too far," Honoré writes. It's easy to agree with his assessment about the dangers of multitasking. (We had plenty of warning on this front: Publilius Syrus, a Roman philosopher from the first century B.C., said, "To do two things at once is to do neither.") But Honoré also documents the negative impact of speed on our relationships, our health, our economy. To reverse this damage, he encourages us to rediscover the off button.

So this month I've turned on an away message on my computer saying I'm checking e-mail infrequently. My friends and colleagues know it's somewhat aspirational—I'm still checking in the morning and evening, and often in the afternoon. But I'm weaning myself off the constant use. Meanwhile, I'm trying to have real conversations in place of staccato e-mail exchanges. And I've set aside time for lying in the hammock and reading novels, for taking yoga for the first time, for drinking wine from the small vineyard down the street and for eating local corn and tomatoes. I'm trying to do some deep breathing and deep reflecting.

To be sure, not everyone has the luxury of slowing down in this way. Traister's point about the expectations of colleagues remains a reality for many people. And even more prohibitive, millions of Americans—when they can find jobs in this economy—don't get paid vacation days or *sick leave*. A single mother can work two jobs and still find herself unable to rise from poverty—much less spend time with the people who are important to her. We should be able to do better, as most other countries in the Western industrialized world do. For starters, affordable, high-quality child care would make a real difference in how families—especially women—manage time.

It's important that we all get at least some time to take stock. If we are to produce not only our best work, but also our best lives, we need to think hard (but with breaks) about developing a different attitude toward time—one that moves us toward saner, more whole lives, and a more humane, more caring country.

# Acknowledgments

To begin at the beginning: I thank my parents. My passion for and fascination with politics and journalism begins with them. My mother, Jean Stein, is an extraordinarily imaginative editor and oral historian; my father, William vanden Heuvel, is a pragmatic idealist whose remarkable career in public life has influenced so much of my thinking.

I am forever grateful to Victor Navasky, whose trust in me, and whose generosity, humor and friendship have shaped my life as an editor and person. I once affectionately described Victor as a man of velvet and steel. It is a combination that I have learned from!

My colleagues at *The Nation* have inspired and informed me. I am especially grateful to John Nichols, Roane Carey, Betsy Reed, Richard Kim, William Greider, Chris Hayes, Richard Lingeman, Karen Rothmyer and Ari Berman for their counsel and ideas and, of course, for their remarkable work and writing in these last years. And I thank Peter Rothberg for first proposing, and then encouraging me, to start my blog, *Editor's Cut*. A group of ace *Nation* interns also assisted with research—Simon Apter, Marc Kilstein, Nicholas Jahr and Roz Hunter.

Ruth Baldwin's wise editorial counsel and superb organizational skills gave this collection a pace and a spine. Thanks also to those at Nation Books, especially Carl Bromley and John Sherer, for their enthusiasm and attention.

Greg Kaufmann has been a valued research assistant, and far more. His humane insights, especially about issues of economic justice and poverty, inform sections of this book. I thank him for encouraging me to trust my gut as a writer.

Robert Borosage is an ally, a friend, a political counselor who, for the last few decades, has ceaselessly challenged the limits of his beloved country's downsized debates. All the while, he's remained a person of humor, brilliance and strategic smarts.

Sherle Schwenninger may be one of the most independent-minded people I work with. His valuable comments and criticism have helped sharpen my thinking in all arenas, and especially when it comes to national security.

Michael Pertschuk, a former Chair of the Federal Trade Commission, co-founder of the Advocacy Institute and longtime *Nation* editorial board member, has been wise and generous, with his editorial and political ideas and comments.

Deepak Bhargava, Executive Director of the Center for Community Change, and a valued member of the *Nation* editorial board, shared his thoughts, and sharpened mine, about the importance of movement-building in these and all times.

Joel Rogers, a *Nation* contributing editor and good friend, understands things that most of us don't. I am grateful to him for sharing his verdant ideas about many things, especially how to craft a more effective progressive politics.

In 2010, the *Washington Post* invited me to write a weekly web column. I thank Fred Hiatt, the editor of that paper's editorial pages, for the invitation—and for including my voice and point of view in the mix. It has also been a pleasure to work with the *Post*'s editors—Jackson Diehl, Helen Jones, Marisa Katz, Stephen Stromberg and Autumn Brewington.

These acknowledgments wouldn't be complete without thanking Dylan Loewe for his savvy ideas and enthusiasm for the project.

No part of this collection would be possible without the love and support of my husband, Steve Cohen, and our daughter, Nika. Steve introduced me to Russia, to *The Nation* and to a life that has been full of shared adventure and passion. Steve has been called many things in his remarkable life and is one of America's preeminent scholars of Russia and the Soviet Union. I think of him as the "alternativist" who wound his way from Owensboro, Kentucky to New York City, and who has never wavered in believing in the importance of alternatives in politics and history. And to my beloved daughter Nika—thank you for your love and patience. Someday, I will follow your advice and "chill!"

# Index